EMANCIPATION AND HISTORY

Studies in Critical Social Sciences Book Series

Haymarket Books is proud to be working with Brill Academic Publishers (www.brill.nl) to republish the *Studies in Critical Social Sciences* book series in paperback editions. This peer-reviewed book series offers insights into our current reality by exploring the content and consequences of power relationships under capitalism, and by considering the spaces of opposition and resistance to these changes that have been defining our new age. Our full catalog of *SCSS* volumes can be viewed at https://www.haymarketbooks .org/series_collections/4-studies-in-critical-social-sciences.

Emancipation and History

The Return of Social Theory

José Maurício Domingues

Haymarket Books
Chicago, IL

First published in 2017 by Brill Academic Publishers, The Netherlands.
© 2017 Koninklijke Brill NV, Leiden, The Netherlands

Published in paperback in 2018 by
Haymarket Books
P.O. Box 180165
Chicago, IL 60618
773-583-7884
www.haymarketbooks.org

ISBN: 978-1-60846-105-9

Trade distribution:
In the U.S. through Consortium Book Sales, www.cbsd.com
In the UK, Turnaround Publisher Services, www.turnaround-uk.com
In Canada, Publishers Group Canada, www.pgcbooks.ca
All other countries, Ingram Publisher Services International, ips_intlsales@
ingramcontent.com

Cover design by Jamie Kerry and Ragina Johnson.

This book was published with the generous support of Lannan Foundation
and the Wallace Action Fund.

Printed in United States.

10 9 8 7 6 5 4 3 2 1

Library of Congress Cataloging-in-Publication Data is available.

Contents

List of Tables

Introduction

The social sciences have always had a fundamental role in the discussions about social emancipation, ever since they crossed paths in the middle of the nineteenth century. Social theory was crucial in this, trying to peer into the future through the traces it left on the present, running ahead of its own time. This is what happened in the past with Marx's theory, Marxisms, other social-ist currents, and continues today with those few other strands, either within or without Marxism, that try to craft a theory with broader reach. Analytical concepts of wide scope emerge as demands of theory itself. But in reality, this commitment to large processes and how to deal with them intellectually has been considerably lost.

There are good reasons for this, since the certainties that Marxism exces-sively affirmed and promoted were shown to be questionable and, in some cases, downright wrong. Historical teleologies are no longer convincing. How-ever, this should not have led us to give up on efforts to read in the present those possibly pre-figurative traits of the future, at least in the sense that they announce possibilities, whose realization implies no necessity, while other possibilities and trends, often more powerful than those that might lead to emancipation, are also at work. It is a matter of sorting out among trends those that could be propelled in the emancipatory direction they may harbor. This would allow for a broader and more productive way of linking what will here be called trend-concepts with social creativity and historical contingency.

Nowadays, the topic of contingency pervades sociology. Creativity is, as usual, rhetorically evoked while issues about directionality have been all but lost. Each piece collected in this book is part and parcel of a larger endeavor to promote this re-articulation, in order to, within the context of the advanced modernity we live in, resume the discussion of social emancipation without remaining attached to no longer workable theoretical schemes or giving in to empiricism and the short-run. The political consequences of remaining locked into schemes bereft of adequate answers and of accepting the accommodation with empiricism are, after all, taticism – short-term political moves –, since a long-term strategy must be guided by a larger perspective of where we want to get to and how to get there. Doubtlessly, it is not a matter of demanding new certainties and exclusive allegiances, but, rather, we should be bringing up the question of large processes, providing the basis from which to reckon with politics.

The junction of emancipation and history, in particular through the re-turn of social theory, points precisely in this direction: can we identify the noteworthy trends in the contemporary world whose power can be harnessed without giving up on the idea of contingency and social creativity? Is it possible to outline some future horizon, as classical theory intended to, although in a far-fetched way? Is there anything in this regard that deserves to be discussed from the point of view of critical theory, in tandem with the possibilities of emancipation of the human species? Are we capable of going beyond empirical description and historical narrative, providing an answer to these queries within critical theory? These are the most general questions that underlie the texts published here.

The book opens with an inquiry into the actual meaning of critical theory today, with a rather severe assessment of the paths it took and suggesting reinvigorating alternatives (Chapter 1). The following texts are heavily centered on the discussion about *trend-concepts*, either generally or with more specific foci. Next, trend-concepts, and their linkages, at least such as understood here, with *collective subjectivity*, are considered in a systematic way, moreover, through the prism of sociological theory (Chapter 2). In this regard, religion and secularization exemplify the scope and reach of the discussion, in a global perspective. The analysis moves on to the status of what several authors, among whom Marx and Weber stand out, attribute to the several "dimensions," as they are usually called, of social life. The question is solved by the conceptualization of what I have called the fundamental *social existential questions of the species* and the several ways to tackle them (Chapter 3). This theme has repercussions, also at a very general level, in the relationship between history and sociology, particularly in the body of work of exactly those two classical sociologists (regardless of whether they recognized themselves as such or not) (Chapter 4).

Two sorts of still very general yet well-defined issues, allow us to move forward in the understanding of trend-concepts. This concerns first of all the construction of political modernity as a fundamental and separated dimension of social life, confronting the specific social existential question of power, with the state at its center. This trend is accompanied by an autonomization of citizens as individuals who are increasingly less controllable by the state apparatus, despite its ever-increasing strength (Chapter 5). There is a crucial axis of emancipation with respect to contemporary life, whether by its concentration initially on political economy and afterward on philosophy and culture, or because the "dictatorship of the proletariat" promised in a simple way, although practically dramatically, to sort the issue in a thorough manner. The epistemology underlying the way to conceive of these trends is once again summoned and expanded in this chapter. Finally, the family in global modernity sets the stage for relevant debates, given its flexibilization and its resolution of one of our fundamental existential questions – the male–female pair, as constituted by the reproduction of the species and sexuality (Chapter 6).

The *imaginary* – a crucial focus of contemporary discussions and in some part the core of the exercise of creativity and which is presented here through a direct dialogue with Castoriadis – offers an analytical axis, which indeed crosscuts the whole book. It is particularized and open to the discussion of so-called "populism" and of the rather influential theory posited by Laclau concerning this phenomenon, which is criticized for its simplifications and problematic consequences (Chapter 7). The discussion of the *basic forms of social interaction* – in which networks of voluntary collaboration, so decisive for any socialist project, must be contemplated, alongside the principles of market and hierarchy – also sums up a number of issues, at a very demanding conceptual level. This is moreover a precise example of what should be understood as a strategy of analytical construction (Chapter 8).

Finally, we return to the longitudinal themes that receive pride of place in this book and the trajectory of trend-concepts in the history of Marxism, as well as in some contemporary theories, such as Negri's and Sousa Santos', providing an opportunity to inquire into the relation between them and the idea of *critical theory* and *emancipation* as such. The goal is to a large extent to once again approach the discussion against the backdrop of what I refer to as the question of "late communism," which is how I conclude the book (Chapter 9). It is a return of sorts, albeit already at another plane, to the thematic introduced in the first chapter. As the book proceeds, themes are deepened and expanded and I can finally resolve issues announced at the outset, relying on the systematic social-theoretical analyses carried out in the previous chapters.

It is also worthwhile noting that, if Chapter 6 gauges how distinct civilizational traditions were brought to bear on the most intimate and basic relations – "primary," according to a traditional sociological strand – and also the influence of religions and worldviews at large, Chapters 5 and 9 adumbrate themes we need to grapple with more systematically, with respect also to practical developments. I refer here to political *mediation*, which, because of new forms of practicing it and collective mobilization, has been brought to the center of experience and of political debate. It depends on the principle of voluntary collaboration studied in Chapter 6 and is projected as an element the possible strengthening of which is a real, but difficult trend, now as much as before.

With this sort of construction, I believe I am capable of going beyond recent works in which I offered a critical view of global modernity, while simultaneously making an effort to take a step back from so-called post and de-colonial theories (cf. Domingues 2012). This choice was not so because they do not raise questions that are in principle interesting, but because they deal too diffusely with the critique of modernity, concentrated as they are in their own discursivity – to the detriment of properly theoretical questions – and ultimately end up unequipped to identify what would be the true key-questions to be critically and, all things considered, politically addressed, in an emancipatory direction.

A systematic theoretical role is therefore attributed to sociology, contrary to what critical theory typically reserves for it, namely, the mere identification of empirical processes, different from what would accrue to philosophy and political economy. I assume here that philosophy has its theories built with limited reference to the empirical world, or at least that it superimposes its rather a priori schemes on it, while political economy deals with only one aspect of social life, in a way, contrary to what Marx thought, perhaps not so central to emancipation in strategic terms, a sphere that seems to belong to *politics* such as we know it today (without detriment to the construction of an alternative world vis-à-vis the capitalist one in which we live). It is theory, rejecting its capture by the specific and exclusive Western cases, that must allow for the overcoming of Eurocentrism and Occidentocentrism, as well as of Orientalism, permitting a critical view of global modernity, in its general developmental trends and, also thereby, its particular regional, national and local expressions, in their actual hybridizations with modern civilization.

These texts and thoughts have been weaved together incrementally, having achieved more precise definitions in the last years. Many people have contributed to their elaboration. In the notes to each chapter I thank them specifically, even though certain names will have escaped me. This project has been carried out in the Laboratory for the Study of Social Theory and Latin America (NETSAL), housed by the Institute for Social and Political Studies of Rio de Janeiro State University (IESP-UERJ). I thank its members and especially Breno Bringel, who co-coordinates it with me, for the discussions we have had. I would also like to thank in particular Wolfgang Knöbl for analyses and conversations in which some of these topics have come up very often, Peter Wagner, who received me in Barcelona in 2013, and Paula Diehl, who arranged my stay in Berlin in 2015. Much of the pieces collected here found their inspiration and were written in some of these environments. I would also like to thank Alfredo Saad Filho and David Fasenfest for the presence of this book, now in English, in the *Studies in Critical Social Sciences* series. My English in several chapters was revised by Thiago Nasser. Judy Pereira was superb during the editorial process. I would like to thank them both. Finally, the research for this book was made possible thanks to the support of CNPq and FAPERJ.

CHAPTER 1

Vicissitudes and Possibilities of Critical Theory Today

Defining Critical Theory

The goal of this text is to evaluate the directions of critical theory today and its relations in particular with sociology, with concrete reference to the contemporary world. It is not a matter of restricting critical theory to the tradition of the so-called Frankfurt School and its offspring, nor circumscribe it to what has been named "Western Marxism." I would rather focus on critical theory in a more ecumenical way, supposing that other authors and currents are included in it more broadly, sharing, however, some common presuppositions. This takes us to a discussion about some trends that could contribute in the direction of a renewal of this theoretical field. Before doing so, nevertheless, it is necessary to define the extent to which and how a theoretical approach can be brought within the critical tradition, without aiming at a systematic discussion of all currents that could at present be seen as part of this intellectual field. Let me concentrate on some fundamental strands of the contemporary debate. Ambivalence in relation to the evolution of modernity, in its multidimensional aspects, which include capitalism, without being restricted to it, characterizes much of European social theory since at least the mid-eighteenth century until, especially, the last decades of the twentieth century. Freedom and domination loom large in several of such analyses as the poles in which modernity is substantiated and frustrated, since its promises are actualized in a partial and unilateral way by means of institutions that to some extent embody the values of the modern imaginary, but simultaneously establish patterns of social relations rooted in new forms of domination (Domingues 2006, Chaps. 1–2). Some, as Weber, take critique very far. This may not, however, really amount to what I want to define ecumenically as critical theory. Weber did not go beyond resignation as to a highly-bureaucratized society, deprived of freedom, in which the values of liberalism could no longer, he believed, be realized (Cohn 1978).

* Originally published in *Revista de Sociologia & Antropologia*, vol. 1 (2011); and, with some changes, in Breno Bringel and José Maurício Domingues (eds), *Global Modernity and Social Contestation* (London and Delhi: Sage, 2015).

Critical theory stands here, therefore, as a strand of questioning of modernity that supports not only its values, against present institutions, but that also
endeavors to find in it, as well as in the agents that move within it, the potential,
the elements and possible subjects of the emancipation promised by modernity. These values cannot of course be merely a derivation of the ideas of the
critical theoretician, rather consisting in conceptual extrapolations of themes
and tendencies that emerge and linger on in the actual social world of modernity in its successive transformations. That is, it is an immanent critique that
aims at transcending social conditions that prevent the actualization of the
values of modernity and the demands social agents effectively critical bring to
the fore of intellectual and political disputes (Benhabib 1986, 328–329; Browne
2008). There are many ways and "models" of doing critical theory even in the
more circumscribed tradition of the Frankfurt School (Müller-Doohm 2005). It
must be clear that it is not the case of abiding only by the conceptions of justice that appear in social movements, nor of looking exclusively for incipient
moral elements that articulate them on the basis of suffering or that may come
to articulate them morally, but all these factors as well as others. This means I
disagree with both Fraser and Honneth (2003). If that demand furnishes clear
criteria, on the other hand it is plain that reality is not pure. More complicated
is Habermas' (1981) straightforward substitution of social analysis and immanent social impulses toward change by the idea that the core of critical theory
resides in the very structure of human communication and by a somewhat
fuzzy idea of a strategy of conceptual "reconstruction," which he has applied
differently to several phenomena.

Nobre (2008) for instance has insisted on a claim of "no competition," since
Marx, but especially with reference to Horkheimer's founding text, between
"traditional theory and critical theory," an outlook that would reach at least to
a certain period of Habermas' work. I see here some ambiguity: it is not clear
if no competition is to be posed in terms of parallel developments, although
critical theory can embody the findings of traditional theory, or if it would be
really superior to the latter due to its cognitive standpoint. Only according to
this last angle do I think that the perspective of no competition would be valid
in Marx and Lukács. More generally, the critical standpoint, linked to emancipation, can claim pre-eminence only insofar as it is rooted in the transcendence of the present through the recognition of the emancipatory elements to
be found in it at least in nuce.

I would like to suggest, however, that it is not in a methodological perspective that we must ground critical theory, but rather on the social immanence
of a core value, which has not lost at all its potential, although it can become
dormant when some social goals of emancipation are achieved. I refer to equal
freedom, that is, the demand that every and each one has the same social

power and is at liberty to choose his or her own path in life, individually and collectively, beyond systems of domination – or that imply control – and the false liberal dichotomy of negative and positive freedom. This has been the substantive historical core of critical theory since Marx, through Adorno, to Habermas (Domingues 2006, Chaps. 1–2).

That said, what about the whereabouts of critical theory in a stricter sense? Twenty years ago, when democracy started to decay in the western world, after decades and even centuries of difficult and conflictive strengthening, its outstanding approaches supported the idea that the expansion of "civil society" or the "public sphere" – and procedural and deliberative democracy – would occupy center-stage in emancipatory politics (Cohen and Arato 1992; Habermas 1992). No capitalism, no neoliberalism, no de-democratizing changes of the state. In this respect, although there were already problems in Habermas' (1981) main work, in particular, due to his adoption of systems theory and a tacit affiliation to neoclassical economic theory, his ulterior discussion of democracy moved to fill a gap, albeit in an arguable way, that was highly problematic for critical theory. Nevertheless, it also meant a retreat from a broader conceptual standpoint. His last relevant intervention in this debate took on important discussions about the encroachment of eugenic neoliberalism upon life politics (with reference to biotechnology) (Habermas 2001a, 2001b); and, more recently, it evinces perhaps the beginning of the acknowledgment of the possibility of de-democratizing processes, exemplified concretely by the present fate of Europe (Habermas 2011). Honneth, after insisting on the centrality of recognition politics – which can offer an interesting middle-range theory, but should not be blown out of proportion – seems to have concluded, in his contribution with Martin Hartmann, that critique lost its immanent transcendent core. This would be due to the capacity of contemporary capitalism to take up the demands of the 1968 generation, with its aesthetic and social critique, at most remaining, as an element of tension, the "paradoxes" generated by the inevitably incomplete and somewhat illusory realization of such values (Honneth 2010), although, in what is his main opus thus far, freedom, as the general principle of modern ethical life, is re- affirmed (without however an at least more explicit recognition of its egalitarian thrust, as a value, in this civilization), and as if it had been basically institutionalized (Honneth 2011). Global conceptions of justice have also recently drawn the attention of authors within this tradition, in relation, however, to individuals, not countries or collectivities, nor in what concerns the dynamic of capitalism or democracy at the national and global levels (cf. Fraser 2009).

In order to weave part of his recent arguments, Honneth draws upon the work of Boltanski and Chiapello (1999), whose diagnosis of modernity holds great interest, when they deal with what they consider the "new spirit of capitalism," although they excessively emphasize morals and motivation (in variance, in fact, with Weber's view). This is a problem that also harms Habermas' and in particular Honneth's works. More seriously, Boltanski, the group's "chef d'école," chose later on an amorphous and unspecific definition of critical theory, which excessively stresses moral issues, his arguments fuming away, moreover, in a rhetoric in which power is absent as an issue (Boltanski 2009). His theory does not give pride of place to, or even vents, crucial developments undergone by European countries at present, the selection of models of critique that he carried out formerly with Thévenot, all egalitarian-meritocratic, leaving no room to relations of domination, which rarely come to the fore morally in modernity (Boltanski and Thévenot 1991). Furthermore, despite their mobilizing of several authors of political philosophy, arbitrarily selected, they do not aim at a "critical sociology" but rather at a "sociology of critique," paying no attention to the main values that we can surely find in the multiple lifeworlds and their daily criticism, which compose the core of the modern imaginary (Boltanski and Thévenot 1991). That is, the polarization of classes, racist demagoguery, the decay of democracy, neoliberalism, nothing of the kind turns up in Boltanski's writings, although crucial aspects of capitalism are actually present in his joint study with Chiapello (Boltanski and Chiapello 1999).

At the same time, some Marxist authors, such as Harvey (1990, 2009), have critically presented interesting and relevant discussions about the contemporary world, proceeding, however, as though it was enough basically to resume Marx's theoretical scaffoldings, something that is not plausible after so much change in the world and in theory in the last decades. Some "post-Marxist" writers jumped into the world of "discourse" and, despite interesting conceptual discussions, have been treading a cloudy sphere, which has limited capacity to understand the present in its multidimensionality (cf. Butler, Laclau and Zizek 2000). A reductive concentration on the West comes out, moreover and once more, also in these currents. On the other hand, there is "post-colonialism." We still have to wait to see which will be its concrete innovations, beyond the idea that it is necessary to thoroughly reinvent social theory, beyond Eurocentrism, as if this had never been carried out and the social sciences and the humanities had never been capable – for instance in Latin America, where in a way or another "critical thought" has thrived, but also elsewhere – of proposing solutions to the problems of intellectual dependency and conceptual lack of adequacy which they denounce. This is patently absurd (see Debés Valdés 2012). More interesting are actual pieces of work in this direction and with a perspective close to post-colonialism, such as those of Nandy (1978), whose work already is – or should be – a global reference. His is a rare example of a partially non-modern critique of modernity, although at the same time it stands as already modernized alterity (therefore as part of modernity), centered around the question of freedom and blending European influence with a transformed heritage of the Indic civilization (Domingues, 2010). Concrete analysis of the contemporary world, about so-called post-colonial societies, are absolutely missing in such approaches – apart from Chatterjee's interventions (1993, 2004), whose fixation on the ideas of "community" and the secundarization of the struggle for rights are rather arguable, indeed close to a sub-repetitious – and unintentional – acceptance of problematic elements of present day status quo. In Latin America, Mignolo (2000, 2005) stands out in this regard. His work is centered on the exclusion, through "coloniality-modernity," of original peoples and the search for a savage rhetorical articulation, against western rationalism and official rationalization. It is the world of discourse, dear to the crisscross of post-modernism and post-structuralism, that underpins much of this restrict "post/de-colonial" standpoint, notwithstanding the relevance of a number of problems they emphasize (a shining example of which is Spivak 1988).[1] In any case, although these are surely relevant issues – diversity of the global social world as well as epistemological and political challenges must be tackled – critique cannot by any means stop at this.

Besides, such a discussion is not an exclusivity of post- or de-colonial thought: many in Latin America and elsewhere, for instance the Egyptian Marxist Samir Amin (1973, 1988), were attentive to these issues, either substantively pointing out the role of imperialism or with a straightforward critique of "Eurocentrism," whether we think he hit the mark or not. There are several relevant elements in those approaches, but they are, in my view, limited. The world faces increasing problems, and modernity is driven in a direction of ever greater social polarization while democracy is sapped, a process which in Latin America we have at least resisted with some success. This is a fundamental aspect of what I have been calling the third phase of modernity, in what it has of more perverse and more connected to the defeat of emancipatory projects. Let us examine the issue more closely in order that we understand what can be said of critical social theory at present. Here, we must speak of an ecumenical theory and of rescuing intuitions, empirical and theoretical, that surfaced in the origins of this tradition. An incisive sociological approach, rather than

---

1 Providing we keep equal freedom as an orienting value, hence do not lose sight of the future as transcending the limitations of the present, and universalist standpoints, Santos' (2002) demand that we concentrate on the present and search for alternatives which emerge across the planet also can help reaffirm a critical view, although he seems to discard too easily the propelling force of modernity as a global and partly frustrated emancipatory telos, which still holds as a horizon, problems to be discussed below notwithstanding.

philosophical, has much to offer in this regard, keeping, in any case, the clash between modern values and institutions at its core. There are obviously other authors, as well as a legion of themes, such as patriarchy and sexism, racism and the destruction of the environment, which have their own critical lineages. I do not aim at dealing with them all here, much less to exhaust the multiple and ever more specific themes that a social life in exponential complexification throws up. It matters here only to outline what would be the fundamental axes of a critical diagnosis of the present, pointing to emancipatory forces at this historical stage, a crucial theme for the very legitimacy of critical theory, as well as throwing light on research alleys that seem relevant in this connection.

Contemporary Modernity

In the last three or four decades, there has been a radical change in the position of countries across the globe. Capitalism has changed its patterns of accumulation and regulation, as well as of consumption; that is, it has deeply altered its "mode of development," to draw upon French regulation school. Neoliberalism is an expression of that, as much as the changes in the form of organizing production and consumption in what has been conventionally known as "post-Fordism." A globalization of such processes came about in all countries of the world, in a "uneven and combined" manner, along with its fragmentation: through just in time and lean production, through outsourcing and networks between firms, by the pluralization and segmentation of consumption markets, as well as by a further concentration and centralization of capital, and by an increased polarization between social classes, or between poor and rich, from a phenomenological standpoint. Social liberalism has also slowly gained strength, with sectorialized and targeted policies (especially for the poor). This has marked, contingently, let me stress, the passage from the second phase of modernity – organized to a large extent by the state – to the third one, of greater social complexity, in which the state draws back to other governmentality tasks, leaving the economy, now much more globalized, to be increasingly regulated by the market, with a predominance of finance capital over it in the framework of so-called "American empire" (Boyer 1986; Harvey 1990, 2009; Piketty 2013; Domingues 2008, 2012, 2015, Chap. 2).

There was, nevertheless, the expectation that democracy would flourish – or there was at least a normative perspective about the democratic question. The hope of the aforementioned dominant sectors within critical theory stemmed from that. This did not happen overall. Instead, the democratic elements of those political systems have shrunk – in relation to the thrust of citizens in the

behavior of state incumbents, as well as in what concerns the space for participation and their protection, when they do participate (Tilly 2004, 7–30; 2007).
It could be suggested that the problem is localized in the countries of the old
"Third World" and in those which lived under "real socialism," China, Cuba or
Russia. However, this is patently false: democracy is restricted and retreats exactly in those countries in which it originally emerged in the West, in Europe
and the United States. Participation, respect to the electoral mandate conferred
by the population, the articulation with the organized forces of society, respect
for human and other rights, freedom of press, tolerance in relation to distinct
ethnic and religious groups, over all this hangs a question mark produced by
explicit electoral fraud, an accentuation of the repressive side of the state, the
indifference to the mandate received by parties and "leaders" to carry out the
policies defined in their campaigns, the official use of torture and kidnapping,
the growth of secrecy and of secret and surveillance services, official and open
racism, the instrumental and selective use of justice, the growing strength and
independence of executives vis-à-vis parliaments (and within these, of central
banks), frontal attacks against the press if it is critical of the establishment,
whereas the mass communication means become ever more monopolistic and
connected to global neoliberalism (notwithstanding the growth of alternative
media). Unfortunately, very little has been, critically or not, theorized in this
regard (for some aspects of this, see American Political Science Association
2004; Crouch 2004; Sassen, 2006; Pierson and Skocpol 2007; Streeck 2011, 2013).[2]
To a certain extent, the formal continuity of liberal democratic systems fore-
closes discussion of the theme. It is obvious that we should not forget either
that what could called the de-exceptionalization of the "state of exception,"
which marks the evolution of liberal political systems since their own emergence in the nineteenth century and today (Agamben 2003), has reached its
pinnacle, underpinning the strengthening of executives to the detriment of
popular sovereignty and the parliament.

   In this respect, although facing difficulties and shortcomings, Latin America
is the only region in the world that has decisively moved forward recently, contrary to most other global regions, toward building and deepening democracy,
developing what I have called a "molecular democratic revolution." It is true
that a "transformist" project has had great sway over Latin American societies, in particular with neoliberalism in the 1990s and that, economically, the

---

2 Curiously and strangely, in his book about democracy, Tilly (2007) does not in any moment
   refers to twentieth century United States and only rarely and obliquely does so as to Europe,
   often supporting, despite the advances his work represents, a formalist position once the
   liberal-democratic institutions are established.

situation is problematic due to processes of reprimarization or "commodification" that reiterate, even in the case of industrialized Brazil, its peripheral or
semiperipheral vocation. It is also true that, overall, the strengthening of the
executive happens in the region.

However, a project of greater "social cohesion" is visible, to a greater or
lesser extent, in most Latin American countries. It has refused the increase
of polarization and differentials of income and wealth, the hallmark of the
contemporary world. This is clear in the case of Brazil, although speaking of a
new middle class, defined according to income only, does not make sense. In
reality, in any case, a general increase of acquisitive power and of social mobility has been going on. This has led to some extent to what may be a new wave
of mobilization, which has started with huge demonstrations in 2013, with a
demand of universal social rights (Domingues 2008; 2015, Chap. 5). This does
not mean that the politico-administrative systems of domination – sovereignty and governmentality – are not powerful in these countries and that their
control by the citizenry has become less important than elsewhere. We should
not forget the Weberian, and also Foucaultian, lessons about domination, even
the rational-legal one that today has the imprint of more or less democratic
elements in the design of the political system, as well as sometimes with good
social-civilizatory intentions.

Where has been so-called critical theory on the face of it all? Adrift, at best.
The critical theory of Marx centered on a discussion of liberal modernity, its
first phase; with Adorno and Horkheimer, as well as Habermas and other members of the so-called Frankfurt School, on the second phase, state organized
originally, in this case mainly on a philosophical level. This was somehow
reproduced elsewhere in the post-colonial or peripheral world more generally through national liberation movements and nationalist and affirmative
projects of various kinds, often harking back to the nineteenth century (Debés
Valdés 2012). Vis-à-vis the third phase, which unfolds brutally and rapidly before our eyes, it was, at least until very recently, with Habermas' intervention
on a more political level, silent and aloof, or at least awkward and self-centered.
In contrast, the expectations and behavior of citizens and semi-citizens in this
changed world are of deep disquiet and rejection of such models of economic,
political and cultural domination, although they face difficulties to translate
this outlook programmatically and into formal political systems. We often
find unruly or at least restless populations, not prone to deference (which, it
is worth noting, not always finds virtuous practices, especially when democracy and well-being are denied to them, sometimes unravelling in criminality
and blind violence). This is as true of France and Spain as of Egypt and Thai-
land today (Therborn 2009; Pleyers 2010; Castells 2013). Overall, the demand of

equal freedom as to democracy, the rejection of neoliberalism, and the defense of social rights and plural social lifestyles has resumed center stage. Demonstrations, new social movements and uprisings have expressed this across the globe, despite the rise of milder social liberalism and the fact that reactionary right-wing tendencies come up in this context too.

While traditional twentieth century social movements have become weaker, this new situation becomes theoretically plausible once we focus on the destruction of ties of pre-modern personal domination (of which the extinction or radical change of the old peasantry is an expression), by the expansion of capitalism, as well as the generalized reach of the state into society, and the loss of legitimation of social hierarchies all over the world. These populations seem to have at least partly fathomed that the idea of "elites" is merely a justification for a bigger and illegitimate power, as well as curbing the equal freedom that modernity has promised. That is, the mechanisms of disembedding set in motion by the radical modernization of the contemporary world, in multiple directions (with western neoliberalism and a variant of capitalism to be found in particular in East Asia standing out), have been promoting the constitution of a popular subjectivity which, despite the use of several models of "governmentality" (implying subjectivization and control), is socially much freer than at any other moment since the beginning of the Neolithic revolution and the fixation of nomadic groups through agriculture. What is left of control are the tough restrictions to global immigration. Nevertheless, this is often a disorganized mass, whose political mobilization and horizons of change are frequently short, without well-defined projects. Hence, some are willing to talk about the "multitude" (Hardt and Negri 2000) with a positive sign, overlooking, however, the serious shortcomings that underlie its movement. In this regard, also Latin America has been at variance with much of the world, since its social movements have been pivotal for democratizing changes, recent events in Brazil perhaps pointing in a distinct direction, though (Domingues 2008, Chaps. 1, 3; 2015). In fact, account taken of the restrictions to participation and the lack of adequate answers to their demands, it is possible to expect even a toughening of the forms of rebellion that marked the closing of the political space in Europe and elsewhere (Tilly 2004, 27–28), with the present decay of democratic practices by the state.

It is important to note that the systems and projects of domination that characterize the first and second phases of modernity to large extent hinged on attempts at homogenization of social life. This happened through the generalization of the market, through citizenship, in its several dimensions, through nationalism, through mass production and consumption (especially in the Fordist era). In the same sense, the projects of emancipation were launched through the homogenization of classes – especially the working class, but sometimes also the peasantry – as agents of change, through the demand of shared citizenship status in social democracy, through a certain emphasis on freedom and the defensive and emancipatory nationalisms of the periphery. Admittedly, a certain level of social pluralism and of projects always subsisted within these proposals, which, moreover, when victorious, could not be thoroughly implemented, above all due to the resistance of society itself. All the critique of Adorno and Horkheimer (1944–1945) as well as of their intellectual offspring, centered on the violent homogenization promoted by the "Enlightenment," was rooted precisely in those tendencies and modernizing moves. They understood this through a philosophical reading of history that denounced its "logocentrism," which reached its apex with the final solution of the elimination of the irreducible particularity (*Besonderheit*) of the Jew by Nazism. Yet, heterogeneity is no longer scary. If it cannot be controlled, in fact it underpins now new projects of domination, segmentation, exclusion and co-optation, by the market, politics and social policy, which we can see as a new phase of modern civilization (Cohn 2003). It can certainly come along with demands of homogenization, as in the populist racism drawn upon by the European extreme-right and now also center-right ruling circles, as well as in the US evangelical right, constituting modernizing moves that contain contradictory tendencies and elements, all articulated, however, so as to reinforce or resume the vigor of state systems of domination that would allow for a new sustained offensive of the ruling groups of Europe and the US on the face of an economic crisis whose overcoming has been difficult.

This is true too in what concerns, for instance, India and China, with fast developments of capitalism, increasing inequalities (notwithstanding the overall decrease of poverty), overarching and very exclusivist nationalisms, the fragmentation of the market, the destruction of nature and the entrenchment of the rich not only as rich, but also of a middle class that moved apart from the poor and lives now the dream of boundless consumerism. The latter is one of the crucial elements of its differentiation, alongside other mechanisms that characterize lifestyles, which have fault lines in dwelling places, habits, attitudes, vis-à-vis the mass of workers and even the lower layers of the middle classes, defeated and connected to services and social rights. Indifference, such as in China, or spite, as in India, for democracy – which is, however, in this last country enthusiastically celebrated by the popular classes and the subaltern castes – completes the framework for the insertion of such middle classes within their countries. This depiction points to the third phase of modernity, cut across by heterogeneity, polarization, market nixes and threats or blockages to democracy (Abaza 2006; Lange and Meier 2009; Domingues 2012).

As already noted, although Latin America partakes in many of these character-istics, it has moved in the last years in the opposite direction. To which extent this is sustainable in the long run is a question that only the future shall answer.

In this regard, it is understandable that the "autonomism" that has affected some Latin American social movements for a good while has led to impasses (Svampa 2008), although their resistance to bend to sometimes authoritarian tendencies even within the left and center of the left is understandable. We need also to question Chatterjee's (1993, 2004) theoretical views, elsewhere in the world, which in principle identifies, indeed celebrates, "political society," which would exist besides law, declining from a demand of rights, and opposed, according to him, to the "civil society" of the middle classes, a line of argument that ends up commending the idea of an autonomous "moral community." To-day this has very little effect on systems of domination that are well pleased to maintain society divided in watertight compartments, insofar as the so-called "excluded," the new "dangerous classes," are under control. On the contrary, for present-day systems of domination such arrangements can be highly favor-able, moving away from any universalist principle of social cohesion, which demands a broader solidarity, as well as several levels of individual and col-lective subjectivity, which cannot stop at the level of micro-mobilizations. It is necessary to avoid the paroquialism of mobilizations which do not go beyond the local level, which are by the way typical of mobilizations carried out un-der more radically authoritarian regimes (Tilly 2004: 30) – making no sense to reproduce such a strategy in particular when there is greater room for par-ticipation, even though democracy may be limited. It is difficult to predict the sustainability of this mode of capitalist development, with markets relatively shrunk by design, especially inasmuch as a crisis of overaccumulation and overproduction charges the horizon, what becomes graver due to the fact that China is an industrial export juggernaut whose internal consumption is, how-ever, rather restricted (its rate of savings remaining very high) (Brenner 2006; Ho-fung 2008).

More interesting, however, is – at the same time that we emphasize emancipatory potentials, at this point expressed in a still defensive way in the West – to draw attention to the issue of real citizenship, in what it is distin-guished from the formal citizenship extant in many countries, in the material and symbolic aspects. It is not a matter of denouncing that actually unequal so-cial agents, in terms of class, gender and other structures, underlie the exercise of such citizenship. This is absolutely true, but I would like to underline that the very exercise of citizenship is threatened by the deepening of social frac-tures and the piecemeal destruction of the common status of citizen. This was the historical achievement of social democracy especially in Europe, which was reproduced in the US by possibilities of social ascension and market inclusion which no longer exist. After all, since this has been a crucial theme for political theory since Aristotle, we must not forget who, concretely, is the citizen, how he or she can exercise its citizenship, with which reach (Dun 1979). Even in Latin America, which present telos is of advancements, we may easily lose the momentum that pushes in this direction, floundering or stopping half-way in the process of democratization that has been unfolding in the last decades. It is also important to think how different countries are placed in the global system today, for which, even though in need of important revisions, the par excellence Latin American critical theory, the structuralism of the Economic Commission for Latin America (ECLA) of the United Nations (UN) and some versions of the theory of dependency, remain a source of inspiration and analysis (Domingues 2008, Chap. 2). This affects all dimensions of social life, to start with by the issue of global justice, from a collective standpoint.

Can we move further than that at present, beyond the imaginary and the institutions of modernity, but also beyond rhetoric? "Trend-concepts" (see the second chapter of this book), for the diagnosis of the times as well as for the identification of possibilities of development beyond modernity – the "real movement of things" as it was once referred to, have always been a staple of critical theory. But such efforts were simply abandoned in favor of a reading of history that places too much stress on contingency, with few exceptions (such as Habermas' former theorizing of new plural social movements, or those which point to that unspecific encompassing agent, the "multitude," as the great emancipator of the post-modern age). This is not at all clear right now, and probably the level of complexity of social life has foreclosed absolutist and excessively generalized statements about agents of emancipation, let alone abstractly globalized affirmations about such far-reaching historical trends (though the power of corporations seems increasingly pervasive and scary, not emancipatory at all). Moving away from certainty, its underlying sociological and epistemological underpins, was indeed necessary. Perhaps, however, we need to resume this more systematically, even if necessarily in more a modest (and not necessarily optimistic) frame of mind. Of course, sociology can and must play a crucial role in this.

Renewing Critique

The multidisciplinary project of Adorno's and Horkheimer's Frankfurt Institute for Social Research continues to offer an interesting model to follow. A general theory of modernity cannot but demand a joint and multidisciplinary effort.

Moreover, the gamut of problems that requires attention of what would be critical perspectives, necessarily plural, is very large and carries on widening. I would like to suggest, however, that, in order to understand this contemporary social universe, there is nothing better than sociology, a discipline whose identity seems to wither away, torn by the colonization of its field by neighboring or adversarial disciplines. It is not a matter of demanding purity of sociology, of course, instead of stressing the analytical legacy of the sociological tradition, in relation to the imaginary, to social practices and institutions. It is to a good extent upon this that I believe it is possible and necessary to search once again for an ecumenical and vital critical theory. It does not have in the restless populations of the planet its object, subject or destination, but rather finds in the broad and decentered collective subjectivity which is critical in actual social life the agents with which it must be capable of dialoguing and whose ways, in its multiple and manifold directions, it can analyze, discuss, criticize, without a claim to superiority, but without uneasily feeling smaller just because it restricts itself to the intellectual practice that constitutes its own continent.

Getting rid of awkward questions, of free thinking, not immediately practical, has in addition been the consistent project of the ruling collectivities of the third phase of modernity. There is no reason to compromise with that. On the other hand, the specific forms that modernity and, within it, systems of domination take on today contaminate all spheres of social life, wherever in the planet, something that requires special attention. It is therefore necessary to move from philosophy, without leaving it aside, overcoming themes and concepts of the critical tradition, recovering others and extracting from them all that remains of their "rational kernel," seriously discard provincialism and the exclusive concentration on a single country (usually that of the author him or herself), trying thus to systematically outline the specific elements of what I have called the third phase of modernity. Sociology, both professionally and publicly (Burawoy 2005), can critically investigate and bring into the open the impasses, iniquities, injustices and possibilities of this social universe. This is necessary whether we use this concept or any other that grasps the far-reaching changes that cut across the contemporary world, its systems of domination as well as emancipatory aspirations and practices, whose core, as argued above, remains equal freedom as an orienting value. Critical theory, despite the historical troubles it has faced and faces at present, can and must renew itself in order to cope with the greatness and misery of contemporary modernity, contributing to its discovery of the alleyways of progressive social change.

CHAPTER 2

Global Modernity: Levels of Analysis and Conceptual Strategies

Introduction

Modernity has time and again been reinstated as a field of debate. This is especially true in sociology, which emerged as a discipline that tried, from different perspectives, to theorize it. It has become clearly global as the focus of analysis has moved from its "cages" in the nation-state more directly to the world level, although this has happened indeed through mechanisms that are connected to states and control of borders. Post-colonialism has been added, in particular in the humanities, to the interpretation of modernity, but has not been able to influence sociology very deeply.[1] More generally, the demise of different forms of modernization theory and Marxism as an overall developmental narrative, despite a seeming comeback in the wake of the debacle of "real socialism" at the beginning of the 1990s, has basically left contingency as a way of thinking about modernity. This was true even of approaches that emerged with the so-called "syntheses" of the 1970s–1980s, which, in the case of Giddens and neo-functionalists in general sociological theory, as well as in much of renewed historical sociology, as in Mann's and Gellner's case (as well as Giddens' too), had already incorporated contingency in their theoretical underpinnings. The rejection of evolutionary theory and the recovery of history were central to their approaches. The exceptions to this were the theories of Habermas and Luhmann. While the former has indeed reached an impasse, the latter's conceptual framework combined a unilinear view of modernization with a stress

---

* Originally published in *Social Science Information*, vol. 53 (2014), this article was developed within the framework of a research stay as part of the Tramod Project, University of Barcelona, coordinated by Peter Wagner. I would like to thank both him and Kathya Araújo for their comments on a previous version of the manuscript.

1 Efforts have been sometimes made to show how post-colonial thinking could be applied to sociology, most recently by Go (2012). But this is hardly ever achieved, other than using it to rethink identity and discourse as such; sociological concepts are barely touched directly by such strategies, while sociology has only slowly opened itself to the study of colonial situations and global power relations (although Marxism and world-system theories never lost sight of such issues).

on contingency.[2] The "multiple modernities" approach, which appeared as a way out of such impasses, is more dubious in this respect, since it suggests some master-trends emanating from the West, but underlines diversity, basically concentrating on cultural processes (Eisenstadt 2001).

More recently, Marxism has enjoyed a comeback in relation to the crisis of capitalism, for which Marx's and subsequent theoreticians' investigations in the dynamic of capital offer by far the most consistent instruments of analysis (with a stress on global capital accumulation and generalized "commodification," as in Harvey 2003). Modernization theory has had a few followers who have tried to revive it (such as Schmidt 2007, 2009, who stresses "differentiation" – with discussions of individualization more diffusely sharing in its outlook), but its more ambitious overall concepts seem difficult to defend, at least in their original form, at either a more abstract or a more concrete level. Thus, the processes that were originally identified by classical sociology, in which we should by now include Parsons' work, lost much of their power. Yet, they have not been replaced by more far-reaching concepts to interpret the development of modernity, especially when it comes to its historical unfolding. Some of them were found wanting more recently also in the West, which has become even more dramatic as those classical concepts were applied outside their social and intellectual cradle to societies in other regions and with different trajectories.

This to some extent vindicates the post-colonial claim and suggests the need for a fresh look into modernization processes across the globe and even the call for new "epistemologies" (without it really ever being specified what this is supposed to mean). But it should not lead us to overlook the fact that many outside the West have long been engaged in such attempts at conceptual revision and adjustment – although their research results have rarely been cast in terms of general theoretical statements. Furthermore, poststructuralist strategies are hardly conducive to achieving this goal. Such a reconstruction of epistemologies, which relies on a proper balance between description, empirical generalizations and analytical categories, should allow us to move beyond the binaries that too often have plagued sociological theory and other approaches to the study of society, especially through the contraposition between the West and the "rest" ("backward," "traditional," etc.) (Patel 2006). The specific, concrete but connected ways through which modernity has developed are what must be focused upon, although its origins in the West should not be disregarded.

---

2 See Domingues (2000a, Chap. 4) for a detailed analysis of these debates and different schools.

In this light, the present article reviews some of the main concepts and strategies of sociological theory vis-à-vis the theory of modernity. It does not, however, recapitulate all possible approaches, a task that has already been carried out in the innumerable overviews of the topic, often in the form of textbooks, which are widely available. I merely want to bring out some central trends and concepts according to the different *methodological* strategies and levels we can call upon and focus on long-term modernizing trends. This has been a much rarer endeavor.

The first section of the article concentrates on the different possibilities of theoretical interpretation we have at our disposal. The first of these is framed by the description of social processes and aspects of modern social life at different stages, although here an initial demand, sometimes sub-repetitious, sometimes more systematic, for conceptual sketches of developmental trends in modernity can be spotted. This includes exercises in comparative historical sociology. As we see later on, these may or may not try to bring out more general trends in modernization processes, stressing them sometimes, being designed to unearth them or looking for answers to more specific questions. The second strategy is placed at a more general theoretical level. This sort of concept can be more static or more oriented to defining developmental tendencies within modernity, which as such characterize it. Trend-concepts can be included here. Finally, two even more general conceptual strategies can be defined. The first one deals with concepts, or systems of concepts, that pertain to all social formations. A second one relates to general patterns of historical development, whether or not we attribute evolutionary characteristics to them.

The second part of the article moves to deepen our understanding of the strategy of description and analytical construction of trend-concepts, which used to be key elements of the theories of modernity. After establishing the main components, this section tries to raise the question of whether such concepts may be defensible in light of both theoretical and empirical advances achieved in the most recent decades. The theory of collective subjectivity is mobilized to help with this task in order to allow us to go beyond structural explanation without collapsing it into interpretations exclusively based on individual agency, especially with respect to historical developments, which are moreover often long run. This is accomplished by revisiting the concept of secularization. A brief overview of problems and challenges, as well as discussion of some further specific theoretical problems, closes the article.

The goal is to inquire into the possibilities for reconstructing sociological theory, taking into account the criticisms of its master frames in the 20th century, but to some extent summing up the main conceptual elements which allowed for a more general understanding of contemporary social life. The aim is therefore one of clarification. I stop short of a precise answer, remaining satisfied with posing the problems and opening up the imagination to further interrogations of such issues.

Levels of Analysis

In this section I set out to define what would be the usual levels of analysis in the social sciences, especially in sociology, although most authors rarely make this explicit (often they do not even have this idea themselves). This is necessarily a reconstructive approximation in terms of actual methodological approaches, insofar as in practice these levels usually appear entangled and in an a-systematic manner. Defining them, though, will help us understand better both what we are doing and what are the tasks of a renewed theory of modernity. Such a division is in some measure merely analytical, since, in many cases, elements of these distinct strategies are found elsewhere, and insofar as the identification of "facts" and descriptions always – but only to some extent and often in an unspecified way, close to common sense – rely on some theoretical background. This was correctly identified by Parsons (1937, 16ff, 28ff) but was understood by him in an almost normative perspective, which claims an inevitable and positive role for theory, with "description," on the other hand, bereft of a proper definition (merely supposedly reproducing what Newtonian physics did).[3] "Residual categories," i.e. concepts that appear to deal with unavoidable empirical issues, without proper elaboration, usually turn up, he argued also, even when conceptual frameworks are systematically pursued. In other words, analytical concepts (of both the middle range and at a very general level, as we see below) are usually present in descriptions, the empirical, concretely-oriented definition of processes and situations, but this does not mean that they are theoretically constructed: this is a task of science, of sociological theory and related disciplines, whereby we move beyond common sense and even beyond several sorts of obstacles to a deeper knowledge of social life.

---

3   In literary theory, where in fact we can probably find a more productive approach for a socio-scientific understanding of the term, description, as a mode of discourse, has usually been opposed to narrative, in that it is detailed and involves no action. But this is most likely an erroneous polarization, since they are in practice largely entwined. See Ronen (1997), for a basic discussion which I do not pursue here. That entwinement is usually found in sociology, at least as moments in the study of social phenomena, except in radical structuralist approaches to social life.

Descriptions

The first level of analysis would therefore be straightforwardly descriptive, often within an encompassing narrative (thereby combining identification of the properties of concrete social objects with the movement that involves them, whether self-produced or externally driven). Aiming at the characterization and particularization of specific social situations, such descriptions imply an interpretation of social tendencies, institutions, practices, hermeneutic frameworks, looked at from an empirical standpoint – although this can be carried out within a broader or narrower (or even reductive) perspective. In other words, they rely on interpretations that entail a *selection* of relevant information and social processes – and may be more "positivist" (empiricist) or theoretically-oriented, hermeneutically flavored or especially quantitative. They are usually infused with a larger or smaller number of systematic analytical concepts, with varying levels of generality, often alongside a large number of common-sense or at least unspecified descriptive concepts.

Take for instance Harvey's (1990) discussion of the so-called regime of "flexible accumulation," which is supposed to have succeeded Fordism in the late 1980s, especially in the United States. Postmodernism as a concept geared to the understanding of the slow demise of Western modernity and its sense of ethics and future, in Bell's (1978) or Jameson's (1991) case, respectively, is another example. These are descriptive sociological accounts which depict a given state of affairs, as well as to some extent conveying also a sense of history and development, almost inevitable in sociological discussions, with many implicit presuppositions, including some related to historical developmental tendencies. In all these instances, a specific theoretical background is present and more or less specific concepts are introduced. These are capitalism (its expansion) and space-time compression, Fordism and post-Fordism, in Harvey's case, which imply a more general Marxist theoretical scheme, with explicit, respectively, Weberian and Marxist resonances in Bell's and Jameson's cases. Beck's (1986) periodization, in which the second of the two modernities he defines is said to be "reflexive," emphasizes the trends toward a global risk society wherein individualization is far-reaching, while Wagner (1994) identifies three phases of modernity with a more contingent sort of development. The latter's specific periods are grasped, however, through very general categories, such as, among others, liberty and discipline, with explanations articulated with a more concretely-oriented scope. In other cases this is very limited, and analytical concepts appear with less intensity and play a minor role. Much of what Mann (2013, 5) says about "globalization" applies very often to specific or general discussions of modernity, since most authors in both cases tend to "describe rather than explain" such phenomena, a charge that, moreover, can

possibly be levelled against Mann himself. There are certainly other, more systematic analytical efforts which evade this fate, such as Sassen's (2007) "scalar"
global sociology, including its identification of trends toward the denational-
ization of the nation-state.

The same sort of issue turns up in historical sociology. Take for instance
Weber's (1904b) discussion of the Protestant ethic and the spirit of capitalism.
While dealing specifically with a "historical individuality" (the ideal-type – see
below – of capitalism), his general discussion was framed within a broader
comparative picture, including what he considered to be the other main world
religions, implying a large number of general categories (such as "in-worldly
asceticism"). Other authors stopped at lower levels of generality. This is the
case of Moore's (1967) and Bendix's (1978, 1964) passages to modernity, with
their agents and alliances, authoritarian state structures and citizenship; Tilly's
(1992) formation of modern states through the workings of "capital" and "coercion"; and Wallerstein's (1974, 1980, 1989) account of capitalism and the state
in the early modern age, and its unfolding. If Weber looked for general tendencies (i.e. "rationalization") and sought explanations for them, others have
pursued more limited descriptions of processes of modernization and also
more restricted explanations for them. In any case, "concomitant variations,"
to use Durkheim's (1897) language, were a key methodological instrument
in all these cases, whether explicitly or not, comparisons spanning centuries
and regions in some cases, remaining at a more circumscribed level in others.
All of the above examples are related to very sophisticated theory-conscious
authors. As observed in relation to formerly presented cases, much less subtle
and conceptually-oriented discussions can be found elsewhere, despite the
wealth of empirical information some studies are able to provide.

Middle-range Analytical Concepts

We reach a higher level of analytical construction – still limited, however, to
certain specific social formations – by means of concepts which are intended
to be themselves the key element in an explanatory framework. The example of
the concept of "disembedding mechanisms," in Giddens' (1990) phrasing, can
be suggested as an instructive one, resumed from the work of Marx, Simmel
and Lerner, among others. In fact, when used to explain the development of
modernity, it permits an explanation of why identities are suppler in modernity, why life changes so quickly within it, and so on. In Lerner's (1958) case,
through an implicit comparison between the West and a modernizing Middle
East, such a concept assumes application to a comparative, if over-determined,
case (as usually happens with 1950s–1960s modernization theory). "Plus-value"
is another. In fact most of the concepts Marx (1867) proposed in *Capital* could

be deemed analytical, operating at a specific historical level. His political economy of capitalism is within the middle range still the most powerful and systematic social science analytical construction, including a great number of other, more general concepts that are not elaborated and spelled out.

More generally, this would be the case for most of the concepts Merton (1968, Chap. 2) introduced as "middle range" (hence the title of this subsection), except certainly his discussion of "manifest" and "latent" functions (Merton 1968, Chap. 3). His study of legitimate ends that are often achieved through illegitimate means is an instance of middle-range analytical concepts applied to specific social realities (Merton 1968, Chaps. 6–7, although the theme of "anomie" and "strains" is very general). They are analytical, refer to specific phenomena, but they aim at explaining them alone, without further ambition, which Merton in fact at least rhetorically refused, since general theory, to his thinking, should be built as a result of more circumscribed conceptual constructions and accumulation.

A further complication is raised by historical concepts proper. Weber's (1921–22, 130ff; 1920b, d) forms of "domination," political or otherwise, as well as relations to the world such as they are found in world religions ("this-worldly" or "other-worldly," ascetic or not) classically exemplify such an issue. They are so to speak *transhistorical*, that is, they are concepts crafted to apply to all historical societies but do not refer to social structures and action *tout court*. This is, however, the case of the Marxian notion of "relations of production," "productive forces" and "mode of production" (Marx 1859). Perhaps, although crafted originally to tackle the development of modernity, this could be the case also of the relation between "civilization" and "region" (Knöbl 2007). In Weber's case, such concepts appear as *ideal-types* (the construction of concepts through the exaggeration of features of empirical instances), and, in Marx's case, as *analytical categories* (concepts which aim at breaking concrete reality down into discrete elements and mentally reconstructing it). But with this step we approach already what would be the core of this article, that is, the crafting and role of concepts which, within modernity, offer a generalization of developmental tendencies at a level higher than that supposed by mere idealtypical constructions.

Such developmental tendencies are writ large in many approaches to social, and especially sociological, theory. Their understanding has ranged from modernization theory and its forebears in Durkheim and Parsons, with afterthoughts in Luhmannian theory, to Marxism, with Habermas offering a strong late version of such a perspective, which can, disclaimers notwithstanding, be read also within Weberian (to start with his own) and even Tocquevillian perspectives. Many concepts have covered developmental tendencies, among which "differentiation" and "integration" on the one hand, and "rationalization," "universalization" and "individualization" on the other, are outstanding. Such concepts further include the development of capitalism and "commodification" (also of labor power), as well as "reification," "democratization," "secularization," "bureaucratization," and so on. The status of these concepts is hard to define, since they may be overtly descriptive, mere empirical generalizations at best, that is, processes that repeat themselves in different space-time coordinates (such as in Collins 1995, Chap. 5), or ideal-typical. Or they may in principle assume an analytical role in a systematic theory of modernity, or be historical or evolutionary, with some attributing or critically identifying underlying law-like perspectives behind them (Boudon 1984, Chap. 3). They may depict and explain regular processes, but on the other hand they are in need of being explained.[4] Their analytical status would depend on a passage from empirical generalizations to analytical categories, which would imply a very subtle operation, usually left undefined in the social sciences, what, for instance, Piaget and García (1983) have called "reflective abstraction," whereby content is preserved but condensed in a category rather than in a description (see Domingues 2000a, Chap. 3, for further discussion). In the next section, I take one specific example in order to enquire into their validity, especially in relation to the development of a renewed theory of modernity.

General Analytical Concepts

General analytical categories have perhaps been the sort of concept whose methodological aspects have been most discussed in the social sciences, since those who work at this level are usually very interested in such issues. They may refer to the basic characteristics of historical processes, but have been proposed in sociology especially in relation to the structure-action debate.[5] Classically this appeared as opposing individual actors capable of causal impact on passive social collectivities (systems or structures). Interaction and collectivities *qua* causal agents, however undefined their status has often remained, have nevertheless seeped through this initial polarization, which is in any case time

---

4 Martuccelli (2010) descriptively defines, in a conscious methodological move, "singulariza-tion" as a contemporary trend of modernity. He uses, in an ideal-type construction, the con-cept of "challenge" (*épreuve*) in order to understand it. Whether this qualifies as a specific tendency within modernity begs the question, though.

5 There are so many revisions of this debate that it would be tiresome to present it here. I shall rest content with introducing only Domingues (1995a, 2000a) as reviews of the endless, and by now tedious, action-structure controversy. The notion of "collective subjectivity" was introduced in these books as a way out of the impasses of the discussion. I draw upon this concept in what follows.

and again reinstated, since it is a powerful element in the presuppositional mode of modern thought by and large (in daily life and in the social sciences) since the Enlightenment and the Romantic movement. In other words, this sociological debate refers directly to the overall polarization between the individual and society that deeply marks modern thought, reappearing in the guise of so-called individualism (or action-oriented approaches) and collectivism (or "holism," structuralism, functionalism). Such concepts, elaborated or not, controlled or uncontrolled, are inevitably present in any social-scientific endeavor. They lend support to the more concrete descriptions and explanations of what happens in social life. At least since Parsons (1937, 1951) they have been the focus of general ("meta") sociological theory. I do not dwell on them here, since they have frequently been in the limelight, but instead I expand on the concepts of *collective subjectivity* and *social creativity* as a particular way of dealing with this issue, also within a theory of modernity, when I deepen my discussion of trend-concepts.

Should we include general evolutionary or historical categories in the general analytical concepts category? That is, phenomena such as the mechanisms which relate the "forces of production" to "relations of production" and their shift toward more advanced "modes of production" in Marx (1859), or such as Habermas' (1976, 1981) two logics of evolution, "cognitive" and "moral" rationalization? Probably yes, of course, however, only insofar as we believe that this sort of general theory makes sense, which today seems more doubtful, although it is easier to make a good case for milder versions of multilinear evolutionary theory (Sahlins 1960).

A Trend-concept: Secularization

We find, thus, that most of what has been written about modernity is by and large descriptive, although this includes a variable number of analytical concepts and explanatory principles, sometimes even underlying evolutionary assumptions and the identification of developmental tendencies. Trend-concepts have been largely absent lately, bar perhaps the expansive force of capitalism in Marxist theories and "rationalization" in Frankfurtian critical theory, while most other such perspectives have been discredited to such an extent that basically they have been simply abandoned without further debate (see Knöbl, 2001, for a far-reaching discussion of these issues, especially regarding the concept of "differentiation"). To some extent an exception has been secularization theory, in relation to which a true battle was waged in the last decades and which, despite very heavy criticism deriving from a theoretical arsenal and from considerable empirical information, refuses simply to die. It will be instructive to consider it here, after which we return to a consideration of trend-concepts as such.

Many would argue that secularization theory began in sociology with Weber's (1904b; 1919) work on the Protestant ethic. We do not need to enter this discussion here. Suffice it to say that this was the prevailing mood in which it was received and read, especially in US sociology. From then on, a large body of literature developed, mainly in the United States and the United Kingdom, in which the thesis that religion would lose importance in social life, which would become "secularized," was overwhelming, and supposedly constituted a theory. At best, religion would be relegated to the recesses of private life. The explanation for this was based on rationalization and disenchantment, on the differentiation of spheres and the impossibility of maintaining such a unified worldview vis-à-vis pluralism and the scientific mind, or rationalization, more generically. Religious dogma had no place in the modern world. Empirical evidence seemed to back this position, especially coming from Europe, where the level of religious attachment was continuously decreasing. Anti-clericalism had often been strong, people were becoming atheists, religion had no grip on public life, so went the thesis. The US presented problematic evidence, the rest of the world even more so, with religious affiliation and the public role of religion remaining high, but, given time, so went the argument, all places would eventually secularize.[6]

Did this happen? For the increasingly vocal dissenters from the theory, the answer was a resounding "no." They pointed exactly to those elements that secularization theorists purportedly solved with the help of delayed time. The US, the core of the West, was visibly very religious, and the world in general even more so. Bearing that in mind, what was the trend to be discerned? None, and certainly not secularization. The consequence is that there was a tendency for the theory to be simply discarded. Yet, some recent authors have also been more vocal about their doubts. Should the trends discerned by modernization theory be merely rejected due to empirical evidence or did its authors have a point after all? Thus theorists such as Casanova (1994, 2011, 2012) started revising the theory and disentangling its elements, that is, breaking it down into its components. Casanova, for instance, is very clear that the differentiation of spheres brought about by modernity did make religion lose overall influence – although he came to see this as more contingently realized than as a simple teleological and uniform process, contrary to what orthodox sociology would

---

6   See Martin (1978), Hadden (1987) and Bruce (1996) for just a few examples of the different and opposed positions.

suggest. But he is not comfortable with the idea that there is a general decline in religious beliefs and practices, or with the thesis that there has been an overall privatization of religion. While retaining the first meaning of secularization is important for Casanova, since it points to empirically verifiable elements across Western societies, the latter two are true only in parts of Europe, namely, where the Church was clearly and openly associated with reactionary forces, this in turn engendering strong anti-religious movements and the decline of faith, as well as decreasing relevance of religion in the public sphere. This should not lead us to think that there have been no changes in religious beliefs insofar as, following Taylor (2007; see also Joas 2012), it can be said that a distinctive feature of modernity is turning to religion as one option among others, which then ceases being mandatory.

If this is the case in the West, in other areas of the world the issue is even more compounded. In Latin America, Africa and Asia, religion continues to be an important force, although (despite a recent religious revival) it has declined in China, a society whose intellectuals were in any case particularly detached from strong religious beliefs, especially when they embraced Confucianism, on top of having carried out a radically antireligious revolution (Weber 1920c; Madsen 2010). Overall, however, except for large numbers of Muslim countries, the differentiation between the polity and religion has been accomplished almost everywhere, although in fact the secularization of the state has taken very different forms, even in the West (Stepan 2009).

In India, this has yielded a controversy that pitted secularists and anti-secularists against each other. A number of intellectuals supported strong secularizing policies by the state and a broader laicization of Indian society, in a radical Enlightenment direction, in order also to guarantee social peace in the face of an increasingly violent Hindu nationalist and exclusivist position (Hindutva) (Nanda 2004; Vanaik 1997). Others argued in favor of what they saw as an Indic tradition, according to which the state should support all religious currents (Nandy 1990, 1985; Madan 1987 – although he later changed his position, moving against religion in Madan 1997). Religious strife was supposed to develop at least in part out of religious people's anguish vis-à-vis attacks on religion. The state should therefore eschew secularism (which is, however, inscribed in the Indian constitution). In fact, the Indian state controls religious institutions and has mixed Western secular tradition with Indic support to all religions. This was a project of the Occidentalizing position supported by Nehru, as well as Gandhi's accommodating perspective, closer to the Indic heritage. It was a conscious cultural-political choice of the leadership of the independence movement, not an automatic development of modernization, entailing a sort of hybridization of civilizational principles (against the creeping radical, homogenizing and authoritarian Occidentalism of the Hindu religious right that has vied to capture the state only for Hindus, against Muslims and Sikhs in particular). India remains a deeply religious country, yet atheism and agnosticism are now wholly valid individual options, whereas the public power of religion has become a contested issue (Domingues 2012, 113–116).

Thus far, albeit conceptually informed, my presentation of religion in contemporary modernity has been mainly descriptive. Now we must pause to consider the theoretical implications of this discussion. In most accounts of secularization, in a move which is typical of modernization theory but which we can find also within Marxist-based accounts, such modernization trends have been presented as resting on automatic, actually functional processes. There is often no causality in this sort of account. Society or the species evolves and this leads to differentiation, complexification, at best differentiation in one sphere implying and reinforcing processes of differentiation in other spheres, as if a neat fit between them was sought by society, or the species, as functional adaptive mechanisms. This seems to be true even of Weberian accounts of this sort of process. In part the reason is clear. Since causality has been attributed to individual actors alone, with at most unintentional consequences of action being accepted as an explanatory mechanism, we are left out in the cold as to macro causal-explanatory variables, which must be at best statistically collected. Further "integration" receives the same sort of treatment: it seems simply to happen.

Yet these are not automatic processes, and must not be reified. They come about only through the *movement* (in the Aristotelian sense of producing change or reiterating stasis) of collective subjectivities, which exert a specific, collective sort of causality. This is not to say that such collectivities should be thought of along the lines of individual actors. They possess different *levels of centering* (based on variable levels of identity and organization), which imply different *levels of intentionality*. A collective subjectivity may be very decentered, and its elements (individuals and sub-collectivities) may even move in opposite directions. This produces a decentered collective causality, though in other instances, when centering and level of intentionality are high, causality may be very centered. These processes are carried out always in interactive processes, and these moves are always somehow creative, even though they also by and large, to different degrees, reproduce social memories (in the shape of shared hermeneutic frames, institutions, practices, etc.). They have no previously defined telos. In history in general, we should thus speak of *episodic moves*; in modernity they become contingent *modernizing moves*. Secularization is just one case of that. It implies a general trend, but this is not independent of the direction in which collective subjectivities move; the telos of modernity is dependent on the way it is regarded. This is not to say either that there are no processes in this regard that escape the designs of each collectivity and of all of them in the long run. Unintentional consequences of individual action and of collective movement are a permanent feature of social life, creating social memories to which we are inevitably tied at the very beginning of our always-creative endeavors (whatever the degree of novelty they contain, and however much this may be constrained by power and perspectives resistant to social change). Nevertheless, differentiation and integration (plus de-differentiation and fragmentation), as well as the cultural and institutional space for changes in belief and the public roles of religion, stem directly from the collective causality of collective subjectivities (see Domingues 1995a, 2000a, 2008, 2012, for the elaboration of such categories).

We see that, in the West as much as in India, the sorts of institutional differentiation, organization of religious and cultural systems more generally, as well as the goals religious movements set themselves, vary according to what people have in mind, at the same time as they deal with the institutional and cultural (symbolic, hermeneutical) elements already generated by previous modernizing moves. This should help us also to move beyond the Enlightenment supposition of an inevitable push toward secularization, as well as the opposite standpoint, both of which at this stage are obstacles to our understanding of contemporary modernity, whatever our normative preferences.

We could apply this to all other trend-concepts enumerated above. There is secularization as a project and a consequence, but it is contingent on its development and can of course be reversed or take future directions we cannot at all anticipate. The same is true of rationalization, which today is entangled with all sorts of irrationalities, even at the instrumental level, democratization, bureaucratization or capitalist development, individualization and changes in family life, and so on. The modernization of social life would therefore be the outcome of trends brought about by a mix of intentional action and movement with unanticipated outcomes. This, for instance, is what might authorize us to speak, in certainly a more circumscribed way, of a "modern project," as Habermas (1980) did, but especially also of the non-intentional collective causal impacts deriving from it. This is where, on the other hand, Polanyi's (1944) description and explanation of the emergence of capitalism, or the "satanic mill," is both warranted and absurd: while he is correct in identifying a liberal modernizing offensive, which took over the state and from there implanted a society largely based on market mechanisms, he took his argument too far: markets were to a large extent a "spontaneous," that is, a decentered development of social relations, and this is what made it plausible to envisage a market society which could include labor and land as commodities, as Marx (1867) realized. That is what also made it plausible to further it by those modernizing liberal moves. Hence, we have to be careful not to superimpose centered modernizing moves on decentered ones, and vice-versa, since it is from their entanglement but from their differences as well that history unfolds – and has to be explained.

While some trends, such as marketization (commodification), are very strong and others, such as secularization, are more mixed, others still must be seen in a more contradictory light. This is the case for instance with democratization. In modernity it surely has advanced, albeit within the limits offered by state domination and the "crystallization" in it of class and other powerful "external" social forces. Yet this is not absolute, since modernity has lived comfortably with several types of dictatorship and implies also, as Tilly (2007) observed, permanent processes of "de-democratization." Both are to be explained as they shape and are shaped by this civilization (see also Domingues 2012, Part IV).

Trend-concepts may remain as descriptive concepts, underpinned by historical-analytical ones and based on process explanations and more general analytical categories that explain why these tendencies of development have been operative in modernity. As such, trend-concepts imply empirical generalization if we suppose they repeat themselves more or less regularly across countries, regions and periods, partly shaping them. They may be taken also merely as ideal-typical, exaggerated concepts that do not actually correspond to developmental tendencies. But it might be especially productive for sociological theory in particular to rebuild trend-concepts as analytical categories, which could themselves, in their interplay as a system of categories (but surely distant from law-like definitions), explain concrete developments of modernity, in their interrelations. Secularization could work in this direction and so could other trend-concepts, beyond the stage in which, usually teleologically, former theoretical currents tried to deal with them. Even if we eventually decide we had better dismiss them, we still need to return systematically to their evaluation.

The above findings are not likely to solve the theoretical puzzles implied by those modernization trends. But they may help to systematize the queries that can be raised in this regard, and suggest a way to begin dealing with the issue.

Conclusion

What is the purchase of this discussion for a renewed theory of modernity? Despite its recurrent enactment, also found under the name of "capitalism" in Marxist accounts, modern "societies" or civilization are time and again reinstated as an object of study, although at present not much novelty nor many credible alternatives seem to be at stake (Wagner 2012; see, however, Domingues 2012).

Of course, the search for a renewed theory of modernity, the staple of general sociological theory, must at this stage strongly resume a global per-spective, which needs, also obviously, to overcome the stark shortcomings of modernization theory and Marxist accounts, especially insofar as they have had trouble understanding different paths, "trajectories," models, variants or the like. We must recognize the general tendencies of global modernization as well as its specific unfolding in different space-time coordinates. Episodic modernizing moves are operative in both aspects of modernization processes across the globe. The attempt to develop a framework for the interpretation (that is, partly descriptive, but with a clear general theoretical goal) of what may be called the "third phase of global modernity," with its heterogeneity and civilizational hybridization as well as its unity, has been cast exactly bearing this in mind: recourse to history and historical narrative aimed at avoiding the pitfalls of a previously set interpretation, with the support of the apparatus of the theory of collective subjectivity. Such a description/interpretation of modernity relies on a significant number of middle-range analytical catego-ries as well as on more general historical ones (such as complexity, differen-tiation and de-differentiation) (Domingues 2012). Yet, in order to offer a more consistent alternative to mere descriptive accounts of modernity, we need to push further and resume the discussion of more general modernizing trends, which include increased complexification but are by no means exhausted by it. Specific as well as general analytical constructs are necessary to move beyond present shortcomings, and among these we must consider the recon-struction of trend-concepts, in a much more malleable way which has to take into account agency – including surely that of "subaltern" individuals and col-lectivities, alongside that of ruling ones.

Some final words on analytical categories, ideal-types and explanatory mechanisms are in order. It is clear that the theoretical strategy privileged here, in accordance in particular with Marx (1857, 1867) and Parsons (1937, 1951), was analytical and implies the breaking down of social reality and its reconstruc-tion by means of concepts, which try to render it such as it is at the level of thought. This strategy is the opposite of ideal-types, which exaggerate empiri-cal aspects of reality within concepts that are approximate renderings of it. These make full sense only when returned to the analysis of concrete social processes (Weber 1913), although sometimes they operate on a very general level (as to action, quasi-analytically, as empirical generalizations with respect to general historical concepts) as well as in the construction of "historical individualities" vis-à-vis specific phenomena. Yet any analytical pretension was deflected by Weber's neo-Kantian concerns with the limits to a deep conceptual grasp of reality (though I believe ideal-types, by a careful process of reconstruction, can be turned into analytical categories; cf. Domingues 2012). Explanation, as Parsons (1951, 10ff, 727ff) realized, is part and parcel of analytical schemes. But he was so obsessed with the supposed schemes of Newtonian physics that when, inspired by biology, he introduced *mechanisms* to explain social processes, he thought this fell short of proper explanation. In fact, explanation in the social sciences is rarely predictive, and mechanisms must not be opposed to encompassing analytical constructs. Most useful and operative explanatory *causal* schemes in the social sciences are achieved thereby. A reconstructed theory of modernity must not lose sight of that, searching for genetic and on-going causal mechanisms linked to the articulation of general analytical categories which can buttress renewed descriptions and interpretations, as well as standing on its own (see Hedström and Swedberg 1998).

Furthermore, historical sociology has had trouble dealing with agency in systematic terms. Either concepts or structures, or individual actors, furnish the causal explicative elements of modernity; however, the latter are hardly concretely operative, which has led to a lot of ad hoc talk of classes, elites and other collective agents, without proper theoretical underpinnings (see Domingues 2000a, Chap. 4). Authors usually do that in denial or use the terms merely as residual, albeit central, categories – they must be there but have no proper conceptual foundation. Breaking with the polarization of modern thought, collective subjectivity can help us overcome this specific hurdle as well.

The present article has aimed precisely to situate accomplishments and problems, challenges and tasks, for a renewed sociology of modernity (thought of in broad and open disciplinary terms), especially methodologically. This project seems to be in need of further development. Historical sociology, which is highly descriptive, is an important companion to sociological theory, and more generally to social theory, but it does not substitute for theory as such, which needs to be constructed via analytical categories. These can help explain (not only describe) the dynamics of modernity, its genesis and, eventually, its supersession, though creativity and surprise, however these come in, are part of the substance of historical developments. Combining both approaches in a productive manner remains a methodological challenge. To some extent such descriptions, richly informed conceptually, are what really matters for the social sciences, since they refer to actual social life, to the concrete problems people face. It is on this basis that the "diagnosis of the times" – as proposed by critical theory (cf. Habermas 1981, vol. 2, Chap. 8) as well as by other approaches (that is, often liberal, cf. Martuccelli 2010, 26–29) – proceeds, even though it must be attentive to other aspects of social reality, too, at other levels of generality (as I have tried to do with the polarization of modern thought between the individual and society). Contemporary modernity, in its global reach, must thus be a focus for our attention, demanding full mobilization of our social science arsenal.

CHAPTER 3

Existential Social Questions, Developmental Trends and Modernity

The Problem

The goal of this chapter is to return to some of the classical and central themes taken up in the early days of sociology, or by the founding fathers of the discipline before its current state of abandonment. We shall here discuss the developmental trends that, particularly in modernity, drive the multidimensionality of social life. Theoretically these themes remain, or should remain, decisive, insofar as they never cease from the standpoint of social practice. All in all, returning to them will allow us to, in some measure, outline a more complex view of humanity, less ethnocentric, in its directly social aspects and thereby situate more precisely the differential features of modernity as such.

The theme of the *multidimensionality* of social life – or, more technically, of social systems – has time and again surfaced in the social sciences since at least Max Weber's critique of Marxism and its brilliant and unilateral definition of material life as the main causal vector in the unfolding of social relations. However, needless to say, the solutions thus far advanced to this puzzle are hardly adequate. Most attempts, even when suggested in analytical guise, or at least in terms of general conceptualizations, are merely descriptive. When conceptually articulated, the solutions have fallen incredibly short of a proper answer.

To be sure, Alexander (1988, Chap. 1), from a neo-Parsonian perspective, phrased the issue from the standpoint of "action," with its normative and conditional elements, but he did not venture much farther than this, leaving aside social systems and afterward embracing a strong sort of cultural idealism. Mann (1986), in turn, tried his own and innovative solution with his social "networks of power," clearly of Weberian inspiration. Yet the outcome is arguable: Mann slips towards the definition of his concepts, sometimes not consistently, posited as "ideal-types," descriptive and reductive, that is, little theorized and concentrated on the topic of power, which is excessively generalized. There is much musing on the "economy," "politics" (also "polity" or more recently "the political"), "culture" (or "ideology"), etc. (by the way, I have done the same myself, though stressing that it was a provisional solution for a difficult-to-solve

---

* Originally published in *Dados*, vol. 59 (2015).

problem, in Domingues 2008). Otherwise, reference is made to specific systems such as the state, family, religion. By and large it has been a matter of
finding answers located in an excessively concrete plane, also in cases when
supposedly strong theorizations are presented, such as the unified "life-world"
and the self-steered systems of the economy and the polity in Habermas' (1981)
neo-evolutionism.

It is necessary, therefore, to revise the very foundations of this sort of generalizing statement. From the beginning, however, let us note that the risk we
face when embarking in a rejection of general concepts is to fall into crass
nominalism, which would demand very delimited concepts (perhaps derived
from some "thick description" that would exhaust itself in itself), refusing theoretical universalisms, in a variably radical way. This is not my goal here, evidently. If I am searching for an approach and a level of generality that avoids
the hypostatization of concepts in the mold of what I think belong only to
modern civilization, my aim should be to take it to a level of generality that is
at once the presupposition and the outcome of more concrete investigations,
although it is worth our while to emphasize that there is no definite rest for
research and the theoretical results it may produce. An endless to-and-fro is
what we must expect. This implies concepts, at whatever level of generality,
that are always shifting, while, on the other hand, the very definition of what
empirical phenomena are changes too as theory as such changes.

As we shall see, the best solutions, or at least the best ways of posing the
question, are still to be found in the works of Marx and Engels, on the one
hand, and, on the other, of Weber. They still furnish general conceptual clues,
alongside a treasure trove of crucial investigations about the themes I want to
bring up here. These authors outlined the general presuppositions of social
life. While ultimately bonded to a reductionism in which materialism subordi-
nates everything to a relationship to nature that affects first of all the organic
basis of life through labor, they at least pointed out the themes that all individuals and collectivities inevitably have to answer to, without a priori defining
how this answer is articulated in terms of concrete and specific social systems.
In turn Weber (1904a, 45), after criticizing the "brilliant primitive meaning" of
historical materialism (more brilliant than primitive, really, though reductive),
did not explicitly raise that question, but nonetheless provides answers, in several points of his body of work through an extremely sophisticated and varied
analysis of its historical evolution. He sheds light upon the several answers human collectivities furnished to the questions that are inevitably posed to them,
in whatever space-time coordinates (although we must draw attention to the
unifying, and simplifying maneuver, that in the end binds together all the
"spheres" of social life in modernity by means of the concept of instrumental

rationalization – see, especially, Weber 1920a).[1] In contradistinction, the idea of *existential social questions*, articulated analytically and so as to harbor the several historical concrete forms it has assumed, will allow us to treat multidimensionality in an effective, systematic and flexible way.

Not only does this constitute a problem of utmost importance in and of itself, lying at the fundamental core of the social sciences and, even more broadly, the human sciences, an alternative capable of going beyond the usual descriptive and concrete solutions would essentially assist in outlining what could be called historical – and even evolutionary – trends of social life (see Chapter 2 of this book). This move is particularly crucial to reintroduce, in an innovative and relevant way, also from the point of view of possible processes of transformation, the developmental trends that led to modernity and the modernization of the planet. This applies to those that unfold inside it, as well as to those that point to its possible overcoming, without clinging to the concrete social systems most authors in the social sciences focus on, whether or not they are theoreticians. Finally, this process must also be understood in terms of a multidimensionality of trends.

Let us stress that the cross-fertilization I am proposing between existential questions and developmental trends is not at all arbitrary. These questions are answered socially only in specific ways. That is, they depend on how they are articulated in each civilization or "social formation." Nor are they static: their articulation unfolds historically, although in each civilization and social formation they maintain patterns that are reiterated in the long duration of history. This is the case of modernity and it is in relation to it that we will discuss in some detail the issue of concepts capable of identifying and grasping its multiple developmental trends.

Existential Social Questions

One of the key statements by Marx and Engels (1845, 18–36ff) in one of the founding texts of "historical materialism," the collection of unpublished fragments of what, already in several versions, later was assembled as *The German Ideology*, was that human beings need to produce and reproduce their lives as a basic and fundamental task. This meant that two elements took priority in their activities. First, the reproduction of the species was at stake, the

---

1   It does not work either to set "culture" as a unifying principle, as did Parsons (1951, 167–169, *passim*), with a value system that is normatively specified in each subsystem, although some of them can exhibit divergent values and norms.

succession of generations (through sexuality, not directly named in the text), with the transformation of infants into full members of collectivities (another theme left implicit, with the family moreover equivocally universalized as the basis of the reproduction). Secondly, they referred to material production, which transforms nature through labor and allows us to appropriate it, consuming it in order to directly sustain life as well as simultaneously producing the means whereby it is possible to keep production going.[2] More than that, these elements would be ontologically more fundamental than any other activities. They corresponded to the actual emergence of the human species, allowing for the existence, with much greater emphasis given to the transformation of nature as such (mentioned, by the way, as exclusive in the first pages of the manuscript) in the argument of these authors, although they directly say also that these three "sides" (*Seiten*) of social life – or "moments," a word one must grasp in order to understand German philosophers, as they jokingly say – are concretely combined. Our "social being" would be constituted upon these activities rather than "consciousness" (*Bewusstsein*), determining its existence and thus meaning that it is the former that determines the latter. This was nothing more than the conscious being (*bewusst Sein*), according to their wordplay in the German language. This was a seminal intuition, although with strong forerunners in economic and philosophical currents that go from political economy to German idealism.

Given the geniality of the authors, it is to some extent intriguing that they opted for such a reductive view. This is explained by the context of the debate against idealism (although it was reiterated in later writings in an explicit way) and by the intellectual excitement such a "materialist" insight surely provoked in them, opening a whole field of analysis that, in the end, implied class struggle under capitalism. The fact is, however, that they left aside the production of meaning, hermeneutic-symbolic in nature – though they point to the crucial role of language –, and the distribution of power as a trait of the species. Or rather, they treated them, from this moment on as causally derived from "material" processes identified as part of, as Marx (1859) would later say, the "edifice" that grows upon the economic basis (as ideology and state, although power as such appeared in his work more widely, starting with the "basis").

Let us not copy these mistakes, which belong to a time in which the social sciences were just beginning, or in fact were to a large extent being founded by Marx and Engels (as the "science of history," according to Althusser 1965), specifically in those volumes whose publication took place however only later

---

2   A thesis later repeated by Engels (1884, 27) in the book in which he drew upon Marx's notes
    about Morgan's work and in which the family has a central role.

and posthumously. In his "reconstruction of historical materialism," Habermas (1976), among others, drew attention to the theme directly, although his cognitivism and moral solution, as well as dualism, are deficient. But the identification of the questions that pertain precisely to the existence of the human species, through which it is reproduced as a species, is a far-reaching conceptual insight. It is this identification that I want to take up, so as to move forward. This must be done, at this stage of the text and of the history of the social sciences, certainly including, however going beyond, the questions Marx and Engels placed at the core of their materialist conception of history. This leads us to embrace those two other, abovementioned elements, namely, the contriving of webs of meaning and of networks of power, which came to assume pride of place in the social sciences in a systematic way since Weber's work.

The concept of *existential social questions* is introduced here exactly with the purpose of allowing us to take this issue to a higher level of generality, prior conceptually to the concrete definition of the answers to the fundamental requirements of human, ontological existence. In other words, I aim at leaving aside those dimensions of the economy, politics, culture, and so forth, in their concrete facticity, retreating to a level in which more flexible and innovative theorization can be reached.[3] I basically assume, following Marx's and Engels' inspiration, that there are themes human collectivities cannot but confront as a species, however, going beyond production and reproduction, I identify two themes: power and the hermeneutic-symbolic construction of meaning. I want to stress moreover that reproduction must open itself to the question of sexuality, that only after Marx and Engels became more central to social thought (Freud was the major, but by no means the only, thinker preoccupied with sexuality and its scientific expression) and that the production of meaning is intimately linked to the very production of language, although practices are only partly determined by them (if it is legitimate to use the expression "language games" to refer to them, the emphasis must be placed on *games*). The production of meaning weaves an *imaginary*, shifting, "magmatic," such as pointed out by Castoriadis (1975 – see also Domingues 2000a, Chap. 2), that offers thereby a much sharper concept than the usual one of "culture," in its several connotations.[4] Finally, power supposes, in many circumstances, force,

---

3 In a more recent piece, specifically about modernity, Wagner (2008, 4–5) suggested we treat some of its aspects by means of the adoption of the notion of "problematic." As it seems, although this is not totally clear in his argument, he tried to escape from the same sort of problem identified in this text and move perhaps in a similar direction.

4 This includes the relationship between "nature" and "culture," such as formulated in the West, which does not have a correspondence in other civilizations, maybe generically

the capacity of physical coercion or of any other kind, as is well-known at least since Hobbes. However, above all, it refers to the "transformative capacity" of human beings, of bringing about results, individually and collectively, something that may include the capacity to make someone do act according to another agent's will. Power thus goes as far as yielding systems of *domination*, with the unequal distribution, socially, of exercising that capacity (Weber 1921–22, 28–29; Parsons 1967, Chaps. 10–11; Giddens 1984, 14–16).[5]

In sum, regardless of how it organizes, location and age, the human species has to cope with four questions that are unavoidable and in their articulation also define it as a species. We must note, to put things in straightforward fashion, that these questions as such only appear as separate in conceptual discourse, insofar as in actual reality they are intertwined at several points. There is no production or reproduction without a symbolic universe or the structuration of power, nor without a material basis, while power and meaning cannot but go together, whatever the forms and specific contents they assume.[6]

We can thereby, at least for the time being, discard the descriptive and concrete concepts of economy, society, culture, etc. But only for the time being since it will be in a way necessary to return to them and reintroduce them

---

understandable by means of more general concepts such as of "identification" and "relation" (Descola 2005). These are questions that are conceptual and practical, and individually and collectively unavoidable. The best solution for their interpretation is not however structuralist, combinatory, neo-Kantianism (even if supposedly connected to the empirical world and to practices). We are perhaps actually dealing with finite possibilities of practically answering the demands of social life. This generates what seem to be invariant structures of the human spirit (though we must doubt whether the answer to this and other questions are as rigid as Descola suggests). Finally, I take the occasion to note that the notion of "culture" is often used in an extremely unspecific and sweeping way in anthropology.

5   The "authoritative allocation of values" (of the systems theory proposed by Easton 1965, 50) must be seen as the mere subset of the distribution of power and as depending upon it (while it must not suppose the universality of *political systems*); and it is only partly "authoritative," since it can be deeply conflictive. This definition echoes that of "economy," of a neoclassic countenance, as allocation of "scarce" resources vis-à-vis demand, especially the market, price signals and equilibrium (Robbin, 1932, Chap. 1 as well 45–46). This in turn makes secondary the central issue of the material interchange with nature.

6   There is a relationships between the more general dimensions of social systems, which I have defined in other occasions as symbolic-hermeneutical, material, of power and space-time, but they are actually general-analytical in the construction of the concept of *collective subjectivity as the general type of social system* (Domingues 1995a), whereas the existential questions refer to the requirements of the existence of the human species as such, although the systems in which it is organized and through which it answers to those questions are crosscut by that basic multidimensionality.

in the general conceptual framework when we focus directly on modernity, alongside other more precise concepts, such as state, capitalism, family, etc., since they are actually the salient elements of how the human species has become organized in the boundaries of this civilization.

I have thus far mobilized Marx and Engels to outline these existential social questions, despite my criticism and the fact that the former, in an often-quoted text, mentioned the necessity of not structuring thought with a starting-point in abstract issues, which are here, in any case, introduced in an only partly abstract way insofar as, because they cover the basic ontological requirements of human life, in some measure they assume a concrete countenance. In the famous introduction to the *Grundrisse*, Marx (1857–58) suggested a systematic categorial exposition of the capitalist mode of production, which he carried out in *Capital*. This should not begin with such general issues as the division of labor, but rather with the full development of these categories in the specific setting of the modern world, in order to rescue it from the typical generalities of the philosophy of history. This makes sense to a large extent, although we must take this affirmation with a grain of salt and note that it took Marx a long time to decide on the format of his final master-piece, and he also established a sort of anachronism when he set modernity as a watershed moment, redefining the "anatomy" of all previous social forms (as much as the moment "man" became something more than the ape). Nevertheless, from the standpoint of a broad, sociologically and historically-oriented elaboration, it is to Weber that we must resort. These existential questions were worked out in his texts, especially in those several sketches gathered in what became known as *Economy and Society* (1921–22), although we now know that those volumes, edited by his wife, do not possess the organicity we once imagined they had.

Weber treats all these questions in a many-sided manner. Sexuality and generational reproduction, power, the economy and the hermeneutic-symbolic universe, as well as the more concrete aspects of the workings of social systems, which include the family and gender organization, capitalism, the churches, religion and the state, other forms of "domination" and the law, as well as many other specific elements, appear in *Economy and Society* and his other works. Curiously and despite the title, in symmetrical opposition in what regards Marx's *Capital*, the sections about the economy are the least interesting.

Take the well-known forms of "legitimate domination" – traditional, charismatic and rational-legal –, which in the official version of that volume of synthesis were followed (and surely in Weber's thought this was in any event the case, see Domingues 2000b) by the "illegitimate" form of domination which found in the medieval city its refusal, with a situation of freedom ensuing for its citizens. Under the definition of these forms of domination, absolutely central in his work, Weber (1921–22, 122–182, 541–868) includes the relations between men and women, old and young, owners and employees, warriors and peasants, absolute religious authorities and those who control the political stipulation of norms and social behavior. But it is only when he refers to modernity that he defines the most general form of domination as based on the "state." It monopolizes the "legitimate means of violence" in a given and circumscribed territory (that is, exerts "sovereignty" over it), as well as functions according to general and abstract rules, relying on a separate bureaucratic body, since officials do not own the "means of administration" (a formulation clearly inspired in Marx's definition of the modern working classes). Weber does not refer to the "state" in other circumstances – which, it must be noted, does not mean that concerning other social historical formations this could not be correct, partly against his argument –, but rather to those other ways of distributing and organizing power, which is the case when he discusses the democracy of the city and its freedom, which were established against domination and eventually perished due to the growth of the absolutist state. Moreover, the forms of domination cut across all the spheres of social life, also in modernity, penetrating for instance the modern rational capitalist firm, although he does not clearly articulate the theme with respect to gender (in which the idea of rational law would certainly help).

It would have been interesting if Weber had done the same concerning religion, a key area loaded with insights in his works.[7] The drawback here is that he did not, however, even question this most Western and modern definition. He could have searched for a configuration of thought and spirituality, of faith in things in this world and beyond it, in a more specific way, crafting concepts at once more general and more historically circumscribed. A more open conception of law, always considered according to a contrast with its modern Western expression, could have gone the same way. If to "contrast" the modern world with previous societies really works as a strategy in the construction of all his "ideal-types" – "pure" concepts that descriptively exaggerate a number of empirical aspects of reality, and are in this regard fictive (Weber 1921–22, 124) –, here it exacts a higher cost with respect to the aforementioned issues, although affecting less other concepts, such as those of "domination," which seem more infused with autonomous historicity.

---

7   Although the thesis that religion predominated in Weber's multi-faceted conception is not
    plausible – such as in Tenbruck 1980. Politics and sexuality – theoretically and practically –
    come up as crucial in his work (the economy appearing, curiously, always in a non-creative
    way in his writings, liberal capitalism taken for granted, as well as individualist methodology).

Let us take as another example sexuality, always a crucial issue in Weber's writings, and the reproduction of generations, a unique and still not well-explored contribution in his thought (see however Collins 1986, Chap. 11). If the nuclear (or conjugal) family is perhaps very characteristic of most social formations, it is not by far universal or more important than other elements of social organization. Many peoples hold in higher esteem the "masculine house" – where mature and young warriors come together –, rather than the ties between man and woman, or uphold familial forms in which the conjugal couple plays no central role, let alone the patriarchal forms in which a family includes many aggregates to the household, slaves among them sometimes, and is articulated under a traditional form of domination (Weber 1921–22, 212–222; 1923, 23–64). Sex and the reproduction of generations take place in several ways, and we do not need to suppose that the family must be their fundamental axis (whatever deviated from this surprised, for instance, another great comparativist posterior to Weber, namely, Lévi-Strauss 1969).

On the other hand, although having approached in detail and historically these diverse themes, Weber did not outline them in the form of general questions. At most he focused on them in terms of their singularity in the general context of his studies on religion. What he did point out in them, in terms of the value spheres of modernity as such (hence multiplying and lending them a modern terminology) was the multidimensionality of the "direction" of "world rejection" by individual actors (Weber 1920b). This is, somehow and within the aforementioned limits, the contrary of what we have formerly seen with Marx and Engels in their consideration of the production and reproduction of life as the fundamental existential social questions that social formations have to tackle. Each of these approaches therefore offers us an element of the solution, while the other one is still missing. In order to advance with the problem, we must acknowledge the existential questions in their four basic dimensions, as well as admit that they were solved in different and specific ways in the course of human history,[8] modernity for us standing out as the present stage of evolution of the species (itself multilinear, let us not forget), whose answers to those

---

8 By "civilization" I understand a very encompassing type of social system, which changes over time, but remains identical to itself, with answers to each of those questions in a multidimensional way through specific social systems. Modernity would be one of them, with its practices, institutions, relations with nature and imaginaries. By "social formation" I understand a type of more specific social system, in which those civilizations appear in a concrete form, often or in fact even generally, mixed with other civilizations or civilizational elements (with the civilizations to which they belonged having disappeared or giving in to another one, which incorporates them in a more fragmentary manner). They are always weaved by individual action and collective movement.

questions need to be rendered relative. We are not interested simply in this generality, or in a static conception of the problem, but rather in how it appears historically in a particular, as well dynamic, way.

Each of these existential questions, at the individual and collective levels, evolves according to its dynamic, raising problems and demanding answers relative to their own requirements. But, on the other hand, each suffers the influence of and influences the way the others surface and are solved. How to produce depends on how reproduction is carried out, on how the hermeneutic-symbolic element is articulated and how power is distributed and organized, affecting also the way these other existential questions are articulated and unfold. The same is true if we relate them to productive processes and among themselves. Let us add that this varies not only in each civilization and social formation but in the course of their specific histories as well. None of these questions and their resolution is totally capable of conditioning the other – some degree of indeterminacy remains in the form they evolve and of how they relate to one another, since answers, moreover and above all, do not simply come up by themselves. These questions are presented to individuals and collectivities and are answered only through their action and movement, which are always creative and open to the future, although the ways they have been confronted in the past linger on in memories of different kinds (in practices, institutions, imaginaries and material aspects of social life), which are the partial starting-point of new solutions.

How this intertwinement and process of mutual influence actually occurs, the weight of each social system that comes forward to face each question compared to other social systems constituted to face them, causally, cannot be determined a priori and generically. Each civilization or social formation, in each period of its development, has in this regard its own specificity. Deterministic exercises or the attempt to establish general causal laws are therefore doomed to fail. This does not mean that only empirical generalizations can be reached, starting from concrete cases. If the idea of general laws of social development holds in what regards these questions as well, this must not prevent us from recognizing that processes of development linked to the existential questions in civilizations and social formations can be analytically and causally established in a very general way. It is necessary to investigate, for each case, how this happens. This is, for instance, what Marx (1867, 21–24; 1894, Part III, Chaps. 13–15) did with respect to the development of capitalism through the identification of the general trends of capitalist accumulation, which would lead this mode of production to a dead end, regardless of whether or not he was correct in his specific conclusions (I refer here to the famous issue of the "tendency of the profit rate to fall," as well as of the concentration of capital in the hands of a few expropriators, with a huge working class on the opposite side).

If it is furthermore possible to lay out the more general trends within large processes, which are nonetheless specific to each civilization, such as the instrumental rationalization that Weber perceived as inexorably unfolding in the West, only research can show in each case. Bearing this in mind critically and at the same time being prepared to recognize its effectiveness in modernity is what, basically, allows us to escape from the hypostasis of the idea that social life is structured by means of economic, political and cultural or "ideological" systems (with always an etcetera that permits the addition of other ad hoc elements, such as perhaps sexuality and the law), whether this structuration is seen as universal or as stemming from a process of differentiation (as in Parsons 1971).

Existential Questions, Developmental Trends and Modernizing Moves

Considering the arguments advanced in the former section, is it possible to say that the answer presented to existential questions is contingent, even if with some caveats? This would be in line almost with the totality of discussions to be found in the contemporary social sciences – with the exception of capitalism, whose process of expansion, at least in the view of Marxist authors deeply influenced by this perspective, is seemingly inexorable. Each individual and each collectivity answers thus to these questions, at each moment, except in what refers therefore to capitalism, in a rather unpredictable way, in principle. However, although we know there are variations in those answers, it is evident that there are patterns in each civilization and social formation, which are reproduced in a more or less regular and homogeneous way. It is not the case here to re-enter the debate about "action" and "structure," which I have done in other occasions, nor to discuss in any detail the theme of social evolution, which can hardly be seized today by unilinear visions, but which should not, just because of this, be discarded (Domingues 1995a, 2000a, as well as Chapter 2 of this book).

Up to a certain point there are continuities in the way existential questions are answered, sometimes heterogeneously, though often showing some cohesion, especially when a civilization arises and those answers influence each other intensely. Overall, this lends some level of coherence to a civilization. However, if and when it expands, this coherence tends to be lost, in that its civilizational patterns mix with those stemming from other civilizations, originating thereby social formations that can be defined as a hybrid or the like. Let me underscore, however, that, if there are continuities in the passage from one civilization to another, there are also strong discontinuities, sometimes radical ruptures. Moreover, within each civilization and each social formation, we very frequently find radical ruptures. In addition, within each civilization and each social formation we encounter reiterated processes. Regardless of how the identity of this sort of social system is kept, intentionally or not, resorting to the concept of "structure" in an ontological sense so as to solve this theoretical question is not the best solution. I suggest that it is preferable to adopt an approach of theorization of practices, institutions and the imaginary of individuals and collectivities in their attempt to the answer to those existential questions, however they are organized.

In order to advance theoretically, let us concentrate now on the discussion about how these questions unfold in a specific civilization, namely, modernity. I do not intend here to empirically decide which is better or even to present in a systematic way the middle-range theories that can deal with any of them. This is important no doubt, yet it is also essential to understand its entanglement, in the original European context and in its expansion, with its own developmental trends, and when it is converted into a global heterogeneous modernity, articulated multidimensionally and encompassing manifold trends (Domingues 2012 and Chapter 2 of this book). In what follows my sole aim is to first sketch the theme in a general way and then consider, in terms of indications only, both the development of modernity – according to what can be defined as its developmental trends – and what concerns their entanglement, as an answer to their intertwined developments. In sum, my goal is propaedeutic. Having reinstated the theme of the dimensions of social life seeking an analytical solution that goes beyond Marx, Engels and Weber, the following step consists of sketching a strategy to move forward with respect to its systematic unfolding in the framework of a renewed theory of modernity.

Modernity has been characterized by institutional elements that appear, in one way or another, in the works of several authors. As an example, I list below some central theses and authors that may help situate the themes at stake (see, among other interpreters, Domingues 2000a, 2006, 2009, for systematic analyses).

In Weber, we find very general theses concerning rationalization and the rise of differentiated spheres, or the division of labor and the appearance of a new form of solidarity, in Durkheim – "organic solidarity." Parsons keenly emphasized social differentiation in a more general way, whereas Habermas followed the same route, but combined it with broader theses about rationalization (in this case both instrumental and communicative). There are intermediate cases, such as Marx's, in which capitalism, a specific institutional sphere, is discussed in conceptual detail, operating at the same time as the element that defines and causally influences all other spheres of modernity.

There is that of Elias too, steeped in the processes of monopolization of power, control of drives and pacification, discrete yet related and decisive for the whole of social life. Giddens, on the other hand, adopted a a multidimensional approach to deal with the theme, with capitalism and industrialization, state surveillance and the industrialization of war, defining his main institutional axes, although several others are added in the course of his argument, which also finds in the "disembeddings" of social relations from more stable and limited space-time coordinates a more general element in the development of modernity. Although forms of consciousness, in Durkheim and Weber, Parsons and Habermas, as well as Marx, are present in all these discussions and the latter underscores the role of ideology, the theme of the imaginary – namely, how people conceive of modernity and conceive of themselves therein or the values that orient them – has enjoyed much less analytical emphasis in sociology. Eisenstadt somehow sought a way out for modernization theories partly through "culture." Castoriadis, criticizing Marxism, shed light on historical contingency and its creativity, by means of the concept of "radical imaginary" (although in his version such a concept was very individualistic).

All these authors, and many others – sometimes at a lower level of generality – treat these institutions or imaginaries, when they do, in terms of a tendency that unfolds within modernity. We find this for instance in the liberal modernization theories of the twentieth century (see Knöbl 2001), as well as in Marxist interpretations of the same period (see Aricó 1976–77, and Jay 1986, respectively for militant and so-called "Western" Marxism). But also, unless they adopt in fact a discontinuous view of history, such as Giddens did, sticking in any case to that first perspective, they try to point out how the elements that characterize modernity emerged in prior social formations, whether more contingently historically, whether as an upshot of even uni-linear evolutions of the human species. In sum, we are squarely situated in the universe of what can be characterized as *trend-concepts*, in other words, concepts that try to understand more or less contingent or inexorable developments within this sort of civilization or even in what regards their genesis in very long-run historical processes.

Contemporary sociology and social sciences seem to be generally uninterested in this sort of question, yet it keeps returning through the back door, since most concepts they make use of, whether today or in the past, are exactly those that were once treated as stemming from developmental processes that led to modernity and that continue unfolding within it, more or less modified. Giving up taking issue with them, they simply hypostatize them, as well as hypostatize the existential questions we have examined in the first part of this chapter. That is to say, they take such historical phenomena as capitalism, the modern state, the family, etc., for granted, whether or not they recognize that they correspond to historical forms, thereby losing part of what are in fact the deepest processes and mechanisms whereby they are constituted and transformed. This is even more radical in the supposition that "society" (as such an already hypostatized and reified concept) possesses the dimensions of the economy, politics, culture, etc. Or else, in what seems to me a desperate alternative to evade the dilemmas of determinism and of historical necessity, researchers in the several social sciences deal with these dimensions and those more specific social systems in such a contingent way that veers towards nominalism. In any case, they leave aside the general meaning of these concepts and their dynamic and longitudinal unfolding (although of course post-modern narratives tend to do exactly the opposite of what they promise, by evoking powerful developmental trends, as in Lyotard 1979).

In order to adequately grasp the answer to these existential social questions it is necessary, nevertheless, to analyze the genesis of its answers in specific civilizations and social formations, as well as reproduction, which always entail a certain level of change and the possibility of radical transformation. We must moreover look into how this happens with respect to the relative autonomy of the answers to those questions, as well as with respect to their intertwinement and mutual causal sway. This must be done in light of empirical, albeit generalizing, analyses. Above all we must identify analytically the *mechanisms* that preside over such processes. I have called them generative, reiterative and transformative, in terms of an analytical construction in which these specific trend-concepts can be articulated as dynamic solutions to those questions (as further discussed in Chapter 4).

Two tasks thus await us before we can resume discussions that seem crucial in the social sciences and in sociology, but also in the framework of a renewed critical theory that intends to understand history overall and the genesis and reproduction of modernity as well as the processes and mechanisms that can lead beyond it.[9] On the one hand it is a matter of historical analysis and of historical sociology. At best these are oriented by general analytical

---

9   While Marx and Engels clearly defined the processes of genesis, development and overcoming of capitalism and of modernity, whatever the ambiguities of their answers (whether they rested upon classes and subjectivities or on catastrophic trends and "structural" or "functional" contradictions), critical theory concentrated increasingly on philosophy and culture, frequently with a pessimistic bias, like Weber, as in Adorno's and Horkheimer's classical book on instrumental reason and "logocentrism" (see Aricó 1976–77; Domingues 2012). This links up, of course, with real problems and the present-day impasses of radical social change, but in social theory we should not let the paralysis go that far.

concepts (or alternatively by ideal-types) and are also committed to tackling modernity or other civilizations. On the other hand, we need to examine how these putative developmental trends, also within modernity, unfold, starting from the same analytical categories utilized to consider its genesis (in reality these are dependent upon their identification by the researcher as the most important elements in a civilization, inasmuch as the processes that push the transition of one civilization to another are far too complex and multifaceted; an approach that includes everything that historically happens is unfeasible, the delimitation and the selection of causally outstanding variables being necessary).

As a result, the modern state, capitalism, the nuclear family in the West, etc. – but also their projection and specific developments in other regions of the world, in their entanglement and hybridization with elements stemming from other civilizations (see Domingues 2012) – can be analyzed more dynamically and in depth. Let us stress that the entanglement, with variable intensity and vectors, of the unfolding of each of the existential questions, often and increasingly articulated, in the context of a complexification of social life, by social systems themselves multiple and complex, adds a huge challenge to the research. The causal tangle becomes thicker and the multiple influences become multifaceted, making it more difficult to discern where things start or end and what is its specific weight in the unfolding of social processes in each social formation – at its several "scalar" levels (local, national, regional, planetary) – and of modern civilization on the whole at present.

This refers to what is possible to define as the methodology of analysis of existential social questions and their organization with regard to specific dimensions and social systems, in particular in modernity, but not only therein. Let us see now what this might mean more substantively.

First of all, what can be made of the traditional division between economy and politics? It expands toward the necessity to introduce culture as another dimension – or, in more sophisticated theories, such the one advanced by Habermas (1981), a "life-world" in which lie "culture," "institutions" and "personality" –, with other dimensions adduced in different theories. On the other hand, that division is real and refers to the separation which modernity introduced between the sphere of "civil society," whose foundations would be grounded, on the one hand, in the economy, but which would also include the family, the press, churches and other entities, and, on the other, the state, in which the complexification of Marxism conducted by Gramsci eventually led to a curious, almost inverted argument, according to which that sphere would be part of the "enlarged state" (see Cohen and Arato 1992, for the evolution of the concept).

That division is not merely fictitious (as Poulantzas sometimes suggests, also in a subtler version of the political dimension in Marxist theory). It actually structures the whole of social life, especially due to the separation between public and private. However, on the other hand, it contains a strong ideological element (in the sense of hiding reality due to bourgeois class interests, as he suggests), since it veils the actual interpenetration of these two spheres and state power and its penetration of this "civil society." To this it must be added that, although at least formally separate from "society," the state was never capable of controlling and molding it as intensively, shifting from a merely "despotic" relation (repressive capacity) in prior civilizations to a significant "infrastructural power," combined with agents of the very same "society," that is, external to it, by means of a normative-generative capability that is not merely repressive and violent (see Giddens 1985, especially Chap. 7; Mann 1986, 1993; Foucault's influence upon them both is explicit).

Evidently neither politics nor the economy develops separately. On the contrary, they are intertwined, although each has its own dynamic (or, as the Germans say, *Eigendynamic*), which unfolds from its contradictions, projects, unintentional consequences and so on and so forth. The same could be said of "culture," a rather strange expression indeed, since all social systems – or those that surge as politics and economy – have as a constitutive element an hermeneutic dimension, symbolically weaved, inescapable, even when its meaning implies, as suggested by Weber and the Frankfurt School authors, its drainage and drying up (see, for a general revision, Habermas 1981, who takes this argument to the limit in what concerns supposedly "self-steered" systems). Note that some authors, such as Castells (1996), even state that "culture" is undergoing a process of autonomization. As it happens, irrespective of possibly interesting elements in his analysis, he is at fault when he elects as a starting-point the reification and hypostatization of the concept, apparently obvious in its facticity, which should, however, be problematized from the outset, with the consequences this entails.

If we target even more specific systems, such as the state, the family, the market, etc., these questions become even more complicated, but clearly require revision. If we speak of the development of politics, what do we talk about? The state? Or, somewhat more broadly, "civil society"? Or do we in fact refer to a set of practices, which cut across both these modern social constructions – imaginary but also very real, since they actually organize, by means of a large set of institutions, the whole of social activities –, without stopping at them? That is, should we speak only about them or the family and friendship, sports, science, religion and so many other systems that must be thought of not only as part of "society" ("civil" or however one is want to define it), as Gramsci piercingly suggested, but as though they were all directly related, in particular ways, to the distribution of power? It seems obvious to me, taking into account that social existential questions are general and open themes, that the answers to their requirements cannot be reduced to one or two concrete social systems. They pervade several of them, in what regards both general and more specific problems (who votes, for instance, at the same time that what sort of sexuality is authorized are objects defined by power relations, with respect to other systems and agents – *collective subjectivities*, that is, men, women, priests, capitalists, feminists, etc., as the latter were pioneers in emphasizing with their famous motto "the personal is political").

The same can be said of capitalism. Is it merely an economic system? Or must it be defined from the outset in multidimensional terms? If at its core lie relations of production and consumption, in their entanglement with nature, mediated by the circulation of commodities, it is not possible to understand it separated from politics, with law playing a role of mediation between these two dimensions and systems and others. Marx himself drew attention to this, although in *Capital* he pursued a more analytically and concretely circumscribed strategy regarding the economy. It was above all Polanyi (1944), however, who underlined, with some degree of exaggeration, that the liberal state had constituted the market or at least disembedded it from the whole of social relations due to a project commanded by liberal forces. It would be absurd to think also that "culture" – or "ideology," if you will – is a dimension unhinged from the economy. This is the mistake incurred by Habermas, although not by Marxists by and large, Marx himself especially to the extent he stressed the role of the "fetishism of commodity," of money and capital as such, as opaque symbolic constructions. In contradistinction, they causally subordinate the hermeneutic-symbolic dimension to the dynamic of the economy, whereby they for the most part deprive the former of its own dynamic, even if this refers, at best, to a "determination in the last instance." It is surely curious to see how Castells, coming from Marxism, tried to run in the opposite direction, incurring in large measure in a mistake symmetrical to the one he formerly used to make.[10]

A whole range of possibilities is opened up with these moves. One is to treat the existential questions and the several responses to it historically, reconstructing their evolution, also concerning modernity, overall and in

---

10 This should not prevent us from acknowledging, as authors outside Marxism do, that capitalism has a huge weight – also causally – in the unfolding of global modernity, although it makes no sense to think of it as separated from the other existential questions, an inclination we find for instance in Chakrabarty 2000.

this specific case giving attention to the processes that led to them and that unfolded therefrom. There is no reason to assume in this regard any teleology, insofar as social creativity always intervenes and lends them unexpected directions, although there are doubtlessly strong elements of what has been conventionally called "path dependence" in these processes, with the starting-point influencing the next developments. This is what authors who adopt discontinuist standpoints (such as Gellner, Giddens and Mann) underscore. This is also what I grappled with, from the point of view of the theory of collective subjectivity, with the concept of *episodic moves*, which in modernity became *modernizing moves*, thereby weaving together social developments intentionally or as unintended consequences of individual action and of collective movement (Domingues 2000a, Chap. 4; 2012).

Comparative strategies, such as Weber's, can be applied with the aim of opening the focus of analysis, within the bounds of a civilization, as well as between them. Analytical constructions are thereby possible, whether regarding the discussion of existential questions – in the framework of a more abstract exposition, though not that much, since these concepts mutually imply each other –, or as to a specific civilization – modernity, in the case I have proposed to consider in this chapter. Both a synchronic, structural-descriptive, and a more complex, diachronic standpoint, which grasps the tendency of development of those questions, can be adopted. In fact, these two strategies stand as complementary. At this stage, the three aforementioned types of mechanisms – generative, reiterative and transformative – are pivotal, so as to not allow that the analysis turns into mere description, even if organized by concepts, whose theoretical power thus becomes limited. It is crucial to *explain* how processes unfold.

On the one hand, it is worth analyzing the trends with some degree of isolation, at least initially, but this must be corrected afterward by a broader analysis that focuses on the – causal – impact of the answer to questions one upon the others. In this respect the task is by no means easy, although it is not necessary to take it to the uncompromising situation of thinking that only totality could solve the problem More discrete and intermediate strategies often pay off, without the vertigo of absolute knowledge leading to paralysis. Finally, it is necessary to consider that if we take the processes of emergence, unfolding and evolution of social life drawing upon the trend-concepts crafted to this end, combining the construction of categories such as politics and economy, state and civil society, capitalism and neopatrimonialism, nuclear family and patriarchy, nation and citizenship, ethnicity and racism, among others (which can and ought to move beyond the descriptive level), with the explanation of social processes by means of mechanisms, this can only be done if we first and foremost reckon with them in their state of conceptual and historical purity. In the very terrain of their emergence and initial developments – Europe – they became entangled with previous forms of answers to existential questions. This sometimes lingers for long, the modernizing moves that take place lending to modernity rather particular characteristics in each place or country in a given region. When we pan out, and consider global modernity, which resulted from the expansion of modern civilization starting from Europe, this entanglement becomes a veritable hybridization, since it encompasses other civilizational elements across the planet. This means that modernizing moves are themselves also hybrid and that developmental trends become even more complex, but by no means of impossible comprehension. That is to say, they can be comprehended as long as we cast the interrogation about existential questions and the development of answers to them in a systematic way.

Final Words

We thus arrive to the end of our conceptual foray, which approached almost unapproachable themes in the social sciences. From Marxist materialism to the demands that they are articulated multidimensionally, through some sorts of approach with a culturalist slant, widespread today, a query has emerged, openly or more fuzzily, as to the relation between the distinct aspects of social life. I have endeavored to look at them from the standpoint of four fundamental existential questions. We could almost say that they refer to actual "conditions of possibility" of existence of the human species and of the social systems in which this is organized, were we inclined to draw upon Kantian language. Yet we should bear in mind that what is at stake are concrete human practices, not the metaphysical constitution of the subject or of reality in general, the outcome of which is known beforehand, hence lacking a simple explanation.[11] They are instead the themes of production and of the reproduction of the species, of the distribution of power and of the creation of meaning, with undetermined directions as well as historical fallibility. Inasmuch as "historical materialism" became ossified and since what has been conventionally called the "linguistic turn" took place in the social sciences, this discussion

---

11   The functionalist perspective is not therefore a good solution, one in which the concretization of those questions appears as "pre-requisite" for the reproduction and continuity of social systems, easily deriving into a problem of "integration" of the social system and of "order"/"motivation" in the version of the issue in Parsons (1951, 26–36, 167–177). The existential social questions are at once more encompassing and more contingent.

went astray. Both simply affirm the importance of the materiality of human life and of its social causality, without being able to progress conceptually. Alternatively, it is claimed that it is in the sphere of language or of "discourse" that the most important processes and causal impulses must be found, whereby the actual advances of the last decades are severely marred. Some prefer, in parallel developments, to lend emphasis to power, whether unilaterally or multidimensionally, a number of approaches taking an absolute view of them in ontological and explanatory terms, whereas the reproduction of the species and sexuality either remained within varied forms of psychoanalysis (or of its critics) or skittered toward mere empirical description.

This proposal launches itself therefore in what today constitutes a rather unusual direction, resuming crucial and very general discussions, which Marxism originally proposed and which the social sciences, outstandingly sociology, once tried to further. It does so, alongside a concentration on those existential questions, resuming other themes that went off the radar of social scientists in the last decades, in which the idea of contingency has taken the upper hand as an inescapable element of social life and of history, pace the expansion of modernity – with an air of absolute necessity, almost like the expansion of rationality as in the terms of Weber and his heirs –, in its entanglement with other social elements.[12] I have tried in other contexts to argue in favor of a sociology of global modernity, as an expansive and now visibly heterogeneous civilization, as one of the paths through which sociology can and should recover its theoretical impulses, that for the time being have been subdued.

I have in addition combined this suggestion with a call for a renewal of critical theory through this route. The trend-concepts that aim at understanding modernity in its dynamic of genesis, development and possible overcoming are indispensable in order to evolve from a merely descriptive level or even more restricted conceptual-interpretive one, to another, more analytical and explanatory. This path would be, by searching for possibilities of social change, the basis for an amplification of immanent critique. This should go beyond that with which agents with diverse constitutions, with social movements standing out, and concrete moral intuitions keep energizing our world in an emancipatory direction.

This depends on broader and deeper currents in social life, represented by these agents and intuitions, in the struggle against exploitation and oppression.

---

12   Although in turn, with a theoretical deficit and a strong normative bias, the radical neo-modernism of neo-liberalism asserts as the global expansion of markets an empirical and normative trend, which is affirmed as inevitable and necessary, preferably but not absolutely and inexorably accompanied by liberal democracy.

However, it does not imply that the social sciences should refrain from contributing in this direction. Yet, to do so, it is important to confront the key problems of social theory, among which we find what I have called here existential social questions. They allow us to situate the present moment conceptually and open the doors to a better understanding of the social systems in which they are organized in modernity. They stress their contingency and variation, but also mutual imbrication, and the varied levels of necessity and cohesion, their multiple developmental trends, in generative and reiterative terms as well as inexorable overcoming, and thus, all things considered, their historicity. If success is not guaranteed in the identification of mechanisms that can lead us beyond modernity, since this depends moreover on how they truly develop today, it is, even in the worst-case scenario, relevant that we grapple once again with this sort of issue, which is perhaps not existential in the sense employed in this text, the importance of which is however doubtless.

CHAPTER 4

History, Sociology and Modernity

Introduction

The goal of this text is to carry out an analysis of the relation between sociological theory and modernity in its global dimension, in the effort to advance from a descriptive perspective toward an analytical construction capable of reflecting on the mechanisms that preside over its genesis, development and possible – indeed inevitable – transformation. Two caveats must be stated at the outset, however. This is the first: my goal, partly, is to take on not only Brazilian modernity, but also, yet without actual concrete references, Latin American modernity. This intention will be present only obliquely, though. This must be unavoidably done tangentially insofar as Brazilian sociology did not take up larger processes of development of modernity – it above all did not attempt to conceptualize what is dealt with here as the developmental trends of modernity, such as capitalist accumulation, state-building, secularization, individualization, that is, the large processes identified by the European and North American social sciences, in several ways –, except in terms of its specification in the particularity, sometimes assessed from a radicalized angle, of its own history. It exhausts itself thereby in a *description* of its historical process, more or less intelligent and from time to time even brilliant, sometimes based on well-controlled concepts, more or less modified, even though the latter is not its most usual approach. This is something it shares with other Latin-American countries.[1]

The second is one is a warning regarding my demarche, since I present the discussion from a specific angle, which I hope to be at least partly innovative. The social sciences are a plural endeavor, there is no univocal and exclusive manner of carrying it out or expressing it, but evidently, I proceed with a certain emphasis that will clash with the work which is traditionally effected

---

*   Originally published in *Desarrollo económico*, vol. 55 (2015); and Maria Thereza Ribeiro (ed.), *Dimensão histórica da sociologia. Dilemas e complexidades* (Curitiba: Apris, 2016)

1   Maybe the theories of the Latin American Economic Commission (ECLA) and the theory of dependency closed in on that, with their notions of center and periphery, but did not elaborate the issue systematically. The same happened to the Marxist theories of "marginality" and with Germany's emphasis on the passage from "adscriptive" to modern societies and afterward from these to post-modernity in García Canclini.

in the social sciences in Brazil (and more generally in Latin America and even other peripheral and semi-peripheral countries such as India). Interesting research is that which can suggest something that challenges us, questioning what was done before. That is what I hope to accomplish here.

From these initial observations, let us move on to a more substantive discussion, from the angle of social theory, especially sociological theory. I have worked at several stages with very general concepts in the social sciences and tried to develop what I have called a *theory of collective subjectivity*, including such themes as *social creativity, social systems* and other concepts of a similar level of generality. But a following step, which in fact links up with former periods of my trajectory, since I have always been very interested in the connection of theory with historical processes, was to resume this sort of investigation with greater centrality (cf. Domingues 2008, 2012). It is worthwhile to highlight that it is not philosophy what we are doing – or should do – when we develop social theory, not even what is sometimes strangely – though in its basic mistake in a justified manner – called "metatheory," which appears actually as a metaphysics, an a priori construction, which would be beyond the empirical world. Sociological theory is an endeavor that must be connected to the world of empirical research, in its several forms or dimensions, which include, more or less intensively and directly, the historical dimension. This is an important issue, insofar as, furthermore, the social sciences cannot but deal with history, since our object of study is necessarily historical. Social life consists of and in a process that is historical in character. It is thus almost a pleonasm to speak of history when we refer to "society." We can even, formally, stop using the word "history," always however bearing in mind that it is necessarily enclosed in the word "social." These two dimensions must go together, conceptually, as much in theory as in life.

The theme of modernity was very important in the nineteenth and twentieth centuries sociology, although today, for generic reasons (which include the refusal of thinking broadly about social life) and due to sociology as such (with some exhaustion of the empiricism and evolutionism that increasingly took over the discussion, with on the other hand deep impasses in Marxist theory), its capacity to intellectually mobilize has dimmed a lot – at this point at least, it may be expected. The discipline is intrinsically tied, in its origins and development, to the problematization of what modernity is, including what global modernity is. In the last years, the only approach to really tackle this sort of issue, although limitedly (see Wagner 2012), is what has been called "multiple modernities," which refers to nationally or at least regionally cut out modernities.

The author who initially set the parameters for this sort of discussion was an Israeli sociologist named Shmuel Eisenstadt (2001). But he was also, way back, an author connected to modernization theory. At a certain point, he started to question the very idea of a unidirectionality in the development of modernity, posing the question in contradistinction of how modernity combined with other civilizations. He suggested the existence of an Indian modernity, of a Chinese modernity, of a Russian, North American, Latin American modernity. Thus, he highly fragmented the concept of modernity as such and, although the idea of a combination of civilizations is interesting, and slipped toward a sort of methodological nationalism, or methodological regionalism. It is true that he conceived of an original, founding "program," of European modernity, which mixed with those other regional, mainly cultural, expressions. This was in fact very much the theme of the multiple modernities question – such that Confucianism and Hinduism, for instance, appeared as configuring the specific cultural systems of these modernities, which he would eventually understand as plural. The problem is, on the other hand, that a theoretical unidimensionality linked to culture creates impasses for a broader conception of modernity, which must be multidimensional.

This was my starting-point in one of my last books, *Global Modernity, Development, and Contemporary Civilization* (Domingues 2012). Approaching this universe of questions, I tried to comparatively understand Latin America. I began with some former works of mine, aiming at confronting it mainly with Sinic and Indic regions, especially China, India, Pakistan. I heavily drew upon history and historical sociology in this project, both however at the service already by then of a reconstruction of sociological theories and in particular of critical theory. That is, I endeavored to treat the diverse themes that appear in the book (economics, democracy, attitudes toward the world, modernizing moves) in a more or less comparative way, nevertheless exactly with the concern of contributing to the reconstruction of sociological theory and of critical theory, rethinking modernity as a global issue and eschewing in fact a perspective that could be captured by a more static view. Instead of thinking of multiple modernities, I preferred to start from the idea of a global, but heterogenous modernity. It has its origins fundamentally in Western Europe, dated from the end of the eighteenth and the nineteenth centuries, with its later worldwide expansion. In this expansion, its hybridization with other civilizations, which were internally heterogenous, really happened, hence modernity took shape as a highly heterogeneous *global civilization*, whose "societies" – or "social formations" – as *modern social systems* having them all not only more or less the same origin, but basically sharing the same characteristics. However, even in the book I have just mentioned, although it is theoretically – and polemically – oriented and seeks moreover to change Weberian "ideal-types" into analytical categories, my goal was not to lay out a systematic expository system, or to charter the developmental trends of modernity (however much globally outspread). This chapter, in turn, discusses how to do it *logically* and *methodologically*.

An issue that concerned me, nonetheless, already at that point and became ever more a central topic was the weight we should give to history in an endeavor such as this. It is not a matter of how the exposition will look like in the organized work. Moreover, it is a matter of how thinking is articulated vis-à-vis the organization of concepts. One way or another, there is a lot of history in the book at stake. It is necessary to move forward from where I stopped, though. It is in this direction that the present chapter will go. Before that it is necessary to open a parenthesis so as to raise two questions, pertaining to the relation between sociology, historical sociology and Brazilian and Latin American modernity (as well as beyond this region). As already stated, the latter will turn up in a somewhat oblique manner, but it is an issue that underlies all the chapter's argument. Finally, let me say that although there are such contemporary writers as Habermas and Giddens who have relevant substantive contributions to the theory of modernity, it will be in the classics – especially in Marx and Weber – that we will find the bases for a methodological articulation of our proposition.

Historical Sociology and Sociological Theory

Historical sociology is a composite theme, a composite expression. Historical sociology: what is there of history and what of sociology in historical sociology? There is actually much more history than sociology in historical sociology, something we need to face in a critical way. This is a complicated problem. If we analyze the tradition of historical sociology that was established basically during the twentieth century, this is not very difficult to recognize. Reinhard Bendix, Theda Skocpol, Barrington Moore Jr., among others, are authors that obviously work with sociology, but in their works the weight of history is much greater than the weight, let us put it this way, of that former discipline. It is especially weightier than sociological theory (see, for a balance, Smith 1992). Skocpol (1979, 36–39), in the introduction to her book about revolutions, her main piece, draws attention to the fact that it rests on what John Stuart Mill (1843, 278ff) identified as two possibilities of comparative method: the method of *agreement* and the method of *difference* (although this seems somehow a rationalization, *a posteriori*, and not necessarily with positive effects, of her strategy). In the method of agreement, we should look for, in the several cases to be compared, shared elements. An effect, something that came about, is identified and the researcher makes an effort to find the causes common to all the events that occur in all the units that are being compared. In the method of difference, we are on the lookout for what is different, other cases in which neither the causes nor the effects are present. Skocpol also argued that the latter is more fruitful, but, in any case, it would be their combination that would provide historical sociology its comparative muscle. In a certain way, she notes (although lacking precision, but we can, to some extent, charitably understand her vision this way) that this methodological conjunction would allow for the identification of empirical reality, but that to account more deeply for these elements, for the processes at stake, would depend on the articulation of an explanatory theory. This would then be, fundamentally, the task of historical sociology: to identify empirically the cases, detect what they have in common, as well as what they have that is different, and upon this build an explanation that may lend meaning to this empirical comparison.[2]

If we consider Durkheim (1897), we see that Skocpol's proposal looks very much like his "concomitant variations"; he drew, by the way, upon the very same Mill to put forward his argument. What does *Suicide* deal with? It identifies the causes of suicide according to its higher or lower rates, relating them to religion and social situations, its higher or lower incidence explained by means of an analysis of the weight of the community (Catholic or Protestant, as a function of the typical agitation of the modern market and its rather radical individualism, among other elements) and, at bottom rock, its links with "social solidarity." We can say that in Weber (1904b) this is also, in some part, the case. Capitalism emerged only in the West, but there was comparable, actually greater, wealth in China and India. Why then did it surge in the West and only there? Weber took one variable, religion, and when he carried out his comparison he looked for what they had in common and what was different. This therefore led to the assumption that the weight should fall, in explanatory terms, upon the Protestant ethic, which showed an "elective affinity" with capitalism (which is not the same as to say that it causes capitalism, the interpretation stops short of that, remaining more diffuse). I shall present below another way of understanding these theses, but more generally this is, so to speak, the official interpretation of Weber and certainly the most usual, as well as, it seems, his own (see Winckelmann, 1995).

Indeed, the tradition of Brazilian sociology is very much to avoid the issue of comparison, with extremely rare exceptions (such as passages in Buarque

---

2   For a historical comparison, also see the four variants suggested by Tilly 1984.

de Hollanda 1936, referring to Latin America, or when the literature of historical sociology or the like brought up the European and United States cases, as
in Werneck Vianna 1975, or Velho 1976). Brazil is a very large country, which
entertains the weird habit of self-absorbed thinking (*ensimesmamento*, as we
would say all over Latin America). Our gaze is cast within, and when it turns
outward, it looks toward the United States, England, France, or Germany; it is
as though as we look around we realize that we lack a classical bourgeois revolution, we lack a state under the rule of law such as it should be, rational individualism and similar phenomenon, more or less reasonable or absurd. The
issue is often what we should be and are not, entailing a confusion between
what I once defined as "actual Westernization" and an "idealized Westernization," as though modernity hovered aloft in the firmament, ready to be brought
down from the heavens to earth (Domingues 1992; 2008, 7). But the comparison is rarely carried out systematically: Brazil is studied and the collation is
carried out through what others have written about other countries (Lenin for
the "Prussian path," Moore Jr. about "conservative modernization," Marx about
the formation of the "consciousness of the proletariat," Weber about "rationalization" or "secularization," Elias "pacification" in Europe, others still about
liberalism and the racial issue in the US). Nonetheless, nobody is truly dedicated to researching the United States, Germany, England or France and how
their cases were formed. Did anyone spend any time in any of those countries
to compare them with Brazil? We read their secondary literature, we carry out
empirical research at home, but this is not effectively a systematic method of
pushing comparisons in sociology.

To be sure, up to a certain point and depending on the objectives, the simple use of secondary literature is acceptable (I myself often resort to this, with
theoretical aims), but it has its limits. A not less complicated task is simply
to carry on using the classics of so-called "Brazilian social thought" as if they
offered an adequate portrait of Brazilian society, without returning to historical analysis, empirically, of the country's reality with contemporary categories
and methods, with a systematic theoretical intention. In order to make a me-
thodical comparison it is indispensable to study the cases with at least some
detail. Even Latin America – Argentina, Colombia, Mexico, Chile, Uruguay –
only now, in piecemeal fashion, has started to play a role in the comparison for
the study of Brazil.[3] The major exception (apart from Buarque de Hollanda's
insights) was Fernando Henrique Cardoso's work with Enzo Faletto, written in

---

3   Our Latin American neighbors also tend to write more history than sociology when embrac-
     ing the endeavors of historical sociology, as we see in the recent, otherwise very relevant
     work, of Ansaldi and Giordano 2012.

Chile, with its discussion, articulated through the ECLA's "historical-structural" method mixed with Marxism, about dependency in Latin America. Since the rise of dictatorships Brazil became more self-absorbed and turned to the United States and Europe. The main references and the authors used to confer legitimacy to arguments are all from those countries, Latin America stopped being a focus of interest for Brazilian researchers, something which only more recently has been slightly corrected.[4]

Theory and Mechanisms

What to do, though, so as to surpass the excessive concentration on histori-cal analysis, which is also one of the problems, one of the more specific ones, of the sociology of Brazilian modernity (within the boundaries of so-called "social thought")? In the last decades, some philosophers and social scientists stressed, from different angles, the identification of explanatory mechanisms as crucial for science, in some cases with a focus on the social sciences. Bhaskar (1975, 1979) is one of them. He has done so as part of his struggle against em-piricism, making use of mechanisms that are steeped in a physical sense, but extending the argument to all the sciences, the social sciences as well, thereby proposing a "stratified" (and rather reified) view of reality. For him, mecha-nisms occupy deep layers. In the specific case of the social sciences, the au-thors gathered by Hedström and Swedberg (1998) tend to see theorizing by mechanisms as an alternative to "grand theory." They confront moreover the ghost of Talcott Parsons, who nonetheless made use of this strategy, although unenthusiastically, since it did not allow for, he believed, the prediction of so-cial behavior (see Parsons 1951, and those who came after him, such a Giddens, Habermas, and, to some extent, perhaps Bourdieu).

Jon Elster has already developed arguments, some interesting, some very problematic and even trivial, about classical authors. In *Making Sense of Marx* he proposed the idea that mechanisms are crucial in the articulation of the thought of the founder of "historical materialism"; he did the same with de Tocqueville (Elster 1985, 2009). It is nonsensical, contrary to what Elster in-tended, to turn Marx into a methodological individualist. Yet, pointing to the

---

4 We are far from possessing a work that has made an encompassing balance of the production of so-called Brazilian social thought. This is a significant and revealing gap on how modernity has been thought of among us; that is, in a radically ideographic way, also in what concerns the treatment of the national authors that have somehow dealt with the theme. The same can be said, more widely, of Latin American thought overall.

conceptual construction of mechanisms as a key component of Marx's and de Tocqueville's theoretical edifices seems to me a very interesting move, exactly, in part, because we can, through this sort of strategy, get closer to a view of historical sociology that has more links with sociology, especially with theory, rather than immediately with history. That is, instead of setting out with comparisons of historical cases and following this route, although this is necessary also to some extent, in particular at the stage of unbound investigation of the theme, the construction of explanatory mechanisms is what would in effect allow us to approach historical sociology with greater weight on the conceptual construction.

To try and articulate this argument in a less abstract way, two very classical examples are worth mentioning, one related to Marx's *Capital*, the other to Weber's sociology of religion. Let us note too that the identification of mechanisms is a strategy deployed by every author in the history of the social sciences, to begin with these classics. Lest one suppose we are inventing the wheel when we resume this line of conceptualization, this would be a falsification of the development of such disciplines. Nor does it make sense to contrapose it to general theory, as I shall argue below. But it is all the same interesting to underline its scope and systematically argue on its behalf. In simple terms, mechanisms are here understood as processes that repeat themselves regularly – not things, as Bhaskar believes. In their deployment they generate other processes – which they can explain –, without a rupture necessarily happening between them both (and without an opposition between "structures," on the one hand, and "effects" or "events" on the other).[5]

Capital is a profoundly historical book, without consisting, however, in a history book. To start with, we must note that it is clear that capitalism only achieved maturity as a "mode of production" in the twentieth century. Take the second volume of book I of *Capital*, which discusses the historical trends of the process of capitalist accumulation, which unfolded in the long duration of history. It must be observed, though, that Marx is not expounding in the vein of a historical work, although there are elements of description and narrative, in some part as illustration, in some part in a more systematic way. Let us remember the "Introduction" to his research notebooks (the *Grundrisse*), written in the 1850s, a difficult but extremely rich text, in which he handled, indirectly, the discussion of Hegel's contribution in particular to scientific thought. In this text, published posthumously, Marx (1857–58, 19ff) traced certain differences,

---

5   It is not a matter of opposing history (or genesis) to structure, as proposed by Godelier (1973), but of, as we shall see below, pointing to reiterated and repeated processes, although always shifting and of different types.

which he would later resume in the "Preface" to *Capital* (1867), between history and theory, narrative and systematic exposition, research and conceptual organization. He began actually by pointing out that we should take the more evolved forms and building upon them organize the exposition of the historical process, that is, so to speak backward, although this was not absolute insofar as some conceptual categories could be well-developed in less complex societies. In any case, what mattered for him was the weight of each analytical category he believed we needed to craft, shaping a "concrete universal" system of concepts that mentally reproduced the complexity of contemporary society, not its piecemeal historical emergence. The division of labor, for instance, has existed for millennia, ever since the social formation of the Incas, among others. But was the division of labor what was most important in contemporary capitalism? No. On the contrary. What was necessary to grasp was not the narrative of the development of these forms historically, but how the capitalist mode of production was contemporarily organized. What are the categories then that really articulate capitalism? What specific form did the division of labor acquire in this sort of social formation?[6]

If we take a closer look, there are two key elements – not the division of labor, though it is present – that organize the systematic category-based exposition that Marx realized in *Capital*: the commodity with which he opens the book and, afterward, the most important category throughout is *plus-value*, which is based on the idea that labor became a commodity that could be bought and

---

6 At this point Honneth (2014) totally misunderstands the issue, stating that in his political writings Marx dealt with the morals of collective actors and of "contingent" events, while in his critique of political economy he excluded them, since it possessed a synchronic character and focused on the "timeless" development of capital, overlooking openings to social change. We can surely disagree with Marx's revolutionary strategies (but Honneth himself asks why the gradual and sometimes innovative reforms he suggests did not materialize), as well as the way he relates capitalism as an ethical system and the economy. This does not warrant statements to the effect of a supposedly lack of historicity in *Capital*, which delves into the long duration in categorial terms and in what concerns mechanisms of unintentional origins and outcomes (curiously Honneth does not deal with the general trends of capitalist accumulation), nor disregard the contingent/necessary role of mores and of proletarian collective subjectivity and the transformative mechanism (which would break with the infinite cycle of the increasingly problematic valorization of capital, given its growing "organic composition" and the "tendency of the profit rate to fall" – see Marx 1894). Several mechanisms are present in Marx's political works, but by and large they are not treated systematically, and even less categorically. Honneth draws upon Sewell's (2005, 6–12, 121–123) work, a historian who tries, with difficulty, to cope with the temporality of history, proposing the ill-defined notion of "event" (although Mann has convinced him that "developmental trends" do exist, without a teleological trust, a point from which he does not draw the concrete consequences).

sold. Capitalism's wealth is thus "an immense accumulation of commodities," with their double character – use-value, and exchange-value – an idea that is further elaborated until we get to the thesis that there is a wealth whose origin is unknown, which Marx eventually explains as labor not paid, carried out after the worker produced a value that sufficed to reproduce his labor-power. The secret of capitalist production, the crux of the matter, is plus-value, which can exist only insofar as labor became wage-labor, in its abstract generality. But before this was possible a long process of historical development unfolded, with its own origins and directionality, providing the fundamentally general theoretical object of the second half of *Capital,* namely, the "historical tendency of capitalist accumulation."

Marx tried to understand how capitalism was constituted as a world of commodities in which labor is also a commodity that generates more wealth, which is not appropriated by the worker, but instead by the capitalist. For this to happen the worker must be separated from the means of production, otherwise he would not sell his labor-power (nobody is inclined, in principle, to be exploited). When the worker has direct access to the land, as was the case in the United States also in the post-colonial period, people were very often inclined to go to the frontier to work on their own, which had the additional consequence of keeping wages higher for those who stayed in the cities since they had more leverage in negotiating their labor. Nonetheless, what is the genesis of this situation? Where shall it take us? It is at this point that *Capital* ends, or at least where volume 1, the only one published by Marx in his own lifetime, trails off, with the idea that "the expropriators are expropriated." Wealth concentrates, is centralized and, at a certain stage, through the intervention of basically the revolutionary subjectivity of dispossessed workers, the bell tolls for bourgeois property. This is therefore a historical trend, yet it is organized by analytical categories, it is not a historical narrative that Marx presents us with. When he asks how we reached the conditions that lead to this development in the long run, the answer is surely historical, but his focus is very specific, entailing the discussion about *primitive accumulation,* to how there is capital, on one side, and only wage-labor, on the other. But Marx did not narrate the history of England or of capitalism as a whole, he dwelt exclusively on the emergence of a class that has nothing to sell but its labor-power, while conversely there is another one that owns the means of production. This means that the historical work carried out within *Capital* is subordinated to the analytical categories Marx crafted: commodity, wage-labor, capital, ground rent, everything is organized with this in mind. The exposition is an analytical categorial exposition, meaning that these are concepts that represent reality such as mentally projected by the researcher and then transcribed to paper. History is therein introduced as an element that helps to reckon with the original and future trajectory of this kind of society. This concerns political economy, but also, to a large extent, sociology. We can even say that *Capital* is a historical sociology book whose history is subordinated to critical theory by means of this analytical categorial exposition, in which the past is examined from the standpoint of the construction of concepts that aim at understanding the present and its future unfolding.[7]

Let us pass to the next example, *The Protestant Ethics and the Spirit of Capitalism* (Weber 1904b). The most usual in the discussion about Weber is for him to appear as an author counterposed to Marx. Therefore, it would not be a question of how "productive forces," in their contradiction with the "relations of production," such as in the latter, play a role in history, but rather how ideas (or, more precisely, their translation into practical life conducts and, more broadly, "material and ideal interests" of agents) do so. This would be implied in the relation between religion and material life, Protestantism and capitalism. But perhaps the issue may not be reduced at least to the comparison between the West with China and India, of Protestantism with Confucianism, Buddhism, Hinduism (and ancient Judaism, as well as, marginally, Islamism and Zoroastrianism). Weber is a very dense author; hence it is possible to approach him from several angles, some of which he was not necessarily fully conscious of in principle himself, but which are nevertheless legitimate and enlightening.[8] What I would like to suggest is that we apply what I have just done with Marx's *Capital* to Weber's work.

The Protestant Ethics and the Spirit of Capitalism was only the first study of Weber's huge sociology of religion, undertaken in the course of many years, and in which there is in particular the volume collected before his death called "Intermediate Observations" (Weber 1920b). There he crafted the idea of the "religious rejections of the world and their directions." If we take the argument

---

7   See also his own *Grundrisse* (Marx 1857–58, 371–372, 376ff), where the argument is perhaps more explicit. In this regard, it seems that it might be useful to incorporate the sketch of a "materialist genealogy" which West (1989, 223–225) adumbrated under the sway of Marx himself and Foucault, beyond the (neo-Kantian) idea of "conditions of possibility" of certain types of subjectivity, according to the latter instead with reference to the historical emergence of certain practices and social relations, as well as concerning the construction of the social symbolic-hermeneutic universe.

8   But note that Weber speaks of historical "selection" (*Auslese*) of "economic agents" according to their "forms of conduct," accordingly to capitalistic requirements, which starts with asceticism and the conception of "vocation" of the Protestant sects and unfolds as a mass phenomenon later, totally as an unintentional consequence of reforms aiming at salvation. See especially Weber 1904b, 37, 81–83.

in its main structure, we understand that he was contrasting three attitudes in relation to the world. One, that of Chinese Confucian literati, is pragmatic, and does not imply tension with the world, since they cope with issues, problems and solutions without superimposing very strong models to which the world had to adapt, while they are the ones, conversely, who are themselves trying to adapt to reality. Weber was somehow more interested in the other two forms. The attitude of the Indians, asceticism, led to a flight from the world, with a tension between the commands of religion, other-worldly realms and salvation, and the world. The agent ends up engaged in ascetic practices of salvation (*Erlösung*), "deflecting" from the world and trying to close the cycle of reincarnations and to totally free (*befreien*) himself from it. In the West, in contradistinction, a type of attitude in relation to the world developed that is at once similar to and different from Hinduism and Buddhism, both Indic religions. There is also asceticism therein and a lot of tension between transcendence (other-worldly) and immanence (this-worldly), but this is sorted out basically through the idea of "world-mastery," intervention into it, and its subordination to the will; whereas asceticism in India would turn to a sphere outside the world, Western asceticism was attached to action in this world. Protestantism consists exactly in an expression of this-worldly asceticism, with its control and transformation, according to Weber. The typical Western attitude in relation to the world emerged very strongly in the guise of Protestant religion. But in capitalism, which in Weber's view evinces an "elective affinity" with Protestantism, one can detect an attitude of intervention in and control of the world, a restless impulse to manipulate and transform, that eventually becomes a phenomenon totally detached from religion, with the world losing its meaning in its most profound sense and taking up an almost systemic character, with freedom having its ground subtracted.

What I want to bring out here, unlike current interpretations, is a possible and specific articulation between sociology and history. One could sustain the thesis that to Weber the Protestant ethic as such is of lesser importance, the same happening to his comparisons with other worldly "religions." That is, most relevant to Weber would not be the "concomitant variations" of religious attitudes in relation to the world – in a Durkheimian sense, those attitudes which separated the East from the West but that in the main "agreed" in terms of material advances between the sixteenth and the eighteenth centuries –, but rather something akin to Marx's operation concerning capital's "primitive accumulation." Whether Weber had this clear or not, upheld this strategy or would not recognize it exactly as his, if at all introduced to it, is beside the point. Of course, an author's goals matter, but maybe what matters more is what we want to do with their work. This is how I am keen to appropriate him by proposing a manner to outline a theory of modernity. What thus comes up in Weber's discussion is an effort to think about this-worldly asceticism, or at least immersed in it, such as it appears in Western culture by and large. The Protestant ethic would be only an originating element, crucial but not exclusive, that he finds as historically given and that allows him to consider the genesis of an attitude that permeates the whole capitalist, Western, rationalized world, hence searching which are the fundamental categories to explain the modern world, with the genesis of capitalism playing a secondary role in this discussion. In my view, it thus becomes possible to modulate the argument so as to inquiry into how that attitude emerged and developed, afterward expanding across the world. The possible historical origins of the phenomenon would be at stake, allowing for a reconstruction of history with the foremost objective of articulating a historical construction that could explain the contemporary world.

We have identified, in Marx and in Weber, two *generative mechanisms* of modernity following the analytical construction of categories that we can glean from the works of these classical authors. In other words, we have an analytical categorical explanation of the workings of the contemporary world opening the possibility of an analytical reconstruction of the *reiterative mechanisms* whereby the modern world is reproduced, although counting on elements of creativity and innovation – whether from the standpoint of the organization of capitalist society or from the standpoint of attitudes in relation to the world –, we can think of the formative elements of this sort of social formation in its first specific steps, before they became modern, as it were, on the other hand, but making a historical delimitation that focuses only on those developments that interest us, dedicated to certain aspects of reality that have brought us to the present. Weber, as Cohn (1978) argued, was resigned vis-à-vis the modern world, incapable of envisaging ways out of the desolate situation of disenchantment in which we find ourselves. As already pointed out, Marx, in his turn searched for the *transformative mechanisms* of the capitalist social formation precisely in historical trends, in terms of accumulation and in the revolutionary intervention of the proletariat.

At any rate, if we contemplate the attitudes in relation to the world and capitalism from the standpoint of explanatory mechanisms of genesis, functioning and change of contemporary social life, we can also clearly see that these mechanisms cannot do without human action and the movement of collectivities.[9] It is not a matter of mechanisms whose causal impact would

---

9 What is at stake here is the elaboration of the concept of collective subjectivity, which I carried out in a number of occasions and is mobilized throughout this book.

come about automatically, rather, they are always intertwined with individual action and collective movement, which implies the reproduction of memories and the creative generation of new patterns, material, political and imaginary, with mechanisms which, having been sometimes associated to this very reproduction, lead in many cases to the transformation of society, with a re-iterative as well as transformative character. Be it as it may, we must hew to an analytical distinction between these facets, as well as in what regards their generative character of truly new civilizational patterns under certain conditions. Methodologically, moreover, it is interesting to steer the issues in this direction, casting our gaze toward the latter with a reference to the mechanisms that work at present, in a reiterative manner, and in the future, in a transformative course (as discussed in Chapter 2 of this book).

This allows us to understand the relation between historical sociology and sociological theory, concept and description/narrative in a very different way and which can propel our discipline in another direction, which is historical, and empirically based, but which is rooted fundamentally in the search for the identification of the mechanisms of functioning and reproduction of contemporary societies and of their trends toward future transformation. We thus get rid of a trivial view of the concept of mechanism as such and assume a stance focused on processes rather than on putative "structures," without the need to look into layers obscurely defined as "deeper" (except epistemologically, due to the inevitable operations in the very production of knowledge and in what regards their ideological occultation). A vision of the relation between sociology and history emerges which is less a narrative reconstruction of the past and more an explanation of the present and seeks to identify its *sui generis* elements in the former. That is, it is not so much the idea of concomitant variations that comes forward to explain the present, nor that much of the method of agreement and difference, but instead the construction of analytical categories that allow us to understand the formative mechanisms of modernity what we would pursue in historical sociology (without in addition a commitment to what is often called the "uniformity of nature" or "regularity determinism," since mechanisms – themselves process-based – do not always generate the same processes and "events"). That is to say, mechanisms are found closely associated to individual and collective episodic moves, which, in modern civilization, become *modernizing moves*, which are reiterated but are also changed as they find their way in the world.

The task is therefore to build theoretical systems that account for the complexity of modernity, in its multidimensionality and in the directionalities of its development. In *Capital*, Marx provided us with the largest and more articulate among them thus far, with respect to its "economic" dimension and within the frame of political economy. We must not take his theoretical strategy as the only one worth cultivating, although its sophistication is beyond doubt, as well as the productivity of his identification of the tendencies of capitalist accumulation (whether he was correct or not as to each of them in particular) and its future overcoming. Be it as it may, it is important to go beyond description, building concepts and aiming at grasping the developmental trends of modernity, in the Brazilian and Latin American space-time coordinates, within the more encompassing framework of global modernity.

Conclusion

I therefore hope it has become clear what the theoretical discussion of this text has to do with Brazilian modernity – and Latin American modernity somewhat more broadly. Firstly, to think of historical sociology in these terms may allow us to get out of self-absorption. That is to say, if we look at the history of Brazil this way, we can change the questions we pose to ourselves and modify the methodological strategy that has often been used, which is to think of history itself, in its completeness, to see where the country has arrived. On the contrary, it may be a question of thinking where Brazil has arrived and looking back from this vantage point, even though it seems clear that modernity has been completed among us and that what matters in a certain way is the present and the future, not, finally, as much as we wanted until recently, to overcome the past (Brandão 2007; Domingues 2015). This does not necessarily contradict what has been done to date. On the contrary, it is necessary to use the very rich works that have been written to think about the Brazilian trajectory in order to deal with this question, without giving up new research that may even help to relativize them. The case of the countries of Latin America as units of analysis and of the subcontinent itself as a whole is also placed in the same coordinates. In order to stay in the Brazilian national framework and to refer to a few examples, authors such as Euclides da Cunha, Oliveira Vianna, Gilberto Freyre and Florestan Fernandes present us with valuable works that can be instrumental in this direction, helping us to think today about modernity, especially if it is put in perspective by new investigations.

Perhaps in addition, if we are to cast away our self-absorption, it will be fundamentally through this effort to think about the common mechanisms of generation, reiteration and transformation of contemporary modernity at a global level that this is worth bearing in mind. I do not propose to return to the quest of something like the "laws of history." Mechanisms are more modest concepts – even if they are inserted in a complex analytical system, as they seem to me to be more adequately and productively conceived –, whether in biology or physics (whether this is actually occupied or not, basically, with general laws). The social sciences are historical sciences, so one must take into account how these mechanisms work historically, although there are mechanisms (as in biology and the physical evolution of the universe) of a more universal nature. In the context of the discussion between historical sociology and Brazilian modernity, it is worth emphasizing the generalizing character – empirically and analytically – that the idea of mechanisms affords us. So perhaps we can see Brazil not as a *jabuticaba* – an expression referring to a fruit that, much like other traits, supposedly, can only be found here, making it a metaphor for out singular trajectory –, that is, that modernity as we know it exists fundamentally in its bounds. We can thus take the discussion to a conceptual, systematic, more comprehensive plane.

Finally, although it is a matter of keeping the focus on new researches, oriented by the issues of the present, returning to classical authors in the way suggested here can also be very productive, as long as we look for the construction of theories rather than more empirical accumulation (even though this may appear as empirical evidence, referred only to Brazil). To be sure, how reality is transformed and how to transform reality must, or at least could, in a critical perspective, come forward as a key element in the very discussion of the mechanisms that preside over the development of modernity, there and elsewhere.

CHAPTER 5

Realism, Trend-concepts and the Modern State

Introduction

Sociology developed, under this or other designation (such as "historical materialism"), mostly combining theoretical insights and empirical evidence, classically concerned in particular with the development of modernity. *Trend-concepts* – such as capitalist development and its consequences, rationalization, bureaucratization, increasing division of labor, secularization, democratization – have been, or used to be, a key-issue in sociological analysis. So-called "theories of modernization" and Marxism stood out in the twentieth century in relation to such processes and the trend-concepts associated with them (see the second chapter of this book). More recently, after a long and eventually not exceedingly productive exchange about modernity and so-called post-modernity, most interlocutors left the field of debate. Moreover, even though it pointed to a long-term trend, the debate was to a large extent descriptive. This was aggravated by the post-colonial turn, which evinces a strong discursive strategy.

There are several ways to think about the social sciences, but the proposal here is to reverse course and resume analytically-oriented strategies, particularly regarding the theorization of modernity. This must go beyond the mere description of Western countries and the almost direct comparison with similar phenomena elsewhere, instead building analytical frameworks within which global modernity can be grasped.

To accomplish this, I initially draw upon the work of Roy Bhaskar. I shall not, however, remain closely attached to any orthodox "critical realist" standpoint. In fact, I critically depart from some key elements in his conception, toward a process-oriented and anti-reification *demarche*. I then return to the key issue of *trend-concepts*, which intend to frame long-term processes of modernization. I want to show that they should not be contemplated according to an empiricist standpoint, which dwells on event conjunctions and the idea of "uniformity of nature" (contrary to Boudon 1989). Explanatory mechanisms can be built analytically, therefore also beyond the often-trivialized form found

---

* Originally published in Filipe Campello and Benjamin Gittel (orgs.), *Modernizações ambivalentes*. Recife: Editora UFPE, 2016. Here with some of the modifications introduced on occasion of "The Imaginary and Modern Developmental Trends: A Conference," IESPUERJ, September 29–30, 2016.

in most of what passes as "analytical theory" today (Hedström and Swedberg 1998), despite its occasional interesting insights. In any case, mechanisms are not exclusive to such authors, featuring Marx, Weber, Parsons and an array of other "macro" sociologists (see Manicas 2006, Chap. 5). The application of this theoretical strategy to the development of the modern state-society system and its place within global modernity concludes the article.

Beyond Empiricism (and Critical Realism)

Bhaskar's principal target in his works on the philosophy of science was empiricism, or rather its mistaken understanding of what scientists do – with reference basically to the natural sciences, mostly physics. Only later did he apply his perspective to the social sciences (wherein researchers, I would argue, actually espouse much more decidedly empirical perspectives, also when using hermeneutical-interpretive approaches). A realist theory of science was the outcome of the endeavor, featuring a "stratified" view of reality in which the "mechanisms" that generate "events" are supposed to exist and endure independently of the latter. Bhaskar most especially attacked Hume's theory of causality and the idea of "conjunction of events" as a necessary and sufficient condition of science. The "real" underpinnings of causal laws are thus provided by the "generative mechanisms of nature." These are "nothing other than the ways of acting of things," causal laws consisting in "their tendencies," which may be seen as "...powers or liabilities of a thing which may be exercised without being manifest in any particular outcome" (Bhaskar 1975, 12–15).

Bhaskar added that "mechanisms" – which at a certain point he equated to "tendencies" and ground "law-like statements" – "endure" even when not "acting" and, furthermore, "act" in a "normal way" when effects are not produced due to "intervening mechanisms" or "countervailing causes." Conjunctions depend on human action and experiments, conducted usually in laboratory settings. Alternatively, therefore, we need, he argued, to articulate an "ontology of structures" and "transfactually active beings," reckoning with "causal powers," in order to develop the "transcendental realist" approach. Science is connected to "possibilities," not "actualities": "tendencies may be possessed unexercised, exercised unrealized, and realized unperceived (or undetected) by men." Events and momentary states of things do not truly hinge on empirical experience – they too are independent of human beings, except when produced under controlled experimental conditions. Against Hume and his empiricist followers, but in the context of a quick (for bad reasons, as I argue below) dismissal of Platonic realism, Bhaskar believed he had a "perfectly logical basis for causal laws": he eschewed their reification as well as the reification of mechanisms yet thought that "...it cannot be wrong to reify things!" (Bhaskar 1975, 16–26, 36, 46, 52, 56).

In addition, Bhaskar stated that the concept of "tendency" implies the idea of "continuing activity" and thus a dynamic conception of the notion of (causal) power. They are possessed and can be exercised only insofar as their possessors remain unchanged. Once set in motion a tendency is fulfilled, unless prevented by another tendency. This is what furnishes the basis for law-like statements. His "conditionals" are "normic," instead of "subjunctive" (against Humean views): tendencies point to what *is* happening, not to what would happen; they generate not "counterfactuals," but "transfactuals," whether or not their effects become "manifest." One direction alone prevails: if two tendencies causally operate, the resultant is not a combination. The "real" or "nominal" "essence" or "substance" of a thing, Bhaskar went on, apparently unaware of the Platonist implications of the affirmation, are its "properties and powers," in passing putting forward that "...structures act..." (Bhaskar 1975, 50–51, 91, 97–98, 100, 109, 189–192, 221).

According to Bhaskar, mechanisms belong to the domain of the "real"; events to that of the "actual," while experience to the "empirical." Taxonomy is thus an issue for science, but so is explanation. Empiricism, however, can only offer a rationale for the latter if based on the principle of "regularity determinism." The idea of "uniformity of nature" is connected to this standpoint, nevertheless it is mistaken, since it refers to the "invariance of patterns of *events* (or experiences)," though Bhaskar accepts it in what concerns the domain of the real: induction is justified if it refers to generalizations assumed as "laws of nature." In contradistinction, for transcendental realism, "normic statements" refer to "structures" not "events," the "generator" rather than the "generated." They furnish theories, explanatory (albeit not necessarily predictive) models that purport to be "real" (Bhaskar 1975, 21–23, 52–56, 69, 101, 104, 141, 212, 247–248, 250).[1]

I consider Bhaskar's rebuttal of empiricism and the identification of mechanisms related to causal powers as crucial for the understanding of science. The same can said of the idea that we need to penetrate more deeply into (social) reality. However, this does not warrant his view of stratified layers of reality. Tendencies are not a hidden feature of reality that underlie events, but rather

---

1 *Induction* for him refers to "reasoning from particular instances to general statements"; *eduction* to extrapolations from the "observed" to the "unobserved" or from the past to the future (and is justified only if the system is closed, an experimental process). He is not sympathetic to "deductivism": it would be closely linked to "actualism" – the necessary occurrence of events looming large in it (Bhaskar 1975, 129, 216, 219).

processes that yield outcomes. These can, in particular in the long duration, configure developmental trends. The latter can be at odds with other trends, stemming from processes that bend in other or even opposite directions. The resultant of this, contrary to Bhaskar's apparently gratuitous statement, is a specific direction of development, a mix or new vector that independent tendencies would not in principle generate.[2] His identification of structures and things with causal powers is misleading, especially in that he proposes a "naturalist" conception of social life (Bhaskar 1979). He falls into *massive reification* as he strongly and without any further ontological argument relies on the idea of social *structure* (regardless of its limited and somewhat naïf dialectical flexibilization through a combination with "action").[3] Maybe – though I doubt it – we can attribute causal powers to "things" in nature. In social life this is patently absurd, stemming from an unacknowledged embrace of Platonist realism with its talk of "essences" and "substances." Not by chance did Bhaskar hush through this sort of view, cursorily and ineffectually criticizing it, actually embracing it. A different sort of realism is necessary.

In the unpublished "Introduction" to the *Grundrisse* (1857–58) Marx outlined what in practice he would do in *Capital* (1867), namely, a massive reconstruction of the "concrete universal" of economic reality in modernity in terms of a system of analytical categories, inspired by Hegel's logic.[4] Similarly, Parsons (1937, 1951) hewed to a guideline and a method for at least some time, namely, "analytical realism," in a more Kantian vein. They both identified the necessity of mentally reconstructing the mechanisms that causally shape reality, starting with more general categories. But they did not make recourse to structures (except as a descriptive and a sort of instant model, in Parsons' case). They both focused on *processes*, woven by individuals and collectivities, and the mechanisms that produce them and how they are consolidated, either intentionally or unintentionally, to prevent or at least control and steer the transformation of reality, even though Parsons put much less emphasis on social change than

---

2 It is interesting to note that in Latin languages, as well as German, tendency and trend are translated by the same words (*tendence, tendencia, Trend,* etc.). Their differentiation in English allows for a subtler understanding of the matter.

3 See also Archer, Bhaskar, Collier, Lawson and Norrie 1998. The notion of structure is fuzzy in Bhaskar, but his critical realist followers are able to turn out more fine-grained versions. It drew upon the natural science (physics) reified view of "things" as possessing tendencies and was then directly transposed to the social sciences. Manicas (2006, 67ff, 115ff) recognized this and adopted instead Giddens' view of structures as "virtual," denying causal powers to "structures" and speaking only of "persons" as causal agents. This is, however, still a limited solution.

4 Jessop (1990, 340–344) stated the need of this strategy regarding the state, without practical consequences hitherto.

Marx did. But Platonism was clearly rejected by both authors. If on occasion Marx employed inadequate words such "essence" and "appearance" (or explicitly connected "structure" to dynamic relations) to speak of underlying realities, this had nothing to do with notions of substance (see Domingues 1995a; 2000a, Chap. 2). He was adamant to bring out all sorts of reification in modern "society," especially through his critique of political economy, pointing to the interactions, recurrent practices and social relations that underlie commodity, money, capital, the "trinity formula" and other social constructs.

In turn, trend-concepts have been important in sociology, but how to theorize them and which status we should lend them has been less frequently a topic for sociologists. Overall, they have been framed by empiricism, that is, their comprehension has been guided according to a mere association of variables, to Humean-like *empirical conjunctions*, of the sort that figure as Bhaskar's main target of criticism. Once A, then B, whence if B is absent one must suppose that A is not present either, while if A is present and B fails to occur the analyst is all but lost. This happens because the explanation of why such associations between variables occur or not is either defective, superficial (mainly the reiteration of empirical issues, at best through empirical generalizations and descriptive concepts) or simply does not figure in the argument. Indeed, some sort of very basic and empirically-phrased "theory" is frequently found in most of these approaches, but is patently insufficient.

I propose to take the idea of trend-concepts to a higher, analytical level of theorizing, instead of treating them through the mere association of variables or even as empirical generalizations that supposedly underpin general statements about modernizing trends (although there is no rupture between these levels of knowledge, with analytical categories modified once empirical issues demand their revision). We can thereby reconstruct mechanisms of modernization that may furnish an explanation as to why such outcomes occur or not. "Tendencies" contained within processes that are typical of modernity must be identified. They must not be seen as properties of "things" or "structures," but rather as inclinations of specific trends construed in terms of non-reified social processes. These are not reducible to individuals or "persons," nevertheless we must not shy away from going beyond the general social character frequently attributed to them.

The Modern State and Modern Society

The state and its relation to society have evidently been key themes in the social sciences. I propose here a specific way of analytically framing the issue and elaborating the idea of modernizing trends connected to it. To this end, some preliminary conceptual issues must be clarified.

Whether or not we can properly speak of the "state" in former civilizations or should rather refer to a more loosely defined "political system" (Almond 1960), since the state does not appear as a separate and centralized form of "domination" with territorial monopoly and of "legitimate" physical violence (Weber 1921–22, 29), shall not concern us here. But let us stress that the political system – the instance where decisions and policies affecting society at large are defined – is larger than the state, with social forces working from without and trying to move within with the aim to eventually crystallize (Jessop 2008, 1–11). In addition, bureaucracy – the administrative dimension – must be distinguished from the political system proper, although it does take political decisions in a more discrete and limited way (something that in Habermas 1981, for example, systematically leads to confusion, possibly following the lack of adequate differentiation already such as present in Weber's work). The state has been a crucial means through which the paramount, social "existential question" of *power distribution* in social life has been answered in modernity, with its specific and unequal, as well as largely independent, features and dynamic (with power relations, in addition, running through social life, in personal or economic terms, for instance). Social regulation through law-making is crucial in this regard, but the state also contains a decisive element of executive power, which is exercised mainly by the bureaucracy. It is important to stress that the particular sort of modern social formation, namely "society," in its tightly bounded shape, is to a considerable extent engendered by the modern state itself, with its sharp territorial power and unprecedented capacity to penetrate and steer it. The formal separation between state and society – real but largely ideological too –, as well as deeper entanglement, is moreover an important aspect of modernity. Finally, although this is not the center of our discussion here, let us note that, since its inception, the state has been placed in an increasingly more globally encompassing system of formally sovereign states (Poulantzas 1978; Giddens 1985; Jessop 1990; Mann 1993, Chap. 3).

With this background, the discussion carried out below is based on the identification of *two main trends* concerning state and society in modernity. Let us first examine the literature on the topic. We can then present an analytically articulated conceptualization.

We have known at least since Weber (1921–22, 122–176, 387–513, 541–868) that the modern state has as one of its central traits its "rational-legal" character. It has therefore been abstractly conceived according to the formal legal system and instrumental rationality (the increasingly more adequate connection between ends and means) possessed by bureaucracy (also including and above all the judiciary). There lies its "legitimacy." Weber's characterization is somewhat problematic since Anglo-Saxon "common law" is customary rather than actually formal, albeit systematized according to the Roman canon. Formalism is above all a feature of the European continental and Latin American "civil law" tradition (despite recent changes). In any case, overall Weber meant that, in their application, modern legal systems are abstract from the specific characteristics of context and the people involved. Bureaucracy also manifests an abstract interest in the state insofar as, separated from the "means of administration" (much as workers are separated from the "means of production" in Marx's account of capitalism), it has no patrimonial stakes, working according to a code of honor, formalized rules and rational efficiency. Weber saw state *domination* as *autonomous*, a particular embodiment and source of power (politics as such remaining ill-defined in his theory). It was a reality extant only in modernity, controlling territory and monopolizing the legitimate means of violence, differently from "traditional" and "charismatic" domination.

In Marxism, at least one key element of Weber's view has been partly present, despite deep-seated divergences: namely, the abstract character of the modern state. Marx (1844) himself opposed it in his early writings to the concrete (class and religiously-based) elements to be found in "bourgeois civil society" (an expression taken from Hegel's philosophy of law). Class domination was of course a decisive element in Marx's (1871) later views. Henceforth the concrete side of "capitalist" state operations has been treated by Marxists (for instance Gramsci 1929–35; Poulantzas 1968, 1978; Miliband 1971) with a more "instrumentalist," "functionalist" or "relational" conception, at times asserting its almost complete, albeit conditioned, autonomy (Jessop 1990, Chap. 12). Agents who manage the executive branch and the parliament, the army and the police, the juridical system and central banks, as well as the "enlarged state" ("political society" plus "civil society") or its "ideological apparatuses" (schools, churches, unions) have been decisive in this regard.

There has not been much development in the Weberian current concerning rational-legal domination. Tilly (1992) and Mann (1993, especially Chap. 3) more indirectly and partly represent recent, heterodox developments, mostly limited to empirical (even if ideal-typical) generalizations about the concentration of power in the state apparatus and its links with capital and society, which the latter conceptualized in terms of "crystallizations" within it (with Evans, Rueschemeyer and Skocpol 1985, stressing state bureaucratic "capabilities" in terms of its exercise of power). In this respect, despite recurrent complaints concerning the unfinished outline of the school's theory, Marxism went further and refined a number of perspectives on the state and society. This is visible in Pasukanis' (1926) theory of law, wherein we find once again the idea of its abstract character as well as his strong contention that the relation with the "owner of commodities" is the key to grasp the whole system, in which the "contract" is the pivotal element. Pasukanis also stated that the "form" of law, with its own "fetishism" – opposing, as a complementary pair, the private and public dimensions, private persons and the members of political society – was absolutely pivotal for both the modern state and society, which are after all interpenetrated. We could complement this and introduce Lukács (1923, 169–186, 271–272, 183–185) connection between Weber's theory of law and Marx's theory of the abstract side of the commodity, the result of which was his thesis about the latter as providing a "real abstraction" whereupon the whole "superstructure" of modern capitalist society is based. Poulantzas (1978, 54–55, 94–99) was also attentive to the abstract character of law in his later theorization.

Therefore, if the separation of state and society was introduced initially as a basic feature of modern social life, the state is still defined specifically by its abstract elements, in contradistinction to the societal dynamic, with its concrete and particular interests and identities. The former is framed and mediated directly by modern law and its fundamental figure, that is, *citizenship* as a *real abstraction*. In this regard, I suggest we somehow invert Marx's, Pasukanis' and Lukács' view of the commodity and the "superstructure," since they attribute causal and categorial priority to the former, while I would like to suggest that much of modern social life depends on the imaginary and institutional scaffolding of citizenship as a real abstraction so as to function and even to produce economic contracts between equally free agents (Domingues 2006, Chap. 3). There is an obvious connection between these two sides of the state and society divide and entanglement which are given by the very idea of a bifurcated system of public and private law, whose agents are to a large extent the same individuals who concretely produce social life at large and are simultaneously abstract members of the state. Drawing upon Marx's view of the commodity in *Capital*, with its use-value and exchange-value, it can be said that the state-society system consists of a *dialectical unit of contraries* whose interplay is crucial for the developmental dynamic of modernity.

Such a conceptualization might lead us however to a static understanding of the operations of the modern state, *pace* the, in principle, dynamic component entailed by that dialectical tension. Let us therefore firmly move beyond the pitfalls that lurk in this limitation.

First of all, we must acknowledge what is already current in the literature: within citizenship, the concrete irrupted powerfully, through its social aspect, certain collective rights, diffuse rights and the like. When it was not through citizenship that the concrete surfaced – or when we went from citizenship toward less universal categories, as within the framework of a nineteenth century or contemporary social liberalism –, its affirmation was carried out by social policies, by creating target-populations and so on, a stark affirmation vis-à-vis the abstract character of both civil and political citizenship. The concern of private and state ruling circles can certainly be indicated as the driving mechanism of this process, but it was in the popular struggles for the enlargement of modernity that the dynamic that led to the relativization of the abstract must be pointed out, although with universal social citizenship this still has great weight in the definition of modern individuals. This can be characterized as both positive – since such citizens have rights – and negative – insofar as they tend to end up as clients and in a *passive* situation. In turn, targeted policies do the same, but single out groups whose entitlements span variable periods of time, let alone more traditional (thin or dense) sorts of clientelism (Marshall 1950; Domingues 2013). In any case, a true historical tendency is found in this whole process of affirmation of the concrete of societal life. Yet the discussion must not stop there.

Karatani (2004; 2005, 147, 276) insightfully resumed the debate about *The Eighteenth Brumaire of Louis Bonaparte*, suggesting that Marx was concerned with "repetition" as "compulsion" in history. This meant a swing between the normal representation (*Vertretung*) of the bourgeoisie in the state (which, once constituted through the ballot box, becomes independent of voters, as "representatives of the nation") and its crisis. Since Bonaparte as well as in Fascism (a form of "Bonapartism," Karatani affirms) a specific societal figure has emerged purporting to unify society and imaginarily overcome its "fragmented classes," implying a "return of the repressed" (absolutist sovereignty). Karatani's contention that Bonapartism and Fascism are essentially the same is totally absurd (and politically dangerous), yet the valid point in his argument is the opposition between abstract representation and the surge of society-based forces – or state-based, we should add. In moments of crisis, they may take over power and reorganize social life, as a dialectical movement intrinsic to modern civilization and not only as a transitional stage before its full constitution and stabilization. Zavaleta (1990) stated a similar point: while bourgeois democracy would be the normal form of capitalist domination, mirroring politically the civil freedom to enact contracts enjoyed by people in the market, in times of crisis "mediators" break through the political field. These "mediators," partly state-based, partly society-based, and who usually operate to perfect domination, are then released from state domination (which values only itself, with its partial autonomy and the ideological obfuscation of its social ties) and may even become state agents which directly represent society, in a reactionary or progressive direction. In Gramsci's (1929–35, vol. 3, 1619–20) progressive or regressive "Cesarism" the surge of concrete extra-institutional elements was also a theme.

With a diametrically opposed sensibility and intent, modernization theory observed similar sorts of phenomena. Huntington (1968) suggested that when modernization processes break down, especially if institutions are weak, "praetorian forces" may emerge as state powers to organize a society that would not otherwise be able to vertebrate itself politically. He was in fact here alluding to military coups in Latin America, toward which he was sympathetic and tried to legitimize (although he also more incidentally mentioned students and the clergy as "praetorian forces"). In any case, this would mean the dislocation of forces within the state, or the emergence of society-based forces, engendering a rupture with both the abstract character of the legal system and the bureaucratic rationality that in principle, ideally, shape its administrative apparatus. The West, especially the Anglo-Saxon countries, having developed in a much larger span of time than the rest of the world, mostly did not have to grapple with this predicament, having gone beyond its dangers. Germani's (1965) theory of "populism" in Argentina, later generalized for Latin America as a whole, stated a similar point, with elites breaking through a restrictive liberal political system and offering only an "ersatz" form of participation for available masses. Weber's (1921–22, 140ff, 654ff) view of charismatic domination already pointed to the personification of power and to extra-institutional elements.

Two further concrete expressions of interests within the modern state must be mentioned before we move further. First, its neo-patrimonial traits. They are linked to both the societal crystallizations identified by Mann and the access public officials and politicians have to state resources, although they are formally separated from them and neo-patrimonial behavior is thus considered corrupt, illegitimate and illegal, which does not mean it does not regularly occur, to a higher or lesser degree, in all modern states (Eisenstadt 1973; Domingues 2012, 84ff). Finally, we need to consider that representation is only one element in the "dialectic of control" established between citizens whose lives are now much more dependent upon its interventions and the strong modern state (Giddens 1985, especially 11). This is all the more relevant the deeper democratization unfolds. More direct contacts between citizens and the state must be also considered in this regard, either personally or through organizations such as associations and unions.

What we find in these contributions, once we synthesize and lend them an analytical character, are *dynamic contradictions*, mostly revolving around the *dialectic of control*, in which *political representation* stands out, *state power* and also around the dialectic between *abstract* and *concrete* elements. These at times converge, but frequently diverge and clash, as Marx (1852) perceived in the *Eighteen Brumaire*, though the idea of *dynamic contradictions*, which played a role especially in his later political economy in terms of mechanisms and developmental trends mediated by agents' behavior, though often escaping their intentions, hence implying a twofold role for collective subjectivity, beyond any crude sort of automatism (Marx, 1867, 1883, 1894).[5] In other words, a *contradictory trend* develops throughout modernity, combining and opposing *citizen control, political representation* and *state power, abstract* and *concrete* elements, with the possibility of acute crisis looming large.

Political systems can be stabilized and to some extent immunized against the potentially disruptive effects of these contradictions, which are, moreover, closely connected to social struggles, class-based or otherwise. Marxism in particular has dealt with this sort of issue, mostly successfully in Gramsci's (1929–35) concept of "hegemony," with the creation of a sort of social "consensus" alongside "coercion," as mechanisms of stabilization themselves. It never went on to the assumption that this is the mere accomplishment of "mature" democracy, due to the development of its "requisites" (literacy, economic development, existence of middle-classes) (Lipset 1959; Dahl 1989) or achieved "functional integration" (Parsons 1971), running henceforth smoothly and peacefully, as in different versions of liberalism. Neither is it suggested that this would be a sort of "legitimacy" that seems to automatically pertain to the modern state (as in Weber's formulation). Alongside the institutionalization of liberalism, the greater independence of political systems (including parties) from the influence of citizens and the degradation of democracy into the mere "audience" politics typical of the West today (Manin 1997) is perhaps more relevant for their stability than actual hegemonic constructions, accompanied by eventual social explosions and the emergence of what many today problematically define as right-wing "populism" (cf. Laclau, 2005). We must also take into account the *bureaucratic thickening* of the state, through complexification and diversification (Huntington, 1968), as well as the "infrastructural" penetration (Mann 1993) of the state in social life, in order to understand this resilience in the face of crisis and the possibility of disruption. This is a long-term trend,

---

5 Namely, the passage of absolute to relative plus-value, concentration and centralization of capital, the tendency of the rate of profit to fall, changes in population composition, etc., leading to the expropriation of the expropriators. The latter's mechanism was directly dependent upon the working class intentional political intervention. The workings of uncontrollable, often opaque, unintended effects are the best way to render contemporarily the concept of "natural law" in Marx's writings, as he was at least to some extent aware of (Marx 1857–58, 127).

adding to state power. Conversely, we must bear in mind that a sort of rebellious subjectivity, intensely *averse to deference* (Therborn 2009), has also been developing, expanding the limits of citizenship and sometimes overflowing it (as in some forms of recent "autonomist" mobilizations). It stems from both a radicalization of the social autonomy of individuals and collectivities in modernity and the unresponsiveness of the contemporary state.[6]

Disruptive and stabilizing mechanisms are therefore at play in the contradictory dynamic of the modern state. Potential disruption and crisis cannot ever be entirely avoided or kept in check, in any phase of modernity, regardless of the changes in the very form of the state, including different sorts of political regime (liberal, welfare states, Keynesian, workfare states, developmentalist) and the issues it tackles.

Should we behave as historians, or as twentieth century historical sociologists, we might be tempted to search for the origins of the modern state and its links with society, even if our more specific focus were the emergence of citizenship, the concentration of power and bureaucratization (as done by Bendix 1964, 1978, for a number of globally situated cases), although other authors were more selective in this respect (such as Elias, 1939, with his Eurocentric reconstruction of the path to the state monopoly of violence and pacification). We may be better off by strategically sticking to the search for the identification of the specific elements that historically led to this conjunction of systemic and dynamic elements (although extensive historical knowledge is necessary to accomplish this narrowing down of formative processes). In any case, the rationale for such a sort of *demarche* must be made more explicit and the historical element further shrunk: analyses must in this perspective be historical only to a limited extent and with a precise intent (as argued by Marx 1857–58, 371–372, 376ff). In other words, the first task at hand is to take the elements I have analytically laid out above and define them in terms of *analytical categories* and *reiterative mechanisms*. The concrete societal dynamic and the abstract character of the state may thereby stand out, even if neither of them in fact established in such a clear-cut way. This is due to the very existence of citizenship as a "real abstraction" and the penetration of "society" by the state as well as owing to "crystallizations" and the impact of the societal dynamic on the concrete workings of the state, whether through representatives, state bureaucratic personnel or other sorts of linkage. Only then must we look for

---

6　The concept of the "multitude" was introduced by Negri (cf. Hardt and Negri 2005) precisely in order to grapple with this, but its ontological, immediate, empirically all-embracing and vague character leads to an inadequate theoretical and political solution.

the *generative mechanisms* that historically engendered this situation.[7] Also, the identification of *transformative mechanisms that might overcome the present conformation of state and society*, with changes possibly developing from reiterative mechanisms, would be fundamental for a full critical, analytical account of the theme and a productive emancipatory perspective.

On the other hand, the legal fetishism identified by Pasukanis, inspired by the fetishism of the commodity in Marx, assumes the expression of an *enchantment*, linked to citizenship and the state. Therein the abstract subject, in its abstract freedom, takes on a role in the imaginary according to which relations between concrete people vanish, although the development of rights and of the state toward concreteness gradually makes these connections. Mediation – crystalized in the state – is superimposed onto that which is mediated, the relations that constitute it. To which extent the unfolding of the demand for autonomy in modernity can go beyond this imaginary and practical framework, as well as advance in the direction of the overcoming of that ontological individual isolation, remains an unanswered question. The same is true for a possible jettisoning of any external substance capable of defining who and what we are, imaginary in the sense that we generate it and end up captured by it (Zizek 1989, 261–263), being that in this case it is the imaginary such as outlined by Lacan that is at stake, however, I must stress, only partially so since it stems from an inexorably processual and intersubjective phenomenon. This substance can appear to us as the state, law or whatever may emerge in the future, since only then will we maybe know whether this is the case and how it can be, if it is indeed, positing itself in a transformed way.

A methodological note must be adduced here. First, we need to definitely separate the concept of the imaginary from the reified idea of "political culture." The latter is ultimately almost seen as a separate sphere, rigid and with simple and direct meanings, as in Almond and Verba (1965, especially Chap. 1), for example. The imaginary is part of social processes, not something distinct and separated from them. If building discrete models of the imaginary is useful, separate from social practices overall and from social developments trends, their concrete imbrication must almost be kept in purview. This means that its development, insofar as the "magma" of significations permeates all social

---

7 This would allow us for instance to avoid the search for "requisites of democracy," whether in economic development, literacy or anything else, typical of modernization theory, looking instead for elements that have contributed to it, including social struggles as well as values, such a *freedom*, that underpin its establishment. In addition, history as a contingent process remains amenable to a more modest sociological approach, a rigorous one, however, from the standpoint of analytical strategies proper.

practices, is linked to the unfolding of the trends that traverse modernity and actually fashion it, including those discussed in this chapter.

When we analyze the imaginary, it is necessary therefore to pay attention to hermeneutics (taken here in general, symbolically interpretive terms – see Giddens, 1976), without overlooking its wider insertion in social processes, which can be characterized by virtuous cooperation or antagonism. In any case, a hermeneutics attentive to the magmatic constitution and symbolically supple nature of the imaginary must be adopted, although it is structured in main nuclei (rationality and equal freedom, among others, as pointed out above). The symbolic universe is thus more adequately grasped – *verstehen* – either from a general or a specific vantage point, including with respect to particularized empirical analyses. There is no reason to oppose hermeneutics and the analysis of trends, or mechanisms and causal relations, in the same way it is dealt with in the discussion of the fetishism of the commodity, without detriment to the "laws of movement" of capitalist society in Marx.

Collective Subjectivity, Mechanisms, Modernization

How do such mechanisms work? Once constituted, individuals and collective subjectivities, operating within both state and society, dynamically and causally, provide the answers. Here we must be careful to avoid two traditional, albeit misleading solutions, namely, reified individualism and collectivism, reckoning instead with *processes*, as already argued above. "Structures" do not really exist and we must avoid any form of Platonist realism regarding ideas or "essences" (as well as renewed forms of this perspective through mental generative mechanisms such as found in some forms of structuralism). Nonetheless, if we do want to eschew individualism, we must not only consider socialized individuals – trivial for sociological, anthropological or social psychological theories –, but also introduce *collective subjectivities*.[8] Marx, Parsons and Mead were particularly attentive to this (pointing, respectively, to "social classes," "collective actors" and "classes" or "sub-groups" more loosely conceived). Some of them imply the intentions and projects of individuals and collectivities, others stem from the unintended consequences that derive from them.

Two elements must be stressed in a more systematic characterization of collective subjectivities. As such, they are systems of interaction, between individuals and also between other collective subjectivities, upon which, through

---

8   This was systematically discussed in Domingues 1995a; 2000a, Chaps. 1–2, 4; 2012, specifically as for "modernizing moves."

reiteration but always amenable to change, social relations develop (and must not be reified as possessing an autonomous existence). They have a specific, *collective property* related to *causality*. Once we acknowledge *collectivities* (a handy way to refer to collective subjectivities) as important and with specific "properties" (albeit not "emergent," an expression that ultimately hints at a sort of underlying atomism/individualism of the theorist), what would be the reason to reductively conceive of causality and attach it exclusively to individuals? This is actually the last ditch employed by methodological individualism. In contradistinction, we need to recognize *collective causality* as a *property* pertaining and partly defining collective subjectivities. However, let us not take up the model of the modern individual actor either (already highly contested, at least since Freud showed that its intentionality cannot be taken for granted, much less a transparency of motivations and ends). We must grapple with the de-centering of the subject (although not with a post-structuralist bias). Collective subjectivities are variably "(de)centered," that is, their identity and organization allows for intentional *movement* (rather than individual "action"). What is more, *movement* is an Aristotelian expression that points to an agent's capacity to produce stasis or change, in this case collective and referred to the social and the natural worlds. This has no relation to their collective causal impact upon other collective subjectivities (thoroughly de-centered collective subjectivities may have a tremendous causal impact, depending on the context in which they are exerted). All sorts of mechanisms, implying the reiteration of social patterns ("memories"), as well as their creative (intentional or unintentional) transformation, are clearly connected to the movement of collective subjectivities, as much as to individual action.

When we think of the modern state-society system, this must be considered. In social and political theory "classes" and "elites" (whether implicitly in "pluralist" and "deliberative" or explicitly in "elitist" theories – cf. Dahl 1972, 1989; Habermas 1992; Schumpeter, 1942, Chaps. 21–23), or more loosely defined collective agents, are usually pointed out as those who weave together the emergence, development and waning of concrete political systems or historically characteristic types. This is true even when we are focusing on authors, such as Weber, who in principle sustain an individualistic methodology (in which case collectivities become "residual categories," in the terminology of Parsons, 1951, 16ff, 28ff: they must be there in order that reality is grasped, but remain confined to a non-systematic level of theorization). We must therefore clearly recognize the variably (de-)centered collective agency of families and firms, social movements, "elites" (an excessively ideologically charged expression) and ruling circles, political parties, unions and bureaucracies, classes, genders, ethnic groups and (socially defined) "races," or whatever collectivities we empirically identify as important in concrete situations, even simple and diffuse opinion currents. They exert a causal impact in social life that underpins the processes that are the stuff of generative, reiterative and transformative mechanisms. Moreover, at less general levels, this sort of general category must be specified in more particular terms, according to the sort of specific issues to be understood and explained.

How does this play out in the modern state-society system? This becomes clear once we identify the reiterative dynamic of that dialectical "unit of contraries" as well as the problems of its generation and more far-reaching transformation. What is required, first of all, is to identify the collective agents of the reiterative mechanisms that reproduce (with incremental, hence socially creative changes, despite possible breakdowns) such divide and the internal functioning of each side as well as those that lead to institutional and imaginary crises, which in turn can entail either the breakthrough of societal forces directly and disruptively into the state apparatuses or the takeover of some forces which actually belong within it, such as the military. In average modern social life, the divide is kept by the smooth running of the political system, with a usually high level of autonomy of the state apparatus, societal "crystallizations" notwithstanding, as well as the confinement of societal forces to the other side of social life.

The generation of such a system must be looked for, as historians did, probably as far back as the Middle Ages and the ambivalent resistance of bourgeois elements to the Absolutist state as well as focusing on the contradictory dynamic entailed by the manifold, but especially economic and political, modern systems of domination and exploitation. More complicated today is to spot the system's transformative elements, beyond the "dictatorship of the proletariat" or the anarchist (sometimes syndicalist) and Bolshevik/Spartaquist/Left communist attempts (in very different ways) to create revolutionary councils that dissolve and reabsorb the state within society (unilaterally, with the partly non-intended consequences of strengthening the state in the first case). Originally party members and the working class (and sometimes the peasantry) as collective subjectivities undergirded the concrete operations of such transformative mechanisms, but today it is not clear "who" would eventually lead the transformation of state and society and the direction it might take, not necessarily emancipatory. A more systematic realist-categorial analysis and exposition must account for these dynamic and contradictory processes, until they are utterly changed in ways that only the future will make clear. To be sure, the self-organization of the popular classes, counting on enlarged and variably disruptive forms of citizenship, remains a means through which an emancipatory path might be taken, against the strengthening of the contemporary state

and actually its increasing connection to global institutions and finance capital (Sassen 2006). In any case, the extent to which the overcoming of modernity will result from intentionally and unintentionally (de-centered) exercised
individual and collective subjectivity is something we can strive to trace but
cannot fully answer, insofar as social creativity cannot be wholly anticipated.

In sum, we are grappling with *contradictory developmental trends*, based
on what may be called *modernizing moves* by collective subjectivities, originally merely episodic (in the sense they did not aim at creating that historical
arrangement), but which, once the latter was in being, to some extent intentionally aim at its reiteration, although this happens partly as an outcome of
unintentional action and movement. They yield a (process-dependent) *causal
tendency*, however dialectically contradictory it may be, insofar as stabilizing
mechanisms such as "hegemony" are successfully at play. They are always present, moreover, with whatever sort of internal (im)balance and mixed or not
with other tendencies we can find in social life. These must be theorized too
when regularly found, as some other type of trend-concept, or, when this is
not the case, as a sort of more accidental, circumscribed process which need
not assume a systematic categorial elaboration. We do not therefore need to
embrace "regularity determinism" or the "uniformity of nature," even at the
level of mechanisms. These are processes that are all *contingent*, including the
very process-mechanisms that preside over the development of more specific
concrete processes. They must be understood in a non-reified manner, as the
analytical rendering of those very empirical processes that are also amenable
to be empirically generalized. Moreover, with this sort of *analytical constructs*
we may carry out more precise empirically-oriented *descriptions* and perhaps
strategically project future developments.

Final Words

This chapter set out to discuss realism in what concerns trend-concepts in
terms of a developmental understanding of modernity. Bhaskar served critically as its starting point and the modern state-society system as its substantive focus. The aim was to show how such an approach, assuming a systematic
analytical intent, should be phrased according to a realist outlook, featuring
a stratified view of knowledge, rather than of reality. This was combined with
a process-oriented perspective. The need to define generative, reiterative and
transformative mechanisms was also discussed.

Substantively, what we have examined here is as true with respect to the
countries that have been entangled in the global expansion of the modern

state-society system as to Europe, where modernity originally emerged. While its origins in the West must be recognized, they were somehow reproduced, as a collectively intentional model or springing at least partly as a consequence of unintended processes. Latin America is closely connected to the emergence of the modern state-society system, albeit in a more restricted and protracted way; Japan tackled it on its own swiftly, and the rest of the world followed suit, initially through colonialism, afterward with national liberation movements. Since then reiterative mechanisms (which are always also partly creative) have been at play.

We still need an encompassing description, a full narrative of this process, as well as an analytically-laden sociological account of its path. Transformative issues and mechanisms apply to them all, despite the impasse and eventual abandonment of alternatives in the deceased Soviet Union and other countries. This is therefore, along with other themes that lie at the core of modern civilization, a crucial aspect of a much needed globally-oriented sociology. Once we are in possession of analytical categories that allow us to go beyond specific cases, we may recognize the problems posed by criticisms of Eurocentrism without overlooking the intended and unintended dynamic of the actual construction and development of the modern state more generally, as well as its internal contradictions, without remaining captive of the specific empirical forms it originally assumed in the West. Descriptions can then become more systematic and the general as well as particular features of modernization in different countries and regions may be more fruitfully discussed, in a critical and emancipatory way.

CHAPTER 6

Family, Modernization and Sociological Theory

Two Intertwined Themes

The relationship between the various dimensions of social life has always been a difficult and complex subject for the social sciences. If this is true in Marx and in what refers to the subordination of the "superstructure" to economic "infrastructure," in Weber and his idea of multidimensionality, or in Durkheim and his sociological idealism, this is no less true in more recent approaches, for example, Parsons' and Luhmann's social system theories. If these theories recognize a relative autonomy of the different subsystems, they often wonder, sometimes in a very concrete way, about the weight of each one in the reproduction of social life as a whole.

Whether they are conceived in a more concrete or abstract way, presented in a more descriptive or analytical way, these "dimensions," whose epistemological status is not always clear, encompass the various aspects of social life. In these definitions, the family often appears as an important element, though not always. If Hegel was the first to construct a theory in which the family was crucial in defining the modern ethical system, anthropological structuralism and sociological functionalism were the first to see in the family a central axis for the study of the empirical-theoretical social sciences that emerged in the middle of the nineteenth century (there are, however, other important antecedents: in Le Play, who proposed a first sociological approach, in the old Engels and his pioneering contribution from historical materialism, in Durkheim and his attempt to reach a general, although limited perspective, and in Weber, who made several important observations, which, however, were not brought together in one text). It is not my aim, in any case, to analyze to what extent the family received the attention it deserves in conceptual terms as the axis of articulation of social solidarity and focus of emotional investment, in a sense close to the one used originally by Freud, saturating the bonds we establish with people and collectivities (Domingues 2006), even when a denser theoretical analysis of this aspect of social life and its historical unfolding is necessary. It is often assumed that the family is a universal phenomenon, or almost, together with kinship relations, of which it is a central aspect (Lévi-Strauss

* Originally published in *Estudios sociológicos*, no. 106 (2016). I would like to thank Kathya Araujo and Juan Pedro Blois for their comments on a former version of this chapter.

1969). We know that throughout history family and kinship relationships have been crucial in articulating all aspects of social life in distinct ways and with multidimensional expressions, something that has been recognized by both anthropologists (as Godelier 1973, at that time clearly Marxist, a position which he now disavows, by refusing centrality to it in Godelier 2010: 645), as well as by sociologists (for instance, the neo-Weberian Collins 1986, Chap. 11).

Not only sex and biological and social reproduction, but also economic and political relations, are intertwined with the family, be it nuclear or extended. Functionalists, in this sense, placed it at the core of modern social life, linked it with the individualism of an increasingly complex society, and assigned it differentiated functions and specialized roles in the reproduction of "society" (according to a patriarchal division between males and females) (Parsons 1955). Other authors, in contrast, pointed that it should not be conceived as a unit totally separate from other units with which it maintains relations of kinship and with which it exchanges tasks and emotions (Saraceno 1976); nor do they obviously assume that patriarchal division as universal and timeless.

My purpose in this text, however, is somewhat more limited. On the one hand, I propose to understand the global process of modernization and its relationship with the family and its transformations in several countries and regions cut across by contemporary global modernity. On the other hand, I seek to analyze the relation of the family to the other aspects of social life – which implies, of course, the definition of these "aspects" as such. As we can see, the two themes or issues discussed here are intimately related in a way such that the response to one will allow us to more precisely situate the other and vice-versa.

Regarding the second theme or problem, a provisional solution can be found in the notion of existential social questions, which we will discuss in more detail in a later section. With this notion, I try to avoid a premature definition, either analytical or concrete, about the problem of the relation between the aspects of social life, thus taking distance from ideas linked to the topic of the "base" and the "superstructure" or those that include "subsystems" or "dimensions" not always defined in a clear and systematic way. Equally, and in a similar sense, it is necessary to search for solutions to the problem of the always dynamic articulation of the family with other aspects of social life. This is necessary if we want to adequately evaluate statements such as Smelser's (1959, especially 158) that the family is a subordinate dimension, that is, one without relevant causal influence in the emergence and unfolding of the social "subsystems" of modernity, being, on the contrary, patient of its various influences, in particular of industrialization, and without being able to react on them.

Regarding the first theme or issue, the relationship between the family and the processes of global modernization, there are not many antecedents, and few authors have faced a subject that demands so much. Goode (1963), subscribing to the theory of modernization, was the first of them. According to his view, in line with the style of the age, at the global level the family would be undergoing a process of "convergence" toward the molds or canons of the modern Western family, a transformation that could occur together with other processes or more isolated. More recently, Therborn (2004) has taken up the theme and reached diametrically opposed conclusions. According to this author, each regional or civilizational family pattern maintains its own separate trajectory, without any convergence in global terms. This is true for him even if he recognizes the impact of the demographic transition that regularly reduces family size (with falling birth and death rates – Therborn 2004, 230–270), and the retreat, certainly very variable, of male domination or patriarchy (which affects women as well as their offspring).

As shall be seen, these reflections will allow us to deal with a set of crucial issues for sociological theory, which are grouped into two general lines: (1) the question of the family within the framework of the modernization process at a global level, a relationship that will also be studied empirically, requiring the consideration of a series of specific cases in order to articulate our response; (2) the more general theoretical problem of the various social "subsystems" and existential questions, more analytically conceived, which here will be treated with special attention to its specific dynamics in modernity and from the point of view of the question of family systems. The articulation of procedural and dynamic causal mechanisms will, as we shall see, be very important throughout the discussion. I believe that the theoretical research I propose, if it succeeds, in addition to contributing to the analysis of each one of the subjects discussed here, could show an additional conceptual value in the measure in which it proposes to articulate these subjects in a systematic way.

What we are asking, on the one hand, is whether there is a process of family modernization that can be attributed to the development of a trend that, although procedural and contingent, has a certain directionality. On the other hand, the relation of this possible trend with other trends that may globally characterize modernity is at stake. In the course of the article, we shall dialogue with the theses and ideas of Goode and Therborn, the two main sociological theories of the family in global modernity.

I start from the idea that the process of modernization, which has unfolded in Europe especially since the eighteenth century, has assumed a global character. This does not imply that the world becomes homogeneous. This modernity – contrary to the modernization theory thesis – merges the elements of this civilization with others, originating from other civilizational heritages, generating hybridizations. The main vector of this process is the generation of a global modernity, which is, however, heterogeneous. This is neither a mechanical process nor does it entail an opposition between "tradition" and "modernity," yet this process does not lead to a fragmented world either, since general trends of modernization can be identified without rigid boundaries separating civilizations – which the recent theory of "multiple modernities" is inclined to absolutize. The effort of this text is precisely, with reference to a specific theme and the study of outstanding cases, to move beyond these sociological perspectives.[1]

Globalization and Modernization

There is a long and wide debate about the expansion of modernity around the world, its emergence in Europe and other regions (more or less sequentially or simultaneously), as well as on the extent to which modernity reproduces in the latter the standards that have emerged on that continent. As indicated in the introduction, modernization theory used to think that globalization and modernization were the same as Occidentalization: to make non-Western societies fully reflect European and primarily United States' standards.

In Goode's extremely subtle approach, this thesis was presented in relation to the family theme. His working hypothesis, on the other hand, also involved the second theme put forward in the introduction. According to his view, industrialization "...does undermine the great systems of kinship" and leads toward "some version of the conjugal family found in Western countries," although, the author explained, there was no simple causal relation between these two variables, especially since under the concept of "industrialization" the most varied and distinct orders of phenomena were grouped together (urbanization among them). In fact, Goode recalled, the family had already changed much earlier in England (seven or nine centuries earlier), a process facilitated by "neolocality": a new home after marriage, independence from relatives, individualization, and low fertility. In the same sense, the ideas (ideologies, values) about industrialization, once developed in England, had spread in other countries even before this process took impulse within their borders, which prepared people and stimulated changes in the family. According to the author, in the global expansion of the modern standard it would have been very

---

1   I have discussed such theses in detail in several publications, especially in Domingues 2012 and in Chapter 2 of this book.

important that in each place, although moving toward the same point of arrival, the process had begun from very different situations. This gave it a wide variety of characteristics and rhythms of development. Finally, it would be very likely that traditional families would have been inappropriately grasped, to which we should add that there might be a confusion of ideals and realities. In any case, in spite of the foregoing, there would be, according to the author, a clear convergence between all types of family (Goode 1963, xv–xvi, 1–4, 368–389, *passim*).

In reviewing Goode's discussion and thesis, Therborn points in a clearly opposite direction: in his view, there is no convergence. Far from this, the standard is divergence, which follows the paths of regions defined according to "geocultural" lines. Although there is a "globality," there is no process of "world revolution" of the family. Demographic transitions, due to the fall in mortality and birth rates, on the one hand, and a male-dominated patriarchy (or male domination) in varying degrees (but never achieving gender equality), on the other, are the only elements of convergence that he recognizes. Thus, while admitting a modernization in relation to diminishing fertility based on a modern tendency to seek a "rational mastery of the world," unlike Goode he does not offer us an organic and clear conception of these changes and processes (his adherence to Marxism had already been left aside as the previous stage of its intellectual evolution). The transformations in the family have, under these conditions, an exogenous origin, politics and law appearing as the elements around which their dynamic gravitates, although it is also sensitive to the religious dimension (Therborn 2004, 10–12, 297–299, 306).

Let us leave, notwithstanding, for now the relations between the family and the other variables of social development and let us focus our attention on its globalization/modernization – a necessary step in any case, so that this theme can be duly confronted, particularly if we do not want to confine our analysis to the Western world. Instead of immediately unpacking a theoretical argument, let us briefly review three concrete cases: India, China and Latin America. I suppose, it should be clarified, that the cases of Europe and North America, in addition to their differences, are fundamentally similar.

India presents one of the most interesting and complex cases of contemporary family. Singh (1986, 174–184), who sympathizes with the idea that modernity is advancing in India, and other scholars (Shah 1998; Patel 2005; Therborn 2004, 108–112) coincide in the main and indicate that in the subcontinent the "joint Hindu family" is still in force (a term that did not exist in this region – which includes Sri Lanka and Pakistan – and was eventually translated from English into local languages). Its validity, it should be clarified, is mainly given at an ideal level, since in concrete terms the nuclear family predominated among peasants and continues to predominate to a great extent. Throughout history, the nuclearization of the family is part of a broader cycle that at other times covered the joint residence. However, it is necessary to bear in mind that the mere isolated location of the family can hide the affective bonds that indicate its joint character, ties that can even be very strong. In this sense, the Indian family was neither nuclear nor Western. Not only do Hindus reaffirm traditional forms, but insofar as they serve as a model for Sikhs and Muslims (in Pakistan we find the same trend), low castes sometimes go through a process of "Sanscritization" in which the family of the higher castes is emulated (there being, however, a wide variation in the specific forms it adopts in each region of the country). Nevertheless, in this family system, as it seems one of the most resistant to change in the world (and in which it is not infrequent that the changes happen only in regard to the public sphere and not within the home), transformations do exist: power and emotional ties tend to greater "nuclearity" and "individualization"; lateral involvements lose force in favor of conjugality and relations between parents and their children; middle-class women, when authorized by their spouses and parents, have the possibility of working outside the home; the selection of espouses depends more and more on the individuals themselves – beyond the changes in the articulations between castes (extended) and the use of modern forms (through the mass media) of seeking candidates for marriage; the power of parents over their offspring no longer has the intensity and generality of control they had in the past, though it remains important. Be that as it may, it should be noted that there are strong and varied tensions and that resistances to change, as indicated, are current.

As though it were a question of showing that Asia as such does not exist – and that the civilizational patterns and concrete dynamics in this vast region are very different –, the family in China has always had characteristics very different from those found in the Indic subcontinent, acquiring others with its modernization, which distanced it further. With the influence of Confucianism, the family in China became relatively homogeneous in the certainly vast territory of the Empire. Among the components of this family system were ancestor worship, filial piety and cohabitation, combined with a low collaterality – summarized in the relationship between siblings (married or not) or concubines. It is important to make clear that both the cohabitation of three generations and collaterality occurred only among the upper classes, with many poor men incapacitated for marriage due to lack of resources. Clans, as extended family ties, played an important role in social life. However, with the process of modernization, first with the socialist revolution and then with the development of capitalism (since the late 1970s), changes have been and are enormous, to a great extent, although not only, originating from state policies (which include limiting the number of children to only one). In this context, while family nuclearity (even when intergenerational housing is often unavoidable due to severe housing problems), filial piety has weakened and patriarchy, although strong, has not remained untouched. It is still up to women to take care of the elderly, including the parents of their husbands; on the other hand, the preference – sometimes murderous – for boys, especially in the countryside, has deepened, due the restrictions on conception. It is therefore necessary to ask: what is the relation of these processes with the traditional variables of modernization theory? While social policies centered on fighting clans (abandoned in the villages) and supporting women seem to be important in producing these transformations, industrialization does not seem to have a significant impact, even when phenomena related to urbanization and market pressures imply arrangements and affective investments in the most elementary family units. It is worth emphasizing, however, that the joint or extended family maintains its importance or presence in the countryside (Zeng 1991; Ebrey 1991; Botton Beja 1999; Davis and Friedman 2014).

Goode (1963, 270–320) saw in the Chinese family an example of modernizing change, driven fundamentally by the communist project of deep renewal of society according to Western models, a process which, according to the author, preceded and indeed facilitated industrialization, in what he seems to be right. Therborn (2004, 119–122), while maintaining a pluralist and non-convergent view of the contemporary family – insisting in this sense that the joint family continues in many parts of China – does not detract from the importance of these processes, in contrast to what he thinks about India and its joint family. Goode (1963, 203–269), as might be expected, was much more "optimistic" about the "direction" of the shift toward family nuclearization (a concept based on a current view among Indian sociologists at the time). In his view, this process did not result so much from industrialization and other transformations of the social structure, but from certain ideological factors. Inasmuch as its "quantity" or magnitude was nevertheless smaller than that recorded in other latitudes (except in the Arab world, where the hamula, the extended family and clan still predominated), his analysis, as he acknowledged, constituted at that moment more a prognosis than a description.

In turn, Latin America appears to be advancing, albeit unevenly, with countries departing from very different situations, toward a powerful modernization and flexibilization of the family that closely follows the Western pattern. This nuclearization, however, has specific characteristics, depending on the case. During the colonial period, and even during the nineteenth century, the region had a wide variety in its types of family, with a pattern that often combined the extended type with male absenteeism in the upper landowning classes but also in the popular classes, particularly in areas of indigenous population (slaves, it may be recalled, could in general procreate but not marry). Although in the twentieth century there was a tendency toward the nuclearization of the family, in a context still marked by the absence of industrialization, but with a high degree of urbanization, the pattern remained complex and heterogeneous, exhibiting nuclear families, often with a woman as head of the household. Separations within this framework are very common, especially in countries such as Argentina, Uruguay and Brazil. If patriarchy, for its part, maintains its rule, particularly in countries such as Mexico, there is generally a high degree of individualization and autonomy, which includes women. Among the various specificities of Latin American families, it is worth noting that around the 1970s the demographic transition was already underway (with some even speaking of a second, more cultural wave) (Medina Echevarría 1964, 33–38; Ariza and Oliveira 2002; García and Lorena Rojas 2002; Arriagada 2002, 2004; Quilodran 2003; Rodríguez Vignoli 2004; Therborn 2004, 18–19, 34–37, 90–91, 157–160; Domingues 2008, 150–152, 179–186).

While Goode seems to simply assimilate the Latin American family to the Western one, Therborn (2014, 72) creates a category that, curiously enough, is fit only for Latin America (and Africa). He speaks of a "phallocracy" as typical of the region, as if the problems he identifies (and which he may create out of a misunderstanding) were not present in other parts of the world (including the United States and Europe).[2]

What can be derived from these examples and the theoretical questions connected to them is that, all things considered, there are general changes of a global character in the structure of the family, which do not imply, it should be emphasized, a plain convergence. What we see is rather a process of hybridization which, in addition to the demographic transition and the weakening of patriarchy, leads to greater individualization and nuclearization, with a certain degree of convergence, which is by no means absolute. These trends, as we have seen, occur in very different degrees according to those regions: in Latin America, they express themselves radically, in China, quite strongly, in India in a much more limited way (as in the Arab world; Japan for its part approaching decisively the Western model). In this framework, it is possible to identify a set of factors or elements from which an explanation can be elaborated, not only of the changes, but also of the permanencies, since they also need to be analyzed. In no case, it is necessary to make clear, are we dealing with natural

---

2 It is worth noting that, as in the West, in Latin America this second transition, which has as a fundamental aspect the pluralization of families, although it varies according to different countries, increasingly includes those based on homo-affective unions.

processes, such as the evolutionary theories of modernization suppose – bar Goode's sophistication –, or as certain authors dedicated to the empirical identification of the different regional patterns of the family – among them Therborn, who proposes no explanation for these phenomena – seem to suppose, albeit in a less defined manner.

In the first place, urbanization presents a more or less direct empirical correlation, although not absolute, with family changes, which does not mean, however, industrialization. An extensive literature (Quijano 1977; Nun 2001; Kowarick 1977; Lezama 1993) on these two supposedly empirical trends in the development of modernity – which after all did not take place everywhere – was produced in the 1970s–1980s in Latin America. A "theory of marginality" was then put forward in which the typical features of capitalism in this subcontinent (with a formidable presence of monopoly capital and the large agrarian property) were identified as responsible for an urbanization without industrialization or with an industrialization limited and incapable of generating the necessary jobs for the absorption of workers from the countryside in the cities. This situation contrasted with what happened in the central countries (although in the European case we should not disregard the phenomenon of emigration). I believe that this theory, which at the time generated deep controversy, continues to be valid for Latin America and also for other areas of the "underdeveloped" world (such as India, Pakistan and several countries in the peripheries and – even today – semiperipheries). It is worth saying that, if this theory has identified a correlation, almost statistical, it is still necessary to reconstruct the generative and reiterative mechanisms that explain or generate it. For this, the concept of disembedding (Giddens 1990; Domingues 2006, Chaps. 1–2) seems particularly useful. According to this concept, in face of the de-structuring, in varying degrees, of the so-called "traditional" patterns of action or conduct, individuals and collectivities experience a situation of openness of identity that demands a re-embedding. In this predicament, the previous patterns maintain their importance as a source of individual and collective memories that must be reworked so that the reconstruction of identity can be carried out.

On the other hand, an equally important factor seems to be, as Goode assumed, values, in particular that of equal freedom. Although the institutionalization of this value has never corresponded to the demands and tensions imposed by concrete social life (which rarely corresponds to what is fixed as a horizon of possibility), its value is crucial in the emergence and development of modernity. Through it, individuals and collectivities find themselves in a situation in which a new – but not inevitable – axiological orientation implies greater autonomy, in a context in which, on the other hand, the expansion of the market and the construction of the modern state, with its central concept of citizenship, generate greater individualization (what in Europe, let us remember, only resulted from a large historical process). If values such as these are in some part, as it were, imported from the West, they are also deeply connected with the effective changes unfolding in the peripheral and semi-peripheral countries, following closely what happened in the central ones (Domingues 2006, Chaps. 1–2; 2008, Chap. 1; 2012, Chaps. 6–9).[3]

That said, let us ask ourselves: why in countries like India, where those elements or factors – urbanization and change of values – are not entirely absent, are the transformations so limited? In these cases, other mechanisms intervene that work as a counterbalance to the action of those elements that lead to the alteration of the civilizational standards mentioned by Therborn, producing their reiteration or reproduction. First of all, it should be emphasized that the family – as well as the religious conceptions with which it is often deeply intertwined – constitute fundamental and extremely intense nodes of concentration of affect, as are more generally what many in the United States since Cooley (1909, Chap. 3) classify as "primary relations" in temporal and proximity terms. This generates, as Freud knew well, memories that are intensely charged with emotions, fundamental to the construction of individual and collective identity (Domingues 2006, Chaps. 6–8; 2008, Chaps. 3; 2012, Chaps. 6–8). The work of creativity (not only individually but also, and especially, collectively) is arduous and costly; its result is often limited. The personality and identity of each person, who was born and bred (or "socialized") in families whose patterns have often hardly changed and/or continue to be sustained as socially desirable, are very sensitive to these changes. Standards, in addition to operating as social models, are reinforced insofar as they are shared with other close (i.e., also "primary," such as neighbors) circles. If adult male power largely accounts for the validity of patriarchy, the intensity and crystallization (always partial) of affections are also a fundamental component in its reproduction (between men and women, boys and girls), making "cultural change" a long, difficult and often painful process. In this sense, it is the reasons for the change that, mobilizing the mechanisms that lead to the nuclear family, must be investigated and not, on the contrary, the reasons that explain why family systems change little. Strictly speaking, it is necessary to consider here a two-way process, formed by trends and counter-trends, which are opposed or complementary, and from

---

3 A warning is needed here. Individualization is undoubtedly a subject as broad as it is central in the social sciences. Within the limits of this work, however, we can only treat it briefly, emphasizing the autonomy of people in relation to the collectivities in which they are involved.

which an upshot is produced that gives account of the concrete processes through which the different countries and regions develop.[4]

Through this strategy, the simple convergence/divergence issue loses meaning, and it is possible, I believe, to explain both the broader and more general as well as the more delicate and subtler variations found in contemporary modern "societies." This means that there are developmental trends, but also others that resist change or lend new directions to modernization. Both trends, which I have termed trend-concepts, can accurately capture, merge, and produce combinations whose direction these concepts cannot predict a priori insofar as they are necessarily contingent (though not arbitrary) processes. There are different types of modernizing, "episodic" revolutions, unleashed by individuals and collective subjectivities, which are the basis of these processes, whose developmental direction is sought here. These moves, it is worth pointing out, are themselves mechanisms that secrete other processes, which can, depending on individual and social creativity, take other directions, never fully escaping from the social memories crystallized in projects, routines, institutions, imaginary elements and values. This is not to say that these moves are always intentional, particularly if we are talking about collectivities whose goals are very dispersed and even internally contradictory, although several of them – as often the families themselves – show a high degree of centering, that is to say, of identity and organization, whose consequences include a high level of intentionality.[5]

Given the above, it is possible to affirm that there is a global modernity in which the family hybridizes, resulting in a convergence that, if often limited, is actually real. In this sense, for example, if we look for the relevant empirical data, it is clear that the functionalist (Parsonian and Smelserian) position could be effectively generalized at a global level since there was in general a clear family specialization (even when a counterexample could be presented). The family, in this regard, no longer performs all the tasks it previously performed (education, work, etc.), or only partially fulfills them, concentrating

---

4 Here I dialogue with Bhaskar's (1975) work and his proposal, mistaken in my opinion, about the meaning of the concepts of tendency and mechanism (which he reifies as a "property" of "things"), and his claim that only one of them prevails in each situation. Against this second thesis, I assert: mechanisms are also processes that tend in one direction and which regularly produce other processes, which must be explained by them (this makes clear why it is not necessary to think that only one tendency is in operation).

5 For the fundamentals of this discussion, to which I will return in later paragraphs from another angle, see Domingues 1995a, 2000a, where a theory of collective subjectivity is fully developed, as well as Domingues 2008, 2012, and Chapter 2 of this volume, where this proposal is combined with the sociology of modernity.

now on the biological, affective and social reproduction of its members. Its "role specialization," however, takes on greater fluidity than that with a strong patriarchal slant functionalism had assumed from the American experience of the first half of the twentieth century. This question of the development and establishment of a globalized modernity is directly related to the second theme put forward in the introduction, that is to say, to the relations or links that connect – or not – the various constitutive aspects and fundamental questions of social life.

The Family, the 'Dimensions' of Social Life and the 'Existential Questions'

As I mentioned in the introduction, the idea that there has been a specialization of the family and that this – which should be thought in the broader terms of kinship systems – is no longer at the center of the coordination of all social systems is widespread. Marxism and functionalism coincided on this point. In fact, in the human evolutionary process (which must always be thought of in a contingent way) there has been a radical complexification of social life which, it may be suggested, has made the family a type of social system among others, neither so central nor so embracing.

If we look more closely, what does that mean? In principle, the family, in its various forms, no longer functions as a central element in the articulation of economics, politics and the religious world ("dimensions" which are usually more or less directly identified empirically). On the other hand, that the family in modern societies no longer maintains a centrality comparable to what it would have before in the biological, emotional and social reproduction of people. Nevertheless, it is necessary to carefully weigh and analyze what the former issue means. To this end, without ignoring its merits, it is necessary to go beyond the functionalist ideas – very widespread and often inadvertently assumed by researchers – that define the family within the framework of the differentiation of social systems and subsystems. Questioning these certainties will allow us to ask ourselves about the link and causal impacts of the different "subsystems," to employ an originally functional vocabulary. The notion of individual and collective existential, historical-social, questions will allow us to take this step. How to organize social life? How to relate to nature? How to reproduce individuals as such and in their social insertion? How to satisfy sexual desires? What sense does it lend to this whole universe and to the individual and collective trajectory? Such are the themes or questions that all individuals and collectivities must answer to. It is necessary to clarify that when we speak of the development of modernity, we must consider that each of these questions has its own concrete unfolding and that, therefore, it is not a matter of searching for a general "package" that covers all aspects of social life. It is necessary to proceed cautiously, looking for how the modernizing moves operate in relation to each of these questions and how the solution or answer to each of them impacts on the other aspects of social life and the solutions that are proposed for the other questions. Thus, we can advance in relation to Marxism, functionalism and even the multidimensionality of Weberian theory, although we all have enough to learn from all these perspectives.

Analytically, it is possible to break social life down into some fundamental dimensions: material, which carries out productive or consumption exchange with nature; that of power, which accounts for the distribution of resources and capacities to intervene in social life and give it direction; the hermeneutic-symbolic, through which the meaning attributed to the world is constructed; the space-time (social even if based on the material one), which defines in a heterogeneous way the unfolding of time in its close connection with space (Domingues 1995a, Chap. 8). All these dimensions are structuring of social interactions, whether fleeting or highly institutionalized (they are "conditions of possibility," we would say in a Kantian perspective, but here referring to concrete social agents and practices, not to abstract epistemological problems). The queries posed in the previous paragraph are always faced or answered by systems of interaction – social systems or collective subjectivities – in terms of their internal constitution and their relationship with other systems. The most important or widespread collective systems or subjectivities tend to be institutionalized, that is to say, to find patterns that are reiterated in time (although the change that occurs in everyday interactions makes this institutionalization always partial and can, quickly or gradually, change it deeply). In all these systems or, in other words, collectivities, we find those dimensions. Family and broader kinship relationships are no exceptions. Indeed, in many of the less complex social forms – although, as we have seen in the introduction, this is neither absolute nor universal – they answered a number of questions very directly. In particular, they responded to the existential questions of the reproduction of life, of human beings, the construction and regulation of gender and sexuality, as well as the place of the offspring in the social hierarchy and the inheritance that belongs to each individual, guaranteeing the transmission of property as well as the hierarchical reproduction of symbolic systems and social ranks (which implies the identification of offspring by men, as Engels supposed, to be dominant). It still does today, but its scope of action has been markedly reduced, with many of those issues suffering only its indirect influence, as well as of kinship systems, especially in regions where the nuclear family reigns, while the construction and regulation of gender, sexuality and material and immaterial heritage remain at its core (Godelier 2010, Chaps. XII–XIII).

Thus, if in the past the impact of the family – and more generally, of kinship relations – was central (although never absolute and always intertwined and often subordinated to a large extent to the dynamics of other social systems), its current influence on political questions is relatively small. Nonetheless, if we consider, for example, the Arab hamula or, again, the ancient Chinese clan, we can see that it still exerts a very powerful influence (which has not diminished, as in the first case, or even in the second). Equally, the family was fundamental for the reproduction of the material dimension of social formations. Today, this continues to be so, but in a different way, perhaps with less intensity. Or is it possible to doubt the importance of decisions, strategies and family ties for the global development of capitalism, whether in the West or in the Latin American, Arab, Japanese or Indian world? In the hermeneutic plane, it continues to be fundamental, through the "identifications" of sons and daughters with fathers and mothers, as well as the transmission of the "cultural" instruments, of a symbolic baggage, contributing to the legitimacy of social belongings and hierarchical contacts. Finally, individual and social reproduction, gender relations, as well as sexual life, are questions that continue to be produced and regulated to a great extent by the family or that find in it the fundamental focus from which they are structured. Even though within the framework of an increased evolutionary complexity, different systems have been concentrated in some of the realms of social life and on the practical answer – and also theoretical, articulated by intellectuals (ideologists, spiritual specialists, "expert systems," disciplinary schemes, governmentality, etc.) – to the existential, individual and social questions, we must avoid the excessively fixed delimitations that make the systems watertight compartments in the name of a supposed functional specialization. Each "subsystem," including the family (whether extended or nuclear), has to deal with these questions one way or another. If in some questions (such as economics and politics), their size seems to matter, when it comes to influencing and effectively exercising their power, in others, more closely related to the realm of intimacy, it does not seem possible to decide generally on the relative impact its extension may have.

On the other hand, it should be noted that the family already shapes a spacetime of its own – dimensions that merge and have variable and specific conformation if we think according to the theory of relativity and not according to Newtonian-Kantian physics (in which space and time are defined separately and as homogeneous), as may be the case in the social sciences (see, for more details, Domingues 1995b). As collective subjectivity, or in other words, as a system of interaction that extends latitudinally and longitudinally across so-cial life, the family forms an affectively charged node, as well as socio-spatially delineated, with specific boundaries and rhythms of unfolding distinct from those of other systems of interaction (which answer differently to the various existential social questions). So too, whether it is faster (as in Latin America or China), or more slowly (as in India, Pakistan or the Arab world), its space-time configurations, depending on whether they are more extended (of a joint type or in similar forms) or smaller (mainly of the nuclear kind), enter into variable relations with other collective subjectivities (the capitalist economic system or the state, experts in psychology or social services) in their interaction and mu-tual causal conditioning. Obviously, this implies recognizing the existence of heterogeneous directions and rhythms of modernization in social space-time. This, contrary to the postulate of modernization theory and Marxism, that if we really recognized a possible momentary lack of synchronicity between the "dimensions," "structures" or "subsystems," generally assumed the existence of a homogenizing or integrating fit at the end of the process (an issue that has always, of course, proved problematic when analyzing concrete situations of social change). Contrary to these theories, we must recognize that discrepan-cies are constitutive of social life, with its multiple and varied configurations and developments.

Taking these considerations into account, what then is the impact of the family as a particular type of social system? Does it not any longer influence other social processes? Many scholars of the modernization process share this view. It is true that one would hardly hold such a position in relation to gender relations, generations, and other aspects in which the family is ostensibly cen-tral. Nonetheless, as I have already suggested, it would be equally impossible to say that politics is not affected by the process of individualization that his-torically accompanies the development of the nuclear family – globally – and which has in fact contributed to the formation of the modern state. In this, the citizen is defined according to an abstract existence that supposes its absolute separation from any extended social tie, even when in the case of women the (partial) civil citizenship did not correspond to political citizenship, and in which however more than the abstractions there were always individuals and concrete collectivities with varied characteristics – including extended fami-lies (which no longer existed in Western countries, except among the nobility, between the seventeenth and nineteenth centuries) (Domingues 2006, Chaps. 3–5; Pateman 1988). Add to this, as already mentioned, that industrialization itself was originally impacted by the nuclearization of the family which, as Goode noted, was decisive in liberating people from the ties that limited their mobility and the sale of their labor-force – a process which, as that author observed, in England occurred in advance, linked to a longer-run individual-ization (see also Macfarlane 1978, 166, in particular).[6]

While it is true that the family often changed under the impact of modern-ization – modern state-building, industrialization, urbanization based on the market (also when industry was absent) – this has not always taken place, as has happened with the joint family in India, in which case it also repeatedly resists legal and formal changes. In other words, it is necessary to complicate the causal relations that occur in the process of family change in global mo-dernity, proposing more refined explanatory mechanisms to account for what can be empirically identified. In this context, the question of individualization and its in principle narrow link with the establishment of the nuclear family is highlighted, and the historical causal impact of these two elements is a tradi-tionally very thorny issue. Perhaps it is possible to have individualization and extended family, but historically this has not happened, at least not yet, what may change in the future – a time by definition unpredictable, about which, at any rate, plausible hypotheses can be constructed, as I hope this is.

In order to advance in the analysis of the global modernization of the fam-ily, these are certainly some questions that cannot be ignored and which I hope will be taken up and deepened, possibly in an innovative way in rela-tion to evolutionary functionalism, temperate empiricism and Eurocentrism. Less implicitly it still predominates in the social sciences – still in relation to Latin America, either as a mere extension of Europe or as a case with aberrant traits. To assume, as some do, that there are social systems whose standards are internally inclined in an absolute and apparently spontaneous way to be immutable is to adopt an unsustainable theoretical bias (even when there are powers and perspectives that resist change). On the contrary, a more dynamic view is necessary since even the hermeneutic dimension of autonomy/freedom is internal to the family and not merely external. Even when focusing outside the West, if this dimension was initially placed largely as an imaginary com-ponent to be imported, it is increasingly rooted in the concrete, those broader and more intimate dynamics. In this sense, it is necessary to emphasize the

---

6   This was also a strong theme in Weber's work. According to this author, Protestant asceticism allowed for the rise of an individualism that broke with extended families – with traditional (taken for granted and rigid) blood ties being replaced by the open community of believers and way of life. These families, which remained in force in India and China, were, according to the author, a persistent obstacle to the development of "rational" capitalism (the modern state also contributing to this). See Collins 1986, 267ff. It is also worth noting that Weber did not see the family in any way as being at the origin of society (although he rejected the idea of savage promiscuity), what today seems somewhat proven, in spite of Lévi-Strauss, as well as in the case of Freud's "primitive horde." See Godelier 2010, Chaps. XI–XII.

fact that not only through law and the state are the changes and the weakening (sometimes very limited) of patriarchy propelled. These processes can also be affirmed from internal conflicts to the family itself, which is not, as we have indicated, an isolated and closed empirical "dimension" in relation to other social systems. Far from this, it is a form of institutionalized interaction in which values have a constitutive effect, as a proper dimension (and not as mere external elements) against pressures and resistances or, in other words, against multidimensional violence applied by power. It is not by chance in cities, in situations in which disembeddings are more present, that the demands for change (in patriarchy, social and psychic mobility, individualization and freedom) enjoy greater impact.

Conclusion

In this chapter, we have investigated the global evolution of the modern family in two theoretical planes: in terms of its globalization/hybridization and in terms of how it answers to certain existential questions and is dynamically related to other social systems. I have sought to affirm, although in a nuanced way, the idea of a global modernization of the family, as well as to complicate the idea of autonomy of the systems and their impossible natural immobility. As we have seen, even when it is not always explicit, the themes discussed here are intimately linked, and it can be said that there is a developmental trend in what concerns the family, which alters and transforms it, with the opposite operation of another one, originating in routine and in resistances, which links it to pre-modern forms. These trends, as we have seen, combine with others, also crucial, in the unfolding of modernity at the global level. For their study, we have drawn upon some empirical examples (India, China and Latin America) not as an end in itself, but as a way of giving support to the conceptual moves we have proposed here.

The family is a key element of social life, a phenomenon with a scope and depth that few other have. It is difficult to understand the scant attention given to it in sociological and social theories. This conceptual neglect is undoubtedly a serious example of the limitations that these theories present today.

CHAPTER 7

The Basic Forms of Social Interaction

Introduction

Social interaction is a central issue in sociological theory. It may be thought of according to an interactionist model, in which it stands out as the most basic element of the social fabric, and from the ontological point of view as well. Social interaction can also be envisaged through the prism of the individualistic perspective, in which it is a mere outcome of the action of individual actors; or, yet, as the outcome of the impact of collective phenomena, in which case interactive processes are a secondary element in the constitution of social life. Interaction may be seen as occurring between individuals alone, but it may be understood as taking place between collectivities too. Different combinations and approaches to this sort of issue can be found in sociological theory. The "dyad" form as well as larger forms, such as explicitly theorized by Simmel (1908) and, to a lesser extent in Marx's (1867) theorization of the "commodity" form and the relations between classes under "capital" (reified as things by political economy and de-reified by his critical theory), as well as Mead's (1927–30) symbolic interactive interchange between individuals and collectivities, are the foremost expressions of this basic social process (to which authors such as Parsons 1951 and Habermas 1981 later on adduced their own contributions). Once they assume the aspect of regular practices and social relations, interactions become social *institutions*, such as phrased by sociological language (at least since Durkheim 1893).[1]

It is not my aim here to deepen the meaning of interaction, even if I do understand that it is ontologically constitutive of social life and that it takes place between individuals and between collectivities will guide the arguments of this chapter. In fact, I will eventually elaborate on the idea of collective subjectivity in order to fully make sense of some questions that stand at the core of my exposition. But the focus here is somewhat narrower.

The chapter is concerned with the *basic modalities of social interaction*, encompassed by what I want to call *principles of organization* and *principles of antagonism*. They aim at mapping out and encompassing, at an analytical

---

*   Originally published in *Miriada. Investigación en ciencias sociales,* vol. 8 (2017).

1   Boltanksi's (2009, 119–123) recent idiosyncratic formulation of the term "institution" is a less than useful deviation from common sociological usage.

level, the ways through which individuals and collectivities interact, with a claim to universal validity. In other words, the principles that I shall introduce here theoretically exhaust what are surely the interactive inclinations of individual and collective subjectivities, but also their concrete unfolding. As they are proposed in analytical terms they may be concretely combined in different ways, within the scope of the principles of antagonism and of the principles of organization as well as between these two modalities of interaction, even though it is possible that they appear only by themselves. Such principles must be broken down into two further analytical components: principles of organization depend on mechanisms of coordination, while principles of antagonism depend on mechanisms of opposition to develop within interaction. Both depend on bases of justification, which may be internal as well as external to the agents that take part in interactions, except when they are forged through violence, that is, completely externally, a rare and extreme possibility, which tends not to apply to, or to dissolve within, concrete interactive processes. Justifications imply validity in logical-symbolic terms, and legitimacy, socially. They may or may not be internalized by individual actors (as, respectively, norms and rules, in the former case entailing psychological motivation and commitment); in any case, they rest upon social adequacy in normative as well as empirical-cognitive terms, that is, they depend on what is socially expected and how these expectations are understood. I shall discuss in what follows all these aspects as well as more specific contents and characteristics that relate to each of these analytical aspects.

These concepts are introduced at an analytical level, in the Kantian-Parsonian and Hegelian-Marxist traditions, as categories that break down social reality and allow us thus to reconstruct it mentally ("analytical realism," according to Parsons 1937, Chaps. 1–2, 19, drawing upon Whitehead, in his first major book, but with a historical trajectory, as noted by Marx 1857, 14ff, in the famous "Introduction" to the *Grundrisse*). They are certainly not a priori categories, but rather derive from the abstractive movement which leads from empirical generalizations to the construction of categories which are in fact suffused with empirical information, regardless of apparently being empty of content. They aim to cover the whole range of possible interactions in concrete social life, wherein they may appear entangled rather than as pure types, as already pointed out. Moreover the "method of exposition" prevails here, whereby the material collected through the "method of investigation" is taken to a higher analytical level (see Marx 1867, 25). It is necessary to note that interactions here are thought of in relation to the dyad as the basic unit of social process, but also as being present in any interactive process, with whichever number and whatever sorts of agents. In order to properly build these analytical categories, we need to break them down, distinguishing and theorizing their several analytical *elements* (which will be successively discussed in what follows and furnish the content of Tables 7.1 and 7.2 below).

Table 7.1, which I will explore in the next sections of the chapter, sums up the concepts herein proposed, illustrating what has been discussed above and will be further elaborated upon ahead, as well as additional analytic details yet to be introduced. This shall be done in the following sections at a more general level, but I will also provide examples in order to ground the exposition and clarify the meaning of these overarching theses.

Two observations are in order before proceeding. One is that the choice of terms above to denote the concepts proposed here either derives from what is widely accepted in several strands of social literature available today about such matters or due to mere convention, so as to make analytical distinctions and clarify further use. Other choices of words would of course be admissible. Although these are deployed here as technical terms, for a long time now many of them have, due to the impact of the social sciences in social life, entered everyday vocabulary.

Second, as to the *bases of justification* it is worth noting that what I propose here is actually an alternative to Habermas's (1981, vol. 1, 44–71) "validity claims" as well as Boltanski and Thévenot's (1991), and Boltanski and Chiapello's (1999) "justifications," related to multiple social "worlds" (*cités*). Habermas's categories are too narrow and were crafted at an exclusively abstract, a priori and rather

TABLE 7.1   *Modalities of social interaction*

	Principles of organization			Principles of antagonism	
	Market	Hierarchy	Network	Conflict	Competition
Mechanisms of Coordination/ Opposition	Voluntary exchange	Command/ Obedience	Voluntary Collaboration	Struggle	Emulation
Interactive Inclinations	Trade	Rule/ Comply	Cooperate	Fight	Outdo
Fundaments of Justification	Interest (mutual, in general)	Authority (mutual, sometimes)	Project (mutual, always)	Interest/ Common good	Interest/ Common good

normative level. The categories put forward by Boltanski and his collaborators oscillate between daily and intellectual justifications, a rather problematic mix (see Honneth 2008). In other words, although they are supposed to be derived from, or applied to, interactions in the empirical world, they were built upon the work of great European intellectuals. Moreover, and in contradistinction, they are closely connected to empirical issues and evince a strong descriptive character. Stated otherwise, they are not sufficiently analytical and ultimately become not more than a classification of empirically-oriented principles of justification, a problem that often comes up in Graeber's (2011) recent and already well-known discussion of "debt."

The demarche I mobilize here aims at avoiding shortcomings, excessive abstractness and a priori normativity as well as the difficulty to surpass the empirical level, including any sort of mere taxonomy. I resort to empirical generalizations – not to singular empirical cases – and to what are already partially analytical categories and some instances which can be found in an array of classical and contemporary authors in the social sciences. These empirical and in some measure partially analytical categories are sublated in the direction of systematic analytical categories whose objective is to furnish us means to return to empirical interactive processes with more consistent conceptual instruments. I shall not, however, pursue this sort of epistemological elaboration at this point but I shall return to these issues in my conclusion.[2]

This chapter has therefore two main objectives. First, to organize in a common framework the different approaches to the modalities of social interaction, bringing together the principles of coordination and of antagonism that have too often been dealt with separately and not very systematically. Second, I strive to do so in a multidimensional way, focusing on the symbolic-hermeneutic aspect of such interactions by tackling and giving centrality to those "validity claims" and "justifications." This is important not because social life is suffused with moral or ethical elements, which often play a superficial role in social interactions. Nevertheless, agents cannot simple eschew them away, not even when they are just paying just lip service to claims and justifications, except in extreme cases which I shall later pinpoint. Hence the need to properly analyze this symbolic-hermeneutical aspect of social life in a more complete manner than hitherto.

---

2   These and other issues dealt with below were discussed at length in Domingues 1995a; 2000a; especially Chap. 3; and, in relation to the principles discussed here, initially in Domingues 2006; 2012, Chap. 2.

Principles of Organization, Mechanisms of Coordination

Social interaction depends on specific patterns among agents in order to develop. In the course of history it has assumed several different aspects. Yet, once we look at them from a more general angle, that multiplicity comes down to only a much smaller number of patterns. One comment by Hobsbawm (1964) to Marx's passages on history in his *Grundrisse* may serve as a starting point. Hobsbawm suggested that there are only three possibilities of labor relations: dependent, bonded labor of different sorts (from slavery to servile relations, of a collective or individual kind[3]); wage (paid) labor; and cooperative, communal labor. To this we may add that the first is basically labor exercised within hierarchical relations, the second is mediated by free relations entertained in the market (although the existence of social classes should not be overlooked in his framework) and the third implies the willing collaboration of the workers themselves, within free relationships (in "primitive" communities or, prospectively, in the "association" of free human beings that Marx 1867, 92–93, called communism). Labor relations are therefore exhausted by three general modalities:

1) *Hierarchy*, mediated by the *command* and *obedience* mechanism in terms of coordination. Thereby one can order someone else to do something, even against his or her will, as Weber (1921–22, 28) famously put forward in *Economy and Society* making use of the word *Befehl*. Servile and above all slave labor are based on hierarchy and thus command, with variable levels of autonomy and obedience of workers in the labor process and outside it.

2) *Market*, mediated by *voluntary exchange* as a mechanism of coordination. In this case workers are at least formally free – in the sense of freed from everything, as Marx and Engels would have it (1848) – and go to the marketplace to sell their labor to the owner of the means of production –, something also true of professionals whose skilled, or even highly skilled, labor can be bought and sold – though we should be wary of adopting Weber's (1921–22, 177–180) individualist position in this regard.

3) *Network*, mediated by *voluntary collaboration* as to coordination – indeed joint labor, as we directly discern the issue etymologically in the word used to refer to it. This is the world of hunter-gatherers, post-Neolithic agrarian, and fundamentally egalitarian communities, or of modern

---

3 Anderson (1974, 21–22) notes that in Antiquity relations of personal domination could be located in a continuum from servitude to slavery.

cooperative endeavors (as represented by experimental socialist or anarchism economic activities or different sorts of solidary economic enterprises, as Wainwright 1994, especially Part III, for one has argued); and of course, of Marx's freely associated producers.[4]

Concretely, however, such simple forms of labor are to be found entangled: agrarian communities in feudal Europe or imperial China implied collaborative peasant communities and hierarchical relations between them and, respectively, feudal lords and the imperial state in collective works (the draining of marshes or irrigation works for instance). Free wage labor ends up in a contractual relation whereby workers "voluntarily" enter hierarchical, even despotic relations under the yoke of the capitalist labor power buyers. Cooperative enterprises often make use of managers and supervisors who, at least for lengthy periods of time, exercise some form of milder or tougher domination over the workers themselves. It is also worth noting that the market can be present in interactions and relations that are not "economic" and that moreover in the "economy" or other spheres of social life debt represents an incomplete process of voluntary interchange, its formalization as such in a contract mattering only in a certain sort of relation, the same being true of its eventual completion (Graeber 2011, Chap. 1, also 121).

I could go on and provide an endless list of examples in this direction. But let us move on from here and generalize the argument of such modalities of organization and their corresponding modalities of coordination.

Since modernity as a specific sort of civilization came about, there has been a tendency to reduce social relations to two modalities alone: market and hierarchy. Or, at least, that was the case until fairly recently, since, for reasons to be approached in the conclusion, network has become a principle of coordination that can no longer be discarded. Polanyi (1944) has clearly shown how a utopian perspective held by liberals has made the market principle paramount in the organization of modern national societies. However, Polanyi stretched this argument too far, as if the overwhelming development of capitalist markets was the mere outcome of utopian moves once they acquired control of the state. Regardless, Polanyi managed to portray how a number of state-led moves actually strengthened the market. He showed thereby how hierarchies remained crucial for modern society, a perspective that can be complemented for instance by Pateman's (1988) conceptualization of the sexual-marriage and the labor contracts as instrumental for the maintenance of command/obedience

---

4 Here, and throughout this text, "network" is defined in a very different – and much more restricted – way from most of the North American sociological tradition (cf. White 1992), in which links between actors more generally are often at the core of the conceptualization.

coordination once women and workers have entered them. In British positivist jurisprudence, from Bentham onward, and from there to other places and debates (including Weber's own formulation), command has been taken indeed as a key issue in the definition of law and of the state in relation to the population (see Austin 1861, 56–57, 86–89).

What is more, Polanyi (1944) showed how the network principle was eschewed by modern blueprints for the functioning of social life, whereas throughout history it had formerly been absolutely fundamental for all social interactions, in the short and the long run.[5] In any case, as a vast literature has repeatedly made clear, starting in the United States and then taken over (with or without explicit acknowledgment) in France, the network principle – as in Castells' (1996) "network society" or in Boltanski and Chiapello's (1999) "world of projects" – has made a triumphal empirical and conceptual comeback in the last decades.

Thus, at this point we have already analyzed the principles of organization introduced in Table 7.1 above as well as the mechanisms of coordination on which they depend to concretely operate. We must now tackle the interactive inclinations and the bases of justification related to them. However, before, let us examine the principles of antagonism and their mechanisms of opposition.

Principles of Antagonism, Mechanisms of Opposition

While principles of organization bring people together, willingly or unwillingly, principles of antagonism are based and lead to situations in which people are at odds with each other. This does not mean that, in a sense, they are not

---

5   Polanyi's (1944, Chap.4) principles of economics ("reciprocity" and "redistribution," "symmetry" and "centrality") are transversally related to the principles of organization discussed here. They may be connected to elaborate forms of the network principle, although they also point to other issues, sometimes of a more ideological nature when they rest on the principle of hierarchy. "Reciprocity" is more horizontal and implies what its name directly conveys, "redistribution" working from the top down as a legitimation for the disproportionate appropriation of resources once social divisions set in. "Householding," at least the way he defined it, does not imply social interaction. In turn, Karatani (2010) uses the concept of "modes of exchange" to move away from "modes of production," while retaining the economic dimension as fundamental for historical developments; he is in fact however speaking of forms of coordination in a potentially multidimensional perspective, although tending recurrently to economic reductionism. On another key, we may think of both the "gift," redistribution and money as means of circulation, while contract may assume different forms, featuring on occasion as one of their aspects, which have to be always considered taking into account all the forms of interaction analyzed here.

coordinated in their action, since patterns of relationship may develop or provide the conditions whereupon such interactive processes unfold, in the short, medium or long run. Yet, it is through an opposition between actors, which may be deadly indeed, that such antagonistic relations take place. Partly resuming issues raised by Weber, Elias (1939, especially 274, 304–306) showed exactly this, although his analytical perspective was limited. This is especially true vis-à-vis what is sought in this chapter, in relation to the processes that in medieval Europe opposed knights and kings in competition, mustering economic, political and military strength, and regularly became an openly conflictive and violent relation, namely, warfare. However, after using his view as an initial gambit, we must move to more sharply distinguished antagonistic relations. They imply two principles. Once again, it is worthwhile stressing their analytical status:

1) *Conflict*, mediated by the mechanism of *struggle*, entails straightforward clashes, consisting in a dispute that is undertaken directly with opposite individual actors and collectivities;

2) *Competition* is a more indirect phenomenon, in which winners and losers do not necessarily touch each other, with the mechanism of *emulation* sending agents in parallel undertakings in order to improve their position to achieve supremacy, without direct confrontation.[6]

Take for instance war: it is indeed, in common parlance, a competitive endeavor, a struggle, literally, of life and death in which individual actors and collective subjectivities aim at defeating their opponents in direct confrontation. Take for instance market competition between business firms: they struggle, as a matter of fact, to overcome their competitors in terms of what they buy and of what they sell. This does not imply a direct clash, though. It is the indirect proficiency of individual actors and collectivities that underpins the possible outcomes of such sort of competitive race. Hence conflict is based on a principle of opposition which corresponds to these more direct clashes, namely struggle, whereas competition rests on emulation, i.e., the effort of each agent to do better than others, more as a means to acquire greater leverage to achieve other goals than as straightforward defeat of the opponent.

Economic theory has been the field in which the discussion of competition such as presented here has been more thoroughly developed, either in

---

6   Weber (1921–22, 20–21) clearly distinguishes (ideal-typically), between *Kampf* (struggle) and *Konkurrenz* (competition). My analytical definition here is similar but actually somewhat distinct from his formulation.

classical political economics, in its Marxist variant, or in the neoclassical current (including shifts toward neo-institutionalism and the recognition of hierarchical relations within enterprises – e.g. Williamson 1983). Firms compete with other firms for market shares, workers compete against other workers for labor posts, professionals want to sell skilled labor in the market in the most favorable conditions possible and thus competition ensues (as, once again, ascertained by Weber 1921–22, 177–180). In order to do so they have to offer the best deal for those who want to purchase what they have to sell. Consumers (and producers consume too) compete with one another to get the best possible offers of what they want to purchase. Competition for marriage partners implies similar patterns of behavior, to suggest another example. That is why some may try and apply the market principle of organization (and, supposedly, its attendant orientation, "rational choice" orientation) to this sort of institution (cf. Becker 1991), however arguable such a move may be (but, again, Weber knew better, not to conflate such different sorts of relation: 1921–22, 20).

Conflict is a mainstay of different social science literatures. Struggles between classes and different social groups especially stand out (for the former, see Marx and Engels 1848; for the latter, in terms of "power" relations by and large, see Foucault 1982). The same is true of the disputes between countries and armies, the object of concern in international relations literature (above all in realism – cf. Morgenthau 1949). Direct clashes and the defeat of the antagonist, its subordination or even annihilation, are at stake in this, with the struggle between contenders shaping social relations, that is, the fleeting or repeated – and potentially and mostly patterned – interaction between individuals and collectivities. While utter defeat is often sought after, a better positioning in ongoing relationships is also frequently at stake (for instance in struggles between workers and capitalists regarding labor contracts).

We must bear in mind that competition/emulation may turn into conflict/ struggle, as different ways of developing interactions. They may be both present all the time in concrete social processes. This was, as already mentioned, one of Elias's themes. Besides, whereas for a long time these landlord-warriors moved back and forth in competition and conflict – in fact these were closely related in their concrete activities –, later Absolutist court society tamed them and gave pride of place to the former. The relation between competition (*gegenseitige Steigerung* of *die Anstrengung*)[7] and open conflict (*Kampf*) is also the main object underlying the problematic of what Clausewitz (1832, 7–10)

---

7 English translations somewhat simplify this complex set of expressions related to attack and defense (resistance) by using the word "competition." The general meaning is correct, but this is not the literal phrasing we find in Clausewitz's original text.

referred to when speaking of the relations between war – a generalized "duel" – and politics, with the former consisting in a continuation of the latter by other means, as a "political instrument" aiming at subduing the enemy, while Foucault (1976, 171–172) inverted the adage, keeping its spirit, yet calling it another name. Mann (1986, Chap.14) in turn observed that, alongside war, diplomacy regulated competition in the geopolitics of the rising European states of the modern era. Yet, the parallel or entangled workings of, as well as passages from, competition to conflict, or the other way around, are not universal. Their development does not necessarily lead to monopoly in any sphere of social life either (although this is what Elias concretely adumbrates): even states and markets may become centralized in oligopolies or monopolies, but this is not a law of development of social life (although the "general tendency of capitalist accumulation" asymptotically might lead to that, according to Marx 1867, Chaps. 21–23). In particular, and above all, within a general theoretical standpoint, the analytical differentiation between these types of antagonistic relations must be sustained.[8]

Coordination, Antagonism

We have thus far dealt with the two encompassing sorts of principles underpinning social interaction as if they excluded each other; no mention at least was made of their interpenetration in actual social life. We saw that this is true of principles of coordination and of principles of antagonism by themselves and now we can see that these are usually entangled too. Whether people cooperate voluntarily or collectivities are built upon hierarchy/command/obedience, they may compete or conflict with other collectivities that are built upon the same or upon different principles of organization. Take a business firm in the capitalist market, for instance: it is usually hierarchically built, though cooperatives may operate in such conditions too; despite being internally cooperative, with outside agents it may however entertain an antagonistic connection mediated by market competitive relations. Yet the same firm may work with other firms in a cooperative, networked relation, or be subordinate to them,

---

8   And of course competition is not genetically-biologically determined, contrary to what sociobiology wants us to believe. On the other hand, even Darwinist theories are attentive to the shifting roles of competition and direct conflict for the survival of individuals and species, the "fittest" among them striving for ecological niches and reproductive success, as well as from time to time engaging in intra-species open confrontation.

totally or partially, in a hierarchically-based relation (take the example of industrial districts in which big, often transnational companies organize, linked to suppliers and even retailers). Coser (1956) even suggested that the (functional) integration of social systems is based on conflictive processes, which may generate identity-solidarity and thus furnish it elements for confrontations with other social systems. To drive this point home: all these categories are analytical, concretely they often appear entwined.

Interactive Inclinations

Agents (individuals or collectivities) are inevitably inclined to uphold some sort of "attitude" or "intention," no matter the actual outcome of the interactions in which they take part, which, in turn, derive from their individual action and collective movement. If they are individuals, we can speak of social action. More generally, however, in order to avoid reification and the anthropomorphizing of collectivities (which, as we shall see, cannot be taken as a mere counterpart of individuals at a collective level), we should say that agents are driven by some amount of *interactive inclination*.

With regard to principles of organization, those inclinations can be defined in three ways in terms of the analytical strategy of this chapter: (1) agents may be inclined to *trade*, given they are willing to take part in market interactions (not, however, because they are fundamentally and naturally inclined to "truck, barter, and exchange," as posited by Smith 1776, 21), mediated by voluntary exchange mechanisms (although whether this is based on barter or mediated by money does not really matter in this particular respect); (2) they must be willing to *rule*, if they are inclined to hierarchical relations in which the command mechanism operates (bringing about, once interactions are stabilized, more or less rigid and more or less encompassing systems of domination), demanding "obedience," as Hobbes (1651, *passim*) explicitly stated, hence to some extent at least implying willingness to comply with those who rule; (3) or they need to be open to *cooperate* if they enter voluntary collaboration as a mechanism related to the network principle of organization (in order actually to develop something together on a more or less equal basis, at least regarding that specific collective endeavor).

In what refers to principles of antagonism, there are two possibilities: (1) agents must be willing to *fight* if they engage in conflict and mobilize its mechanism of opposition, only becoming satisfied after the defeat or submission of their opponents, with some "hostile intention," as suggested by

Clausewitz (1832, 8); or (2) they are required to *outdo* other individuals and collectivities if they are in competition with them, emulating their behavior and going beyond their accomplishments in order to achieve their goals and overcome their opponents (a sort of more indirect victory or at least a better positioning vis-à-vis one's adversaries).

In the examples above some of these elements are already present, and therefore they can prove useful according to the terms used in this section. For instance, in Polanyi's view those liberal elites were interactively inclined to rule – thus imposing the market principle on society, which, willingly or unwilling, had to comply, meaning that individuals would be interactively inclined to trade with and outdo others. For Marx, instead, the increased division of labor in capitalism pushed people to trade as well as to outdo, in terms of their interactive attitudes. This is true both for individual motivation and collective inclinations. For Weber and Foucault people were inclined to fight within conflictive relations and to rule insofar as they aimed at social power, the same occurring to the warriors depicted by Elias. In turn, Marx emphasized future cooperative inclinations in communism, which are prefigured in the organizations they form to fight against the bourgeoisie in capitalist society.

This does not mean that in the actual course of interactive processes the initial inclinations of one agent will be met by others. This inclination may change or remain the same, prevail in its entirety or to some extent, prove itself misplaced or even be instrumentally used by others who take part in the process, especially if an individual or a collectivity is inclined to organization (through market, hierarchy or network), while their interactive partners are inclined to antagonist relations and may manipulate the openness the former evinces. Even within the processes that are based mainly on the principle of organization one may be prone to voluntary collaboration and end up – knowingly or unknowingly – subordinated to command or mere voluntary (in this case in fact involuntary) exchange. In addition, one may be prone to engage in voluntary exchange but be fated to a relation of command/obedience after having sold some sort of commodity (such as labor power). Once again it is necessary to bear in mind that all these categories are analytically built and presented here, therefore rarely operating in actual interactive processes purely. This demands from the analyst an acute perception of the possibilities that appear concretely in interactions as well as regarding the interactive inclinations that turn up within them. Moreover, this impinges and hinges on issues, especially regarding motivation and veracity, as well as social adequacy at the cognitive-empirical level, that will be dealt with later in this chapter.

Bases of Justification

As noted above, validity claims and justifications have been in the last decades in the forefront of the discussion about the legitimacy of social relations and the processes of interaction whereby they unfold. While, as already mentioned, these two views belong to Habermas and Boltanski and his collaborators, the idea of "legitimacy" was absolutely central in Weber's (1921–22, 19–20, 122–177) work, with the difference, in relation to those two approaches, that it did not mean internalization by the actors of an underlying normative perspective and was related to systems of *domination* whereby interactions and regular relations were crystallized into institutions.

Such claims can thus be grasped by means of the category of bases of justification and the legitimacy connected to them. That means that justifications must be offered when demanded in the course of interaction – more or less explicitly and more or less systematically, usually being very fuzzy and incomplete, but possessing a degree of logical consistency. The legitimation of patterns of reproduction and change of social systems – the functioning of institutions and their change – rests upon the plausibility and validity of such justifications. They apply to all the principles thus far discussed. Systems of domination definitely demand a justification and legitimation insofar as, as it is usually the case, dominated individuals and collectivities must be somehow encompassed by such claims and especially those who dominate need to make themselves worthy of those positions in their own eyes (a point elaborated especially by Gramsci 1929–35). Such justifications must be more or less consistent internally and make some sense in relation to what happens in reality (therefore being plausible), possessing some degree of validity, that is, corresponding to some extent and somehow to reality, even though inconsistencies, incompleteness and contradictions (internal and in relation to social practices) may spring forth – as they usually do, especially when domination and exploitation lurk inside them.

Thus, the principle of organization of the market and the voluntary exchange through which it is mediated, as well as the trade interactive inclination, are founded in the open recognition of the mutual *interest* of the interactive partners (whether the baker, the butcher or whoever else). This is a justification that entails the legitimacy of a social process based on those elements. It is further enlarged by the idea that this is beneficial to social life at large, including the spontaneous emergence of a social order based on "private vices" leading to "public benefits" and virtuous outcomes (see Swingewood 1991, Chap. 2; Halevy 1901–04, Chaps. 1, 3). Of course, inequalities of power in the market – hence hierarchy – may be hidden by such arguments and deeply influence the perception of agents (for instance, unequal positioning and control of assets in class societies). Hierarchy, command/obedience and rule/compliance are usually justified by the *authority* borne by an individual or collectivity due to its placement in a position from which it can and must operate from the top down. It usually implies, however, systems of domination with more or less permanent features, entailing sometimes the view that this is based on a mutual, shared perspective, which is usually, at best, partial. Precisely because both imply explicitly unequal, asymmetrical relationships, they must be paired with different positions and inclinations that arise in their analytical definition. This distinguishes them from the other, analytically even, symmetrical relationships. Once again this entails a justification that makes legitimate the workings of elements that may be hidden rather than exposed, argued and legitimated. *Projects* based on the network principle, voluntary collaboration and cooperative inclinations relate even more strongly to the mutuality of the enterprise. This may be true indeed as long as individuals and collectivities stick to the elements comprised by this modality of interaction, although, as formerly suggested, cunning may cut across its concrete realizations. We thus come full circle as to principles of organization.

The same kind of issue and reasoning applies to principles of antagonism and mechanisms of opposition. Conflict, struggle and fight are based on the idea that the interest of participants is justifiable and legitimate, often the common good resulting from such clashes. Nevertheless, subordinate individuals and collectivities are not necessarily addressed by such justifications and the legitimacy of the patterns derived from such interactions may not be seen as relevant to the dominant collectivities that carry them out. Hence we can say that ultimately there is no need for shared justification: sheer violence, force, suffices, without legitimation in the eyes of those who suffer it. Competition and emulation, as well the interactive inclination to compete, are justified also in the validity of each one's interests, which turn out to result in the common good.

These justifications are elaborated and apply in daily life, the staple of phenomenology and ethno-methodology. They are usually related to "ideal-types" whereby agents typify each other in the "life-world" such as discussed by Schutz (1962–66) and Habermas (1981, vol. 2, Chap. 6, in less individualistic terms than the former, thus with the issue of legitimacy indirectly present in the idea of "validity claims" such as they can be mobilized by the actors). They may be the object of challenges and proofs such as suggested by Boltanski and co-workers (Boltanski and Thévenot 1991; Boltanski and Chiapello 1999, 61, 154–235), as well as other authors (Martuccelli 2006; Araújo and Martuccelli 2012). Yet, intermediary and great intellectuals, individually and collectively, play a decisive role in this regard too: they collect, invent and systematize the bases of justification of interactive patterns, in more general or more particular terms, lending them social legitimation. This is why those works by Boltanski can draw upon the ideas of Adam Smith and other main intellectuals as well as on the vulgar and huge management literature of the 1970s and 1980s–1990s. However, Boltanski does not seem to understand the relation between the hermeneutic tissue of everyday life and the role of intellectuals at different levels of operation. To be sure much of what appears in the major and lesser works consulted by him and his associates is ideological, that is, they imply justifications that hardly correspond to actual history and practices (as in the case of the cooperative undertaking that supposedly underpins the modern social "pact" or "contract," voluntarily enacted by free agents, that has given rise to the liberal or republican state and beyond – see Riley 1982). But this is also true of lay ideas and actors, who are in a constant relation of "double hermeneutics" with intellectual specialists (Giddens 1976, 79).

We must also reject what is a deeply ingrained perspective in Western philosophy and social science. Many approaches, including those of Habermas and Boltanski, stress that such claims are not only external, that they become part of the personality of actors. The latter even reads Weber's (1904b) protestant ethics thesis as though social action necessarily required motivation (Boltanski and Chiapello 1999, 41–47). A better interpretation would in my view suggest exactly the opposite (including the fact that capitalism needs no "spirit"), namely, that external compulsion and merely "instrumental action," bereft of motivation and commitment to the values that supposedly underpin it, is what actually steers actors in modern-capitalist society once the protestant spirit is overcome. Perhaps this thesis is also wrong. It may be that actors, collectivities and interactions move in modernity, as well as in other civilizations, in a much more composite situation. In this regard, a perspective that merely underlines the external character of the normative horizon, with actors not internalizing such norms and dealing instrumentally with them, should not be accepted either. Whether we are speaking of trading, ruling, cooperating, fighting or outdoing as interactive inclinations, we must bear in mind two possibilities, located within a continuum. The justification for interactive inclinations as well as concrete action and movement (at the individual and the collective levels) may appear to actors as internalized and consisting of *norms*, otherwise they remain external and thus instrumentally dealt with, as *rules*. Only the former implies *motivation* and necessarily the subjective *veracity* of individual actors and of collectivities, while they all need to be socially consistent and successful, entailing *empirical-cognitive adequacy* to the interactions in which they come to bear. Table 7.2 below summarizes these ideas:

TABLE 7.2   *Socially-oriented individual action and collective movement*

	Social adequacy	Veracity	Motivation	Sanctions
Rules	Empirical-Cognitive	Absent	Absent	External
Norms	Normative	Present	Present	Guilt

universalism..particularism

The issue of veracity is especially important with respect to the justification based on projects – that is, within interactive systems premised in particular on the network principle. However, even in this case it must not always
be expected that actual behavior will correspond to conviction. In principle,
however, insofar as cooperation is at stake, the opening of agents to one another is to be truthfully anticipated, whereas cunning is at the service of hierarchy, conflict or competition. And it is only when norms are internalized
that *guilt* appears as a *sanction* to the individual actor, as an aggression to one-
self that results from not abiding to the standards one actually believes in, although it may be collectively shared (contradictions with other internal bases
notwithstanding).[9] Otherwise sanctions remain external only. Stealing in the
market, abusing authority established in formal or customary rules, cheating
in cooperative endeavors may lead to guilt only if the values that underpin the
justifications related to principles of organization are internalized. The same
is true too as to competition as a principle of antagonism and even conflict
when normatively regulated. Expressive individual and collective behavior
are present, more or less intensely in all social interactions, even when agents
(purportedly, but not necessarily truly) make an effort to dampen them down.

These categorizations apply to individuals and collectivities, and they are
always the properties as much of the former as of the latter. Yet it is only in
the case of the former that we can speak of motivation and guilt in the sense
of their being internalized by this sort of actor, although this must also be
seen as a property unevenly shared by collectivities, similarly to those other
elements that are shared by other individuals that make up and are made up,
ontologically, by those collectivities.

Parsons (1951, Chaps. 3–5) famously wrote in one of his major books
about the orientations of action, with a sophisticated and possibly excessive
proliferation of categories. Delving deeper into this is not the case here, but

---

9 Parsons (1951, 36–48) theorized both components but emphasized the internalization of
   norms, "introjected" in the personality system. See Domingues 1995a, 101–104; 2000a, Chap. 2,
   which also dialogues with Bourdieu and Giddens.

it must be stated that since the self-interested inclination of agents and their justification must have as a counterpart the benefit of partners in interactive processes, particularisms can appear in self-interested action and movement, as much as the mutuality of benefits may fall short of encompassing the totality of agents to whom such interaction matters. Thus, networked firms must sustain projects with a mutual interest, but they are limited insofar as they exclude, particularistically, those that do not belong to the joint venture (see Castells 1996). Networks can be much more universalistic if they encompass all the oppressed groups found in a society, as in the case of recent Latin American networks of social movements (Domingues 2008, Chap. 3). Self-interested individuals populate markets, but they do not solely respond to the partners in interaction: the whole of society and even the world should benefit (or at least this is what is argued) from their unfettered functioning (Hayek 1944). Hierarchies, when institutionally crystallized in systems of domination, supposedly do not benefit or not only benefit the rulers, but also those who are ruled (unless those beneath do not matter for those at the top) (see Weber 1921–22, 122–177). Competition and struggle are in turn legitimate when resulting in the common good, except when, in limited cases, those attacked and defeated are ignored by their aggressors. Interest and the common good thus also relate to particularism and universalism, as we see for instance in the justification of most colonial enterprises, in Africa as elsewhere (Cooper 2005). Of course, as usual in war, conquest and domination, this is far from corresponding to reality.

Conclusion

The dream of a social science that would be capable of discerning the regularities of the world, in history as well as in a diachronic perspective, held a great many researchers in its grip from the nineteenth century to at least the 1970s. Newtonian physics, with its elegant set of analytical categories and the establishment of regular patterns of behavior of the universe, down to its most elementary components, was the model for that. Parsons (1937, especially 36) carried out the main attempt in sociology to craft this sort of concept and seek for invariable causal relations between them, in other words, he attempted to establish general ("analytical") laws that could operate deductively and even predict future courses of action – as Newton did with nature. Even when Parsons (1951) adopted a temporary, "second best" strategy, based on biology, the ambition remained, discarded partially only later through a firmer commitment to functionalism, though the idea of the uniformity of the social world, and nature, likewise, followed him to the very end, including the identification of socio-evolutionary mechanisms (Parsons 1967). Marx's (1859) thesis about the relationship between "productive forces" and "modes of production," as well as his view of the relationship between the "economic basis" and the "edifice" built upon it was another way of phrasing the issue, even though his main analytical construction attempted to grasp the workings of the capitalism system, that is, a specific historical period and its tendencies of development, which would not be the same in all societies or civilizations. Future, true history was an open venture. Today claims and attempts of this sort have become much more questionable, since (especially empirical) uniformities in social life and its historical development seem more difficult or simply impossible to identify, and therefore interpretive approaches tend to prevail (economics in particular raising nonetheless claims that reinstate that sort of view) (Wagner 1995). This does not mean, or should not anyway, that we cannot identify historic developmental trends, although this would have to be done more carefully and with a stronger theoretical orientation than was often the case before (see the second chapter of this book).

Regardless of the extent to which some of these perspectives could still be resumed, here we have focused instead on the analytical categories (namely, those two sorts of principles) that would necessarily furnish the underpinnings of such sort of general theoretical system, without aiming at law-like formulations and without any necessary connections with tendencies or trends of social development, although this may also be a promising path to follow. Even if we reject a law-oriented, deductive perspective in the social sciences, there is no reason to discard the construction of sets of analytical categories. These allow for a theoretically-oriented description of social life, at different levels of generality – either referring to specific space-time coordinates or aiming at a more encompassing perspective. The basic forms of social interaction discussed here aim precisely at that. And last, but not least, this set of principles allows us to think when and where there is consensus and if and when the – multiple – antagonisms of social life unfold, legitimately. In the same way, a supposedly theoretical simplification that might reduce social life to hierarchies and the market is rejected here, opening room to networks as a fundamental form of cooperative social interaction. It is unlikely that a powerful trend leads us toward it. Yet it may stand thus as a patterned sort of social interaction that humankind would someday eventually choose to embrace in a more far-reaching manner and adopt as a strong normative perspective.

A critical theory of society cannot simply suppose, suggest or demand that all relations be horizontal and that they rest on voluntary collaboration. Apart from the fact that it is pointless to imagine the complete disappearance of social antagonisms, as well as of hierarchies and markets, in the world we live they have a determining weight. In the egalitarian construction of a different world, the networks, in the precise sense I have defined them here, cannot but play a crucial role, although, at least from a more general standpoint, especially in what refers to democracy and rights, they cannot forego being ever more inclusive, which is not always the case, by any means. We must therefore be careful when a basic – "daily" – "communism" is assumed, as Graeber (2011, 94–102) does: if it is possible to say that the network principle turns up in a rather diffuse way in social relations by and large, not only do they concretely get entangled with market and hierarchy, it is also true that only if it affects social life in a generalized way and with a truly egalitarian tendency does it make sense to speak of communism (which obviously includes what we have known as politics and the economy in modernity).

If the construction of an egalitarian world – in which voluntary collaboration would be central, since hierarchy is restricted in it and the market is rejected as the general principle of organization – is not posited as the direction of social development, at least it is associated to a trend toward the autonomization of individuals in advanced modernity, despite the increase in the hierarchical power of the state and the expansion of market-oriented relations right now. In order to build what some are wont to define as the "commons" (Dardot and Laval 2014), actively, networks, as a way to resume indeed the very idea of socialism – more restrictedly or even writ large, depending on the arenas they are built – may serve as a normative horizon in terms of mechanisms of coordination, in their practical realization and with their patterns of justification. This would be, today and in future, the way that best corresponds to the association of agents that the growth of autonomy in modern society engenders.

CHAPTER 8

The Imaginary and Politics in Modernity: The Trajectory of Peronism

Introduction

Culture has been at the core of many recent developments in the social sciences, particularly after the so-called "linguistic turn." This has also been seeping into discussions about the relation between culture and politics. The present chapter proposes a specific theoretical approach in this respect. It mobilizes Castoriadis' concept of the "imaginary," as well as those of "collective subjectivity" and "social creativity." It also makes use of the rich case of "populism," more generally, and Peronism, more specifically, so as to make clear its workings in a sociological strategy that unfolds in both the theoretical and the empirically-oriented domains.

I shall start by discussing the main contemporary approaches to culture, especially political culture, as well as those related to Castoriadis' work, and argue in favor of "collective subjectivity" and "social creativity" as key sociological concepts. I will then be in a position to tackle the trajectory of Peronism. Finally, I will move toward a reconsideration of the notion of "populism" and "popular politics" in a more general way.

Theoretical Background

Two strategies have stood out in the last decade in terms of the analysis of political culture, those of Jeffrey Alexander (2003, 2006) and Ernesto Laclau (2005). Whereas post-structuralism has had enormous philosophical impact, it had not been the case in the discussion about the relation between politics and culture. Derrida (1966) elaborated the most general standpoint of post-structuralism, with significations achieving in his view a supple status, labile indeed, insofar as "structures" would be capable of generating their internal movement, through the "surplus of significations" they embody and produce – implying thus the plurality, fluidity and instability of meaning. This meant a real breakthrough in the discussion, despite remaining drawbacks. Yet this has not been the case for Alexander, who clings to the more traditional view and problematic polarizations of structuralism, consequently

---

* Originally published in *Thesis Eleven*, vol. 133 (2016).

relinquishing in practice his former multidimensional perspective for an exclusive focus on culture. Social life appears to be necessarily divided into two
different and opposite symbolic fields: sacred and profane, a conceptualization in which Durkheimian heritage, he argues, is crucial.

Although Laclau sees meaning as floating, he also reintroduces those
structuralist binaries in a more convoluted way, with serious consequences
for his theory. Even though he does not propose a general view regarding the
role of culture in social life, his construction of politics suffers from the same
binary structure that Alexander followed. More so, Laclau holds a reductionist
perspective of social life overdetermined by politics, even when he adamantly
tries to avoid Marxist economic essentialism. Relevant to this chapter is his
focus on "populism," which I will discuss further on.

Castoriadis' seminal work, *The Imaginary Institution of Society*, appears
as fundamental for an understanding of the symbolic dimension of social
life, far beyond structuralism. He introduced a theorization in the center of
which he placed the "imaginary." His contribution has not been tapped into by
any approach to culture, not even to culture and politics in sociology. It suggests, however, a way out of the binary perspective through a more adequate
understanding of "culture," as well as avoiding the problems associated with
post-structuralism: namely, the neo-structuralist bias regarding the absence of
agency, in addition to the tendency to read social life as a text, a theoretical
strategy that appears patently deficient in sociology.

The two conceptual pillars of Castoriadis' theory (although the second
is somewhat unclear in the original formulation) can be articulated as: the
"radical imaginary" and its institutionalized social embodiment, alongside
a "magma" of collective significations (representations composed of images
and words), as argued by Freud for individual subjectivity.[1] The radical imaginary leans on the somatic body, just as theorized by Freud but more freely
than in the original psychoanalytic version,[2] consisting now in the systematic conceptual locus of creativity. For Castoriadis, the individual "id," with its
non-identitary logic, would be responsible for the indeterminate and creative
character of symbolic life. The "institution of society" would in turn be socially shared, mediated by the "ego" and identitary logic, with certain elements

---

1   In Castoriadis, representations can be expressed in objects as well.
2   From this author's vast body of work, whose contribution to the discussion of the social
    imaginary (including its derivations in Lacan and Winnicott) I have examined elsewhere
    (Domingues 2000a, Chapt. 2), we can single out Freud (1900, 1915, 1923). We find therein the
    successive formulations about the "unconscious" and the "id" (*Es*), about "representations,"
    as well as about "condensation" and "displacement." See also the useful work of Laplanche
    and Pontalis 1967.

remaining diffuse in the magma, blending and turning into each other. It may be suggested that this would happen because the non-identitary logic of the "unconscious" pours into social representations. More precisely, such logic belongs to the "id," which Castoriadis equates to the "unconscious." Like Lacan, he mixes the two Freudian "topics" (two phases of theorization, in which the primary dynamic of the psyche receives different formulations), which must be distinguished. That non-identitary logic is not, I submit, only internal to the individual subject but broader, with the social imaginary as such appearing in principle extremely amorphous, except when agents (individual and collective) try to rationalize it – make it systematic. That is, when they try to rid it provisionally of its intrinsic ambiguity and fluidity, where one thing can be also another regardless of the contradictory character it may assume.

The "id" works through two mechanisms: "condensation" and "displacement." They alter the symbolic elements by mixing them or finding other symbols to replace some original ones which, according to Freud, would have been "repressed," its operations linking up with dreams, daydreaming and neurotic symptoms. Since the "magma" of the social imaginary – in other words, the stock of socially constructed memories – cannot be isolated from the workings of the "id," insofar as the ego that is built upon it is incapable of rationalizing everything, it is permanently under the influence of condensation and displacement operations, decisive for its conformation. Affect is crucial in Castoriadis' formulation as much as in psychoanalysis, variably invested in representations, individually and collectively. Affect and representation together weave the "primary process" that, according to non-identitary logics, is at the core of the id.

A limit in Castoriadis' approach is that it circumscribes his theory precisely to the polarization between a creative individual – with its radical imaginary and exclusive creativity – and institutions (alongside the social magma), although he suggests a dialectical relation between them, a heritage of the Marxism he critically absorbs even if he goes beyond Marx's materialistic quasi-determinism. Social life – the "social-historical," as Castoriadis (1975) liked to put it –, social memories and creativity cannot be forced into this polarization between individual agent and social institutions, which is typical of modern thought and should be criticized.[3] For that, it is necessary to introduce two

---

3   Castoradis seems to realize that social creativity is missing in his account of the radical imaginary. His mere introduction of "creations" by society (apparently in the realm of institutions) does not suffice, since the continuity between the individual and social life is broken, also due to the lack of identification of mechanisms responsible for creativity and the reification

concepts of general reach in the discussion. First, that of "interaction," which from Hegel, through Marx, to Mead and Habermas, has played an increasingly salient role in social theory. More encompassing or more limited in scope, it is in the unfolding of institutionalized or fleeting interactions that the individual imaginary exercises its productive creativity. Thus, an interactive social creativity is produced. Second, that of "collective subjectivity," partly present in Marx and Parsons, as well as in Mead. Social interaction happens between individuals as well as amongst variably (de)centered collectivities. Nevertheless, the latter should not be understood as the ensemble reproduction of individuals, although sometimes they have a higher level of centering which implies identity, organization and intentionality, similar to the individual conceived by modernity.

We can say that the imaginary has, therefore, a multidimensional (not only symbolic) history (not an essence or substance) embedded in social relations, including institutionalized interactions such as those between classes, political forces, genders, races, ethnic groups and so on. It suffers inflections and ruptures that result from the exercise of creativity; that is, new symbols and new significations do not appear from nowhere, but rather from the broad social processes – including social struggles – interactively woven by the individual and collective subjectivities that constitute social life and the representations linked to images or words that are enmeshed in it. It does not imply a substantialist view of social life, either as the sum of individuals or as reified collectivities: it is a permanent creative and interactive process.

A full and systematic analysis of such themes at the conceptual level can be found elsewhere (Domingues 1995a, 2000a, especially Chapts. 1–2). Here I want to put such concepts into operation using a concrete case that may allow me to argue for their potential, presenting the discussion of social creativity and of the imaginary in their entwinement with the concept of collective subjectivity as an alternative approach to culture in sociology. To note how the imaginary as magma is reproduced and historically changes, a case of continuity seems instructive. The reader will see how it is woven in the long duration of history by individuals and collectivities with distinct, conflictive or cooperative inclinations and projects. At stake is a contribution to sociology that has at its core the hermeneutic, "cultural," dimension of social life, entangled with social institutions but also with other dimensions, specifically the political one. Thus, the autonomy of culture is merely analytical. Besides, it should not be reified in "structures": the latter are at best a descriptive device.

---

of "society" as such. See Castoriadis 1994 as well as Adams 2014. For an attempt to link Castoriadis' theories and sociology see Leledakis 1995.

The history of Argentina is often seen, in the country and even more so abroad, as marked by continuities. It is in this regard instrumental for our discussion. Peronism is certainly the most outstanding case, especially because those who claim its heritage relentlessly make recourse to the elements of its imaginary. There are those who speak of an "endless Peronism," with a political productivity that seems inexhaustible (Svampa 2005), while others preach the arrival of a "post-Peronist" era (Sidicaro 2010). Others even consider a chameleonic Peronism, capable of meaning anything in its several incarnations (Martínez 2003, 46–47). There is a bit of truth in all these statements, yet there is something artificial in the polemic. After all, there are other political forces across the world which show a notable level of continuity (it should be enough to recall the political parties in the United States, the British Labour Party, German Social Democracy, the Indian Congress). Nevertheless, the capacity of the forces that claim to be Peronist in order to attain power should not be overlooked. Alongside such imaginary memories, we must stress a social creativity whose impact is evident in the trajectory of Peronism as well as in other currents intertwined or opposed to it. I shall now sketch a portrait of Peronism, emphasizing its imaginary. This will furnish landmarks for the conceptual labor of the last section of the chapter.

Historical Peronism[4]

The so-called Argentine "infamous decade," spanning from the 1930s to the early 1940s, was characterized, defensively and without a future-oriented project, by the attempt to prevent the integration of the popular masses into the political system by means of repression, savage exploitation of workers and the fraudulent manipulation of elections after President Hipólito Yrigoyen was brought down by a military coup. Already in his second term, Yrigoyen represented the first attempt to answer moderately to popular pressure (electoral and unionist, as well as cultural), beyond stiff agrarian-mercantile oligarchic domination. The ensuing regime, with scarce legitimacy, was overturned by another military coup led by middle-ranked officers organized by the

---

4 I draw here especially upon Rock 1987, James 1990, Auyero 2001, Sigal and Veron 2003, Senén González and Lerman 2005, Svampa 2006, Sidicaro 2010. One of the most celebrated polemics of Argentina's social sciences, between Germani (1965) and Murmis and Portantiero (1972), refers to the role of "traditional" internal migrants and of organized unionism in the origins of "populism." We can say that Peronism corresponds also to the "second phase" of modernity in Argentina, in which the state integrates the popular sectors and assumes centrality in economic life (see Domingues 2008).

GOU – United Officers Group – among whom featured Colonel (later General) Juan Domingo Perón. Vice-president after the coup and head of the new "Secretary for Labor and Prevision," Perón moved close to the unions, with increasing insight about the challenge that the integration of workers represented for a new social pact. Coerced by conservative forces to give up power and sent to prison, he would be propelled back onto the political stage by those same masses. The date sanctified as "Loyalty Day," 17 October 1945, was its most dramatic expression of the rise of the movement, with the more or less spontaneous confluence of "multitudinous" masses at the center of Buenos Aires. Perón was elected president the following year and re-elected in 1951. If he showed an ambiguous outlook toward the legitimacy of popular mobilization, even at the initial moment of the clash with the "oligarchy" (always recommending the move home-workplace-home, while the issue of "barbarism" – explained below – was not foreign to him), once in power the regime evinced increasing authoritarianism, with a corporatist and disciplinary attitude toward the working class, although counting on the active presence of the unions, widely broadening social legislation and pushing industrialization. His government would be finally brought down in 1955.

Eighteen years of the general's exile followed, known by his followers as the period of "Peronist resistance." Whereas unions had become stronger during the former period and a cornerstone for Argentine politics, new organizations formed within Peronism with a left-wing orientation, frequently of a revolutionary and socialist character. Several of them embraced armed struggle, especially the Peronist Youth (JP) and Montoneros. While abroad, Perón kept an ambiguous position, particularly due to the prohibition that his word had been publicly censured. His return to Argentina in 1973 forced him to take a stand in the dispute: he opted for the unions and the most conservative forces within the Peronist movement. With his death in 1974, the situation degenerated into an open conflict interrupted by the brutal military dictatorship that took power.

The return of liberal democracy in 1983 took (to the astonishment of many) Raúl Alfonsín's renewed Unión Cívica Radical (UCR) to power, but his government had to give way due to the economic crisis, having as a successor, before the constitutionally defined period, Carlos Menem. Initially featuring as a traditional Peronist, soon enough within the terms of what O'Donnell (1991) baptized as "delegative democracy," the new president oriented his government in a diametrically opposed direction, toward neoliberalism and a new social basis of a transnationalized business class and finance capital.

But what would be the imaginary of Peronism until then? The theme of justice and a "plebeization" of social life and of culture were crucial. A new construction of the nation was at stake, incorporating the masses of workers and the *descamisados* (literally the "shirtless," a term initially used by the opposition to refer to emerging Peronism and re-signified in a positive way by Perón), and leading to a confrontation with what was being seen already as the imperialist power of the United States, which substituted for the decadent British power. If his wife Eva Perón embodied justice and plebeization, the defense of the *descamisados* (as an extension of the "Colonel," identified but subordinated politically to him; Navarro 1977), what the slogan of the first Peronist electoral campaign – "Braden or Perón" – did was to express the claim to national autonomy. The power of workers in the new society was crucial, actively representing their integration into the political system. Thus, the "national-popular movement" was crystallized. Germani (1965), a brilliant anti-Peronist sociologist, recognized that the issue of freedom, fundamentally connected to the dignity of workers, cut across the Peronist question. It was misunderstood by liberals and the socialist and communist lefts, which felt totally disoriented. Important turns such as the approximation of Perón to the Catholic Church (the nation being thereby defined as very conservatively Christian) and later rupture with it (when Peronist symbols displaced Christian ones) must be taken into account here, as well as the sacrificial element, present already in Perón's imprisonment and later widened with Eva Perón's death, assuming centrality in the popular Peronist imaginary (probably related to a metamorphosis of the Christian beliefs of the popular classes with regard to Jesus's own sacrifice). Moreover, although always placing himself as an outsider – that is, he himself did not exactly belong to the people, although being part of it as a member of the armed forces, which he initially described as sharing the same situation of exteriority – Perón managed to build an identification between himself and the Fatherland and between the latter and the People, which was in turn identified with Workers. They were all opposed to the oligarchy and the politicians who, usurping the place of the former, had misgoverned the destinies of the nation. When he returned from exile, however, Perón tried out a conciliatory discourse which broadened the nation beyond its identification with Peronism.

The creative role of Perón and his wife "Evita" cannot be overlooked in this process, but it was based on elements which were pre-existent. It is crucial to underline the whole of workers' interventions – with their apex in October 1945 – whether launched by the unions (hence with a high level of identity and organization in the conformation of intermediary collective subjectivities) or propelled by a more general and spontaneous popular movement, not very organized but with a reasonable level of centering by means of a shared identity which allowed for an unprecedented mobilization. As part of a larger creative collective subjectivity, they were decisive in the conformation of the new face of Argentine society, culture and politics, in its interactive clash with other collective subjectivities – especially liberal-conservative, but also socialist and communist.

From at least Yrigoyen's government, the plebeization of the country was at stake. With the publication of Sarmiento's founding book *Facundo* (1845), "civilization or barbarism" had become a dichotomy applied to the several cultural modulations of Argentine society. If at first the countryside "gaucho" and its "caudillos" were the expression of barbarism, against Europeanized Buenos Aires, the immigrants, originally envisioned as the solution to the problem, were soon thereby also characterized as barbarians. Finally, the popular plebeian Peronist masses incarnated this figure, then positively taken up by the movement with an inversion of its valuation. Evita, more than "the Colonel," was the utmost representation of this popular Argentina, not by chance so deeply hated by oligarchic groups and a large swath of the middle classes. Both saw in the popular takeover of Buenos Aires on 17 October an actual "zoological flood" (an expression that defined the popular masses in animal, very racist terms), which they could barely recognize as human, let alone understand and by no means accept. Unionism had been repressed during the "infamous decade," but remained active, with a renewal of its leadership. On the other hand, several rightist and leftist nationalist currents had appeared in the 1930s. All of this was taken up by Peronism. However, it combined such elements with a personalist and authoritarian political theory which, through the direct and immediate identification between Perón, the Fatherland, the People and the Workers, gave rise to a view of "political conduction" with foresight attributed to the leader alone, who could not be (openly) questioned. During the period of resistance, this view came to ruin on the side of the renewed Peronist organizations of the JP and Montoneros in particular, when Perón returned to the country and rejected their revolutionary positions.

In sum, an uneven amalgamation of elements was present in the imaginary of Peronism, with an equivalence between Perón, the army and Evita; the nation and workers plus popular, plebeian citizens, all against former oligarchic history and domination. Peron stood, however, in a position of superiority. These elements lingered in the Peronist imaginary during its first two governments, resistance and exile, Peron's return, military dictatorships, constituting a strongly and socially shared memory with fluctuations during the period. Since democratization, stronger changes have occurred: with nationalism demoralized to a great extent by the desperate and disastrous adventure of the invasion of the Malvinas Islands (the last attempt of the military to keep power); unionism weakened and the left decimated by repression; a middle class impoverished by the 1980s economic crisis; a youth that found in rock music a new form of expression; and an atomized country without Perón's presence. Thereby the power of that dichotomy – marked by total exclusion of its terms: civilization or barbarism – sank to very low levels. The appearance of a countryside caudillo that Menem displayed when he became president seemed to resuscitate this element of the national imaginary: he had been governor of La Rioja province, the same place that Facundo Quiroga, attacked as archetypical by Sarmiento, had once governed. But he quickly made it obscure by changing his social bases, opting for clientelism (particularly, but not only, in Buenos Aires province), looking for national reconciliation concomitant to his embrace of radical neoliberalism and the offer of unfettered consumerism to the middle classes. Menem lent the idea of plebeization a different meaning, having transfigured it by kitsch aesthetics and social climbing, by the mixture and permanent partying with the rich, empty of its former "national-popular" conflictive character (Svampa 2011, 119–120). Nothing seemed to remain of the opposition it once crystallized, made positive by Peronism through the contraposition between the "people" and the "oligarchy." If the 2001–03 crisis made it reappear with the "cartoneros" (the people who looked for survival in the garbage of big cities) and *piqueteros* (social movements of unemployed workers), piecemeal this became less relevant.

Another element present in Argentina's imaginary, more connected to liberalism but larger and more democratized in scope, has become crucial since the last military dictatorship. It found pride of place, alongside new issues and themes, with the rise of Néstor Kirchner to the presidency in 2003.

The Argentina of Kirchner and Fernández de Kirchner[5]

Kirchner took over with a very small percentage of votes (22%) and practically by indication of the last interim president, Eduardo Duhalde, former ally of Menem, who refused to participate in the second round of elections since he would surely be defeated (in this election a curious political engineering allowed each party to launch more than one candidate, since Peronism could not achieve a minimum of internal cohesion and Menem could possibly win the candidate selection process). His legitimacy was very low, something Kirchner did not overlook. The Justicialist Party, of Peronist characteristics, had already

---

5   I draw now upon Svampa 2005, Delamata 2008, 2009, Sidicaro 2010, Sarlo 2011, Maneiro 2012, Aboy Carlés 2014, as well as Argentina's newspapers and direct observation. Here it is the third phase of modernity – more plural, as I shall argue later on concretely, and counting again more on the market but also often with collaborative networks – that is at stake (see Domingues 2008). Kirchnerism as such carried out, from the state, the networked articulation of these movements, rather than them doing so directly between themselves, differently from what has recently happened in other Latin American countries.

become almost a nominal association, a regionalized machine based on clientelism and personal loyalties which its provincial governors could muster. On
the other hand, although he had not openly opposed Menem during his gov-
ernorship of Santa Cruz, Kirchner and his wife, Senator (of the same province)
Cristina Fernández de Kirchner, had (or pretended to have had) historical ties
with the Montoneros. Thus, he symbolically mobilized from the very beginning his links with the "70s generation," the Peronist radicalized face of social
justice. At the same time, he was skillful in searching for allies from the presi-
dential power position, vis-à-vis a fragmented party and a Congress humbled
by the crisis and the rejection of politicians (the 2001 "they should all go"). Step
by step, while keeping a politics of "transversality" – namely, alliances with all
parties – he also reorganized Peronism around his power project. A major electoral victory and the defeat of former president Duhalde appeared as crucial at
a certain point, achieved in the parliamentary elections of 2005.

Among the alliances he wove as president featured an important and
implicit one with the business groups, who saw in Kirchner the continuity of
the policies of recovery begun by Duhalde (Roberto Lavagna was kept as min-
ister of the economy and steered the successful negotiation of foreign debt after the default of December 2001). But from the symbolic standpoint foremost
were those which Kirchner sealed with the *piqueteros*, the face of social justice,
and the human rights movements, the mothers and grandmothers of Plaza
de Mayo, re-opening the processes against the military and other forces, tor-
turers and murderers of the dictatorship period. He maintained the alliances
with provincial governors, who adhered to his project decisively after the 2005
elections, and even with the weakened unions, which saw in the recovery of
economic activity and the level of employment a feasible goal, as well as giving
continuity to the compensatory social plans of former governments (Menem's
and Duhalde's). Thereby he guaranteed fast economic growth after the crisis
(7–9% per year), the rise of purchasing power and the decrease of poverty,
grabbing the banner of social justice. He introduced, however, in the imaginary projected by his government, a key element which had never featured
centrally in Peronism: human rights.

Peronism, despite pronounced authoritarian tendencies, never broke with
the liberal-democratic political system. To civil and political rights it added
social rights, which lent new content and efficacy to the former. But this was
never really its center of gravity. Having taken over after the downfall of the dictatorship, Alfonsín, a lawyer and human rights activist, embraced the theme,
which was, however, frozen with the deals he and then Menem struck with
the military, ending the processes for violations of those rights. It is surely true
that, as an idea, human rights emerged before citizenship rights (nationally

defined) in their civil aspect. Over the last decade, they have tended to be superimposed on the latter in scope, as well as morally and juridically. Their liberal matrix, individualistic and connected to the Enlightenment, is clear, though. They need, moreover, a positivization in national states, although they claim today once again universal reach.

An approximation was operated thereby in the national imaginary between the "national-popular" themes and those of liberalism, which were always at odds in the 20th-century history of Argentina. This was of course not an invention of the Kirchners: Alfonsín tried out this entwinement in his attempt to transform the UCR into a social-democratic party; Menem meant a pause in the process, but it was a much deeper movement of democratization carried out by popular struggles and mobilizations before, but especially during, the period of bloody military dictatorship, from 1976–82 (see Domingues 2008), that fertilized the soil for this new and virtuous encounter in the history of the country. The shrewdness of the Kirchners was to lend it "political productivity," giving expression to a process of social creativity larger than that which was focused in their political project, rooted in several social movements and political and cultural perspectives, rebalancing thereby the national imaginary, without letting go, on the other hand, of the element of concentration of power and superiority of the leadership that is typical of Peronism, although democratic institutions in Argentina are not amenable to personally despotic exercises at present. Cristina Fernández's easy 2005 election and 2010 re-election, as a carrier of the couple's common project, reaffirmed its main elements, possible inflections notwithstanding.

In fact, Peronist symbols remain strong in the discourse and the iconography of "Kirchnerism": to the sacrificial and leading figures of Perón and Evita was added "He," as President Cristina Fernández usually refers to the ex-president, who died unexpectedly in 2010 (even though N. Kirchner did not often quote the founding leader and nor does she). Unionism, justice, the "people" remain important references in the popular and Peronist imaginaries. But they are no longer amenable to the construction of a polarization capable of fashioning a "popular field" simply opposed to another one, negatively defined. The attempt, in the first semester of 2008, at using the "conflict of the countryside" in this way, a prosaic matter that dramatically circled around increased taxes on the export of agricultural products, evinced the lack of "productivity" of such an approach. The government and the ex-president banked on it, by design or inadvertently, which was clearly expressed in the empty sentence of Luis D'Elía, a *piquetero* Peronist leader brought into government: "I hate the oligarchy." The result seems to have been, however, detrimental to their project, working in fact to fuse discontents in relation to their governments, rather than mobilizing the popular sectors. The Argentine countryside has actually little to do with the oligarchic period. "Transformist changes" maintained the power of the great property (today highly internationalized, whether by the ownership of the soil or through the control of inputs and buying markets) and the pattern of commodity exports, with nevertheless a diversity of situations that cannot be pressed into that dichotomy. Thereby the power of that dichotomy – marked by total exclusion of its terms: civilization or barbarism – sank to very low levels.

Furthermore, the fragmenting of the working class by contemporary economic processes (outsourcing, widened service sector, etc.), and with new issues coming up, means that polarization does not hold. Themes such as the formal marriage between homosexuals and the ecological question – such as expressed in the conflict with Uruguay, centered on Gualeguaychú, due to the installation of a cellulose plant in the neighboring country – have assumed a new centrality, the "people" being defined much more as plural and through the civic element (which evidently incorporates the issue of social rights[6]), rather than through a clear and exclusive "popular" belonging. Others will come up – some to the left, some to the right, some neutral in this regard. The issue of security has assumed the frontline sometimes, recurrently emphasized by right-wing forces, which aim to lend specific meanings with authoritarian and excluding tendencies to the issue of civil citizenship, and re-articulating once again the idea of civilization as order, although without its previous oligarchic guise (see Murillo 2008, especially Chapters. 8–9).

Peronist symbols and many of its themes, founding stones of the history and the popular memory of the country, will surely live on. But it would probably be unwise for a political force to bet too much on them. Those new themes and the intertwinement between "popular" and "liberal-democratic" politics are there to stay. Besides, the contemporary government's legitimation comes also from economic growth and income increases, much as across the whole planet. This depends on the cultural definition of a kind of utilitarian "interest" in the very beginnings of modernity (Hirschman 1976), beyond the permanent and universal issue of the use and distribution of material resources, and has been radicalized to a great extent by the influence of neoliberalism and the defeat of more collectively based political alternatives, although recognition still plays a role, in terms of having some more general, if not universal, access to goods and services (García Canclini 1995). We are therefore past the

---

6   In this regard, even the Universal Child Assignation (of October 2009) tends to be more a universal approach than other cash transfer schemes (to the poor) found across Latin America at present (see Neri et al. 2010).

heroic days of an actually "national-popular" Peronism, although in Argentina, as more generally in Latin America, wealth distribution remains a central issue in the political agenda.

The Imaginary and Politics in Modernity

Let us now reflect about two questions that traverse this article. First the notion of "populism," a political and symbolic issue that has been crucial in Latin America. This will be indispensable to move forward in the conceptual articulation of the imaginary more generally, as well as in what concerns its political constitution in modernity.

My argument was directed toward thinking of the imaginary as a kind of "magma" of floating significations, which change characteristics and mix up, condense and are displaced, acquiring new meanings in this process. This magma, as we have seen, certainly has a history (previously and afterward); it does not appear from nowhere nor suddenly, woven as it is by individuals and collectivities in conflict or cooperation. This is true to the opposition between civilization and barbarism, an ideology that works (as ideologies do) similarly, and banks on the defense mechanism that Freud named denegation, by means of which unpleasant elements are banned from consciousness, in this case almost to the point of denial of the very humanity of the working classes (treated as a "zoological flood"). This is also what happened to Peronism. Recovering controversial and conflictive symbols from Argentina's history and linking them with the concrete situation of the country in the 1940s, Perón strongly glued them together, condensing them through addition with the representation of himself, as "conductor," with the notions of People, Fatherland and the movement for which he operated as a catalyst. The ideas of social justice and plebeian culture lay at the core of this specific sort of condensation, despite his ambivalent view of civilization and barbarism. Evita's role in this is more ambiguous, for she took part in this addition, standing directly for the people (the *descamisados*) and barbarism; but, just like them, she was always politically subordinated to Perón. It is worth noting that, for Freud, "repression" worked in displacement and condensation. It had the task of hiding any sexually problematic object of desire, thus remaining unconscious. Nevertheless, we can think that the construction of a system of social representations usually happens affirmatively, without necessarily discarding disparate elements, bringing them together instead of making them vanish under a single symbol. This allows representations such as Fatherland, People, Workers, Perón, etc., to be affirmed and combined by means of what can be called condensation by addition, instead of by subtraction, as could be suggested in relation to the original Freudian thesis.[7] In the beginnings of Peronism this was probably less problematic since the role of fantasy pointed to the future, as a means of overcoming the frustrations of the Argentine working class, although from the very beginning ideological elements and defense mechanisms mobilized by Perón were present therein – for instance, with the role of leader counterpoised to the affirmation of equality (with even the passivity of workers being preached) and the ambiguous permanence of elements of liberal ideology, including the very idea of individual rights which harked back to bourgeois individualist thought. After the establishment of the regime, with its controlling and disciplinary drive, fantasy assumed more strongly the character of a defense mechanism and the role of workers as protagonists was substituted (or at least restricted) within the frame of a corporatist state superimposed upon them – even with regard to the identification of the historical protagonists of 17 October, in which the role of popular organizations underwent a sort of partial "retroactive annulation." In all these cases of ideologization, rationalization stands out as a "secondary defense mechanism" systematizing but at once defending sectional (not general) "interests" (broadly defined conceptually), distorting the perception of reality and offering (dubious) moral reasons for its operations and practices.[8]

These symbols have suffered inflections. This has taken place either toward the left or the right, in particular meanings, in its extremes, either strong integration or a revolutionary rupture with the dominant system; they blend in strange ways with neoliberalism and linger on, more fragmented today in Argentina's national imaginary. More importantly, they were instrumental formerly to polarize the social field in an antagonistic duality, the "people" versus the "oligarchy," but no longer possess the social strength and the plausibility – a fundamental factor for the efficacy of new representations – that may allow them to operate beyond the sheer daydreams of ideologists and

---

7   This condensation did not emerge through only one symbolic element and even less so through an "empty signifier" that might condense all others, as could appear from a direct use of Freud's theses and as, with respect to the second possibility, Laclau (2005, 69–72, 97–98, 105, 123, 171, 217–220) would have it, such an element consisting in the core of a chain of equivalents that articulates "hegemony." In any case, this does not seem to me the best understanding of Freud.

8   I draw here for these Freudian theses, already articulated to a larger view of social life, upon the important book about "captive reason" by Rouanet (1985, especially 122–138, 147, 182ff, 199ff, 238). Other defence mechanisms are reactive formation, isolation, inversion, identification and projection, which should be utilized analytically in a deeper study of Peronism and of Argentina's political culture more generally.

militants. What may be arbitrary for the individual psyche must have a more intensely shared character socially. With new movements and imaginary elements, particularly in what refers to human rights and the liberal-democratic tradition, as well as the wide range of issues that emerged in the last decades, it has become more complicated to articulate political alliances, melding and condensing their symbols. One could even suggest that we encounter a situation – that should not, however, be seen as inevitable today – with elements suspended in a "colloidal solution" (Sidicaro 2010, 258), which do not actually mix, instead of a condensation in which their meanings fuse or at least articulate (adding up) directly, although the theme of citizenship and rights looms large in all these representations.

This seems to be characteristic of contemporary societies: their level of actual pluralism does not allow so easily for homogenizing offensives based on a simple logic of "equivalences" of "popular demands," which for Laclau (2005) is typical of so-called "populism."[9] This is, for him, after all the real name of the political dimension – "the political" – since it clearly defines two antagonistic social fields, founding – and generating – thereby the notion of "people" as such, indeed as if the collectivities that conform them did not already exist, albeit with somewhat distinct characteristics. But if it is usual to see such dualisms being actively constructed with a clear political function, this is what the modern history of Argentina evinces. We should not think that this is an absolute and necessary ontological condition, much less that leaders have such a transcendent power and that especially those who strongly condense affects are always needed, as Laclau also suggested. Once again the meaning and the conceptual usefulness of what is usually called "populism" is questioned.[10] Rather than as a category of analysis, it may be more sensible

---

9   What Laclau (2005, 74, 110, 127–128, 225) strangely calls "democratic demands" – as against the "popular demands" already totalized by "populism," which originate in the former – are actually demands inscribed in the field of politics as citizenship, although there is in the framework of liberal politics always an impulse to depoliticize them, something which, within the movement of the Latin American "molecular democratic revolution" unfolding since the 1970s (see Domingues 2008), is just not possible.

10 Germani's (1965) original thesis about populism pointed to "available masses" manipulated by emerging "elites" in the transition from "traditional" to modern society. His references were Argentina and Peronism, but the idea was generalized to other Latin American countries and other political phenomena. Problematically (and in my view fundamentally wrong) the thesis for that period, the expression degenerated into a mere term of abuse in the last decades, notwithstanding some efforts to conceptually update it. On the other hand, there is a strange resemblance, despite opposing valuations, between Germani's and Laclau's theses as to the role of leadership.

and useful to treat it as part of the Latin American imaginary, as a means of representing that which may look problematic or deviant in the forms of popular mobilization and popular leadership in this subcontinent (or elsewhere), an issue to which I shall return below. Nor does the dynamic of the Argentine imaginary and politics lend itself to a polarization between "sacred" cores (of consensus and of the "good") of civil society, as the site of solidarity, and the "profane" world (potentially of "evil") that supposedly surrounds it, as we might think with recourse to Alexander's (2003, 2006) cultural sociology. This does not mean, certainly, that some values and institutions are not shared. But not only is their meaning heterogeneous, the power relations that underpin them must be brought out too, especially when such polarizations are proposed and crystallized. Yet, in a sense inverting Laclau's theorem, Alexander sees in representation and representations merely the expression of the civil sphere – also through candidates as "collective representations" – without recognizing how they actually contribute to generate societal collectivities, although we should not attribute absolute creativity to political forces, even less so to political leadership. Both theories of representation – political and symbolic – are one-sided and defective, missing the creative interplay between those agents as well as between them and other social collectivities.[11]

It is really curious – but not by chance, as we will see soon – that Laclau and Alexander in a way express the elements that appear in tension in the Argentine imaginary: the elements of radical popular sovereignty and civic commitment, along with those opposed to them – both intending to grasp the dynamic of modern societies in an exclusive manner with their own dichotomies and ending up supposing a binary social ontology. Laclau at least more clearly perceives this as a social construction, although he prefers a structuralist approach. Subjectivity comes in thereby in an unspecified manner, substituted by the idea of "demands." However, these appear even in his concrete illustrations of "populism," submitted to the political game in which collectivities with specific histories are the protagonists, being in part pre-constituted, although the dynamic of social interaction, in its multidimensionality – and not only at the level of "discourse" – permanently reconstitutes them. In his original work, Laclau and Mouffe (1985) had not really proposed such a simplification of chains of equivalence that build hegemony, especially in an era of great social complexity such as that of contemporary Europe and in view

---

11   The classic review of the theories of representation is Pitkin 1967. See Panizza 2005 for
      further discussion of Laclau's work – including Carl Schmitt's friend-foe dichotomy in it,
      but not the idea of "radical democracy," which was swallowed by that of "populism" as
      popular politics.

of the "new social movements," both issues working as a backdrop for their analysis. It was only when Laclau took over Argentina as a starting point, even though this is not totally explicit, that the imaginary of radical Peronism and its polarization of the country captured him.

Why does this sort of dichotomy seem to have such strength in the social sciences and the humanities? It was central for structuralism (but not for post-structuralism, with its thesis of an "excess of signifiers" and floating meaning), it could also be found (but only partly) in Durkheim,[12] and it is claimed by Alexander and Laclau, in different ways. It is possible to think that this happens because it corresponds somehow to reality, which is translated conceptually in diverse ways, but often assuming this direction. I do not believe this is a correct perception of what occurs. On the contrary, it is a matter of efforts to rationalize – that is, make systematic – the knowledge of social reality, something doubtlessly necessary and inevitable in the development of the social sciences, but that assumes in this case the character of a simplifying operation which has as a consequence the impoverishment of our knowledge through the introduction of certain dichotomies. At best this replicates politico-discursive strategies partially constitutive of their very reality. It does not mean that there are no symbols strongly infused with affect, that are central for identities and institutions, "sacred" if one will – including the identification of the "ego ideal" represented by great leaders.[13] Moreover, such symbols undergo fluctuations and mutations, as supposed by Castoriadis' concepts of the radical imaginary and magma, being fiercely contested at times. The contingent consensus generated by them should not be exaggerated, for it is to a great extent rooted in power relations and systems of domination, for example in the use of coercion by the state or its challengers in an interplay that cannot be focused unilaterally. After all, this is what stands out in Gramsci's (1929–35) concept of "hegemony," notwithstanding his tendency to subordinate culture to politics and the latter to the economy. As we have seen, Peronism made a big effort to build Argentina in binary terms, a strategy whose pay-off is more dubious today.

The literature on "populism" often points to its anti-institutional, sometimes authoritarian bias and demagogic ideology and discourse. If we can find such traits, in fact unevenly, in innumerable political movements and politicians – as we saw particularly in historical Peronism – and in the whole gamut of political ideologies which appeal to the "people," it can surely be suggested

---

12   Durkheim was much more aware of the ambiguities and ambivalences of social symbols when he drew upon R. Smith, as did Freud (see Agamben 1997, 83–89; Riley 2005).

13   Although placing themselves and being placed far above the identification of citizens as equals, with authoritarian elitism in its several versions, implies a non-trivial issue, contrary to what Laclau (2005, 51ff, 221) seems to suppose.

that they define varied political phenomena by the "degree" to which they are present (Diehl 2011). The same holds true when thinking of "populism" as the "internal periphery of liberal-democratic politics" and a "symptom" of its limitations (however, in this case seeing it as a negative phenomenon of "representation," as in neurosis; Arditi 2005, 77ff). But there are other denunciations of the limits of liberal democracy and, in the end, by choosing to focus on that symptomatology we are bound to overlook the variety of challenges to such a system by popular and oppositional forces. In particular, one may be permitted to ask what we gain with the definition of "populism" as a substantive – that is to say, a concept with true analytical purchase – while it could be used in fact, at best, as an adjective, as it is usually conceived in daily parlance, in which demagoguery and the personalization of politics feature as a prominent aspect (as Arditi 2005, 76 himself notes). Again, this is not always the case when appeals to popular will and sovereignty are voiced: a variety of answers have been historically articulated in this regard.

Finally, it is worth considering some of Margaret Canovan's (2002) theses, instructive in this respect and also more generally. Her definition of populism starts from an (implicit) elitist theory of democracy and in fact smuggles the idea that, conceived as popular participation and sovereignty, the latter is actually impossible in complex liberal societies. They are, for her, literally "lies" to be swallowed by the population, which in the end is not sovereign at all – a reasonable empirical insight which she, however, transforms into a normative statement. No wonder whoever disagrees with that or makes use of such notions to define democracy is immediately classified as a "populist" – that is, implicitly a liar (even if such a lie is also self-inflicted) and a demagogue (as she charges Rousseau when speaking of popular will). The whole notion of the imaginary is squeezed thereby and we are left without the elements we need to make sense of it. In what follows, I want to sketch an alternative perspective that avoids the extremely biased jettisoning of such a crucial feature of democracy, by elitist and minimal definitions of democracy which Canovan expresses in a rather direct way, with bad consequences also for a theory of the imaginary and its application to political phenomena.[14]

Modernity implied the "disembedding" of individuals and collectivities from their firmer and more circumscribed space-time locations, throwing them up onto the broader and more fluid coordinates of the nation-state. The

---

14   This does not imply a substantialization of popular sovereignty – even less its identification with the state. The acceptance of an intersubjective view of democracy, such as suggested by Habermas (1992), is important but should not lead to a reproduction of his actual, though partial, acceptance of elitism and excessive reliance on liberal political theory, including his difficulties in dealing with conflict.

fundamental "re-embedding" that modernity introduced (not historically, but in regard to the more general conditions of existence of this civilization, theoretically grasped) was configured by citizenship, civil and political (with well-known restrictions toward the working classes, women and ethnic and racial groups). This re-embedding, at the imaginary and institutional levels, appears as a "real abstraction," since individuals are thereby thought of as "disembodied." It implies a de-substantialization of power as such, which consequently appears as virtual (when it originally was almost apolitical in liberal theory), to be filled through rotation (rather than as actually empty, as suggested by Lefort 1981, Chaps. 1–4). Citizenship is, however, too rarified to assure the insertion of individuals and collectivities in the new "societies" that emerged from the 18th century onward, first in Europe and in the United States – even in Latin America – and then piecemeal across the whole world. New re-embeddings, more substantive and concrete, took place at the same time with class, ethnic, religious and racial features, in terms of nationalism, gender and so forth (Domingues 2006).

This is true by and large and with respect to politics, too. In societies in which liberal citizenship was bent on excluding the popular masses, this led indeed to an antagonistic relation between the liberal forms of politics and popular mobilization and identities. This was the case in Argentina, of which the trajectory of Peronism was an expression, whereas in several European countries social-democracy integrated these popular masses. In the United States the issue was to a great extent diluted, while in other European countries fascism and Nazism were eventually a reactionary answer to such tensions (problems relative today to their resurfacing should be credited precisely to a process of actual de-democratization in Europe and elsewhere). A would-be partial imaginary re-substantialization of power, concretely incarnated in individual leaders, has always been present somehow in politics, and is not an aberration (contrary again to what is suggested by Lefort). This configures equivalences between the leaders and the nation (regardless of how this is conceived), insofar as these leaders, in one way or another, more or less ideologically, more faithfully and "rationally" or demagogically, abiding by institutions, struggling to change or trying to stand above them, represent or intend to represent the nation, filling in the virtuality of political power or falling short of that. Perón was extremely successful in this regard, whatever his democratic shortcomings, with an appeal to the workers and the nation, even when the specific articulation between them varied over time – with Peronism always returning, selectively and creatively combining these memories with other elements. This re-substantialization can, doubtlessly, assume a radical and more permanent character, in particular when the system of limitations to the exercise of power that liberalism projected is broken, up to the point in which the deep penetration of society by state power goes unchecked.

Alternative solutions have been found in other countries and regions, combining specific identities, based on different political regimes, liberal or closed, in a continuum to what has been called "totalitarianism," with different types of imaginary re-substantialization of political power. We cannot examine this diversity here (see partly Domingues 2012). What is clear is that, as a possibility of modern politics, there can be a liberal conception of citizenship that incorporates the idea of a decentered, abstract individualized people (oriented by interests) that is also substantively plural. The idea of a homogeneous people, possessing an imaginary common substance capable of action as an absolutely centered and transparent agent, fighting against an antagonist that is exterior to it, with a possible (and partly concrete) substantialization of political power is another possibility, although its plausibility has become more dubious precisely due to the complexity of contemporary societies. Thereby the people, class, religion, race, ethnicity, poverty and wealth are representational elements creatively combined in varied and contingent ways with the idea of a citizenship of liberalism – embraced in some part by socialism and "real socialism" – counting on the traditions (memories) and trajectories of the societies which compose global modernity in a heterogeneous manner. Individual and collective "interests," framed in a modern utilitarian vein, and "elites" are usually added to this amalgam, the latter consisting in actual power groups whose leadership and domination find support in hierarchical visions that remain in being in modernity, in its several paths of development and implying another sort of re-substantialization.

It is not a good idea to try and force all the diverse modern political solutions, in their varied combinations, within the narrow framework of an ontologization of social life based on a partial experience of modernity, even less of a binary view stemming from structuralism. A sociology that seriously recognizes the proper place of the hermeneutic dimension of social systems is surely necessary.

It is precisely an interpretative sensibility that it must embrace, so as to grasp the fluidity, multiplicity, combinations and partial crystallizations of the social imaginary, as deposited memories and in what concerns the exercise of social creativity, in its entanglement with the other dimensions of social life – whether that of power (examined here), or any other. The exercise carried out in the present text was precisely an attempt to offer an alternative to the study of the cultural-hermeneutical dimension of social life in such terms and, at the same time, to furnish a different reading of what is usually referred to as "populism," in which case that methodological and conceptual strategy was put to use.

CHAPTER 9

Critical Social Theory and Developmental Trends, Emancipation and Late Communism

Introduction

The nineteenth century and most of the twentieth were the heyday of the social sciences that believed to hold the key to historical development, the evolution of the human species. This was a handover from the Enlightenment, whose ideals were translated into sociological terms, whether or not the authors who dealt with these problems referred to their intellectual output as sociology. That said, let us look at some well-known examples. Although he still spoke occasionally of the role of "Providence," de Tocqueville emphasized the march of equality and democracy, which he reckoned irresistible. Marx pointed to the development of the productive forces and the tendencies of capitalist accumulation, as well as the gradual awareness of the working class of its historical role as the gravediggers of exploitation and oppression. Durkheim stressed the growing division of social labor and the development of the new "organic solidarity." Weber, though more cautious as to the directionality of the historical process in general and of one-dimensional determinations, nevertheless pointed out (instrumental) rationalization as a unifying historical entelechy in the West. Functionalism and theories of modernization, on the one hand, and the various interpretations of Marxism, on the other, kept these conceptions alive, often hardening, sometimes softening them. In sum, these were developmental trends of modernity that often went beyond it, conceived in a more or less deterministic way, with the concepts of the emerging social sciences designed first to account for this type of process (as seen throughout this volume).

However, since the 1980s, with postmodernism, the crisis of "real socialism" and, paradoxically, the reassertion of capitalism and liberal democracy, perspectives that bring up long-term processes with immanent, internal logics, fell in disrepute in the social sciences. For many, this result was teleologically conceived, that is, they were created with a clear and predefined

* Originally published in *Sociologia & Antropologia*, vol. 6 (2016). I thank María Elena Rodríguez for comments on a former version of this text and Cunca Bocayuva Cunha for the discussion of the works taken up here.

purpose, as well as inevitably and decisively leading to the "end of history." The crisis of the perspectives that emphasized the processes of development also exited the field of socialist thought, which had largely been based on them – implying the contradictory and self-destructive development of capitalism –, despite the emergence of neo-Kantian ethical perspectives, such as Bernstein's, to which we shall return shortly. In fact, the facticity of capitalism and the modern, bureaucratic-legal and more or less democratic state guarantees tacit plausibility for liberal views, while on the left Marxism can no longer mobilize arguments that go beyond the description of some aspects of reality, without being able, beyond rhetoric, to identify processes that, as a trend, may lead to the overcoming of modernity.

Apart from the pure and simple apology of the present, two consequences have become evident in social theory. On the one hand, contingency has gained centrality in almost all explanations of historical development, putting for example Habermas' (1976, 1981) "reconstruction of historical materialism," with its strong modernist teleology, in an uncomfortable position, as a last exemplary perhaps of the typical narratives of the nineteenth century. No direction could, supposedly, in the extreme formulations of this kind of vision, be pointed out. On the other hand, left-wing politics withered away and lost legitimacy, and, along with Marxism, became mired in the small contingencies of immediate reality, without long-term projects (Therborn 2008), while others have tried to make virtue out of necessity, rewriting, in post-Marxist fashion, for instance Gramsci's notion of "hegemony" in a fundamentally contingent perspective (Laclau and Mouffe 1989), even if certain philosophical discourses, stridently yet superficially, claim for revolution.

Socially, it can be said, in a summary way, that a two-pronged process conditions the current situation: to the defeat of the left, the social complexity that characterizes the present phase of modernity – which is not merely an invention of neoliberalism – was added; hence the situation became even more confuse and opaque. Thus, on the one hand, whether in the spaces of real socialism or in capitalist countries, the restructuring of labor relations, the shrinking of the public sphere, the change in the roles of national states, the strengthening of utilitarian individualism and the commodification of everything and everyone, under the aegis of neoliberalism, characterized the victorious offensive of a renewed global right, which was accompanied by the loss of capacity of the left to formulate alternatives and some social isolation. Superimposed upon this impasse, we witnessed the multiplication of productive processes, market niches, identities, social movements, and different ways of seeing the world, coupled with the intensification of globalization and the stronger presence of this global sphere in the daily life of people, and, finally, the accentuation of communication processes. This shifted the cultural and political debate onto another terrain and increased the scope of the issues that the left needs to address. Its historical conceptions are however too narrow to deal with many of these novelties and it suffers to understand and confront the complicated problems that already beset it in the past. Finally, due to the process of self-isolation and closure of the political system and the capture of political parties by the state, including those of the left, especially the European Social Democrats or similar forces elsewhere, there is a growing gap between the desires for democratic participation and the means that would enable it, consequently leading a growing stratum of the population to reject politics and how it plays out today.

There would be several ways to intellectually address the reconstruction of these themes and more general trajectories (see, for example, for central aspects of the discussion, Domingues 2000a, 2006, 2012). My intention here is initially to investigate only certain aspects of Marxism in this respect – bringing out the main trends of development that Marx and Engels identified in modernity, as well as the mechanisms of their overcoming, according to them. In addition, I shall revisit some central debates of this theoretical and political-practical current of thought. Next, I want to inquire about the alternatives to these conceptions, which seem to have been hopelessly exhausted, even though Marxism as a discourse remains central to several currents of the left, in a systematic or diffuse way. I will briefly review two of those alternatives – which are few and far between –, present in diametrically opposed ways in the works of Santos and Negri, the latter in the company of Hardt for a few decades now. Marxism in general does not show any recent significant theoretical advance, whereas Frankfurtian critical theory has practically dissolved, at best contenting itself with a theory of democracy in the framework of modernity itself, without intending to overcome it, that is, accepting capitalism and the modern state. Finally, diagnosing them as problematic in order to respond to the challenges of the present, it will be a matter of restoring the questions at stake and inquiring into the possibility of articulating more appropriate responses to them. I must emphasize that special attention is given to the identification of trends within and beyond modernity, as well as the concepts that allow us to apprehend them. Unfortunately, the contemporary debate on these issues is extremely limited, including and especially from the point of view of theories that aim at emancipation.

I must also emphasize that this paper falls within the framework of what can be defined as critical theory, although in a much broader sense than what is commonly linked to the Frankfurt School. It begins with the work of Marx, but today it has a much broader ecumenical character, so it is not restricted to Marxism either. In my view, in any case – and in that of the authors discussed here, whether I agree with their substantive conclusions or not –, it is a question of looking at the concrete tendencies of social development and the emancipatory impulses that contain the elements that can lead us to a future beyond the reproduction of systems of domination and exploitation. In other words, it is based on an immanent critique of modernity. Ever since Marx and Engels, critical theory has been rooted in the idea that modernity has made promises that cannot be fulfilled within its institutional frameworks. In a broad or ecumenical view, not necessarily a Marxist or even Western-minded one, its practical subjects may be several, provided they follow, however, the criterion of egalitarian freedom, the crucial value of modernity, without which criticism goes astray and may end up colluding with other systems of domination and exploitation. Critical theory must dialogue with those agents, without allowing itself to be reduced to them, thus maintaining autonomy, its own dynamic and internal impulses, beyond the experience of the actors themselves; it must seek to penetrate aspects of social life that tend to escape the interpretation of the daily experience of the subjects themselves that can be carriers of projects of emancipation.

Capitalism, Accumulation and Communism

It is in the *Manifesto of the Communist Party* that Marx and Engels (1848) publicize, with enormous theoretical and rhetorical force, their view of the trends of modern society (which they explicitly associate to capitalism). Two things were crystal clear. First, these was a proletarian population – free in terms of civil citizenship and free from the control of the means of production – expropriated by those who, in turn, became capitalists. If among them there was a petty bourgeoisie that owned its means of production, capitalism's developmental trends led to a social polarization in which it would disappear, going up or down, with capital becoming concentrated in the hands of some powerful bourgeois and constantly increasing the size of the mass of workers (who are synonymous with proletarians in the manner in which they articulate the theme) that would absorb the more numerous among them, who originally stood in between but had been defeated, the fallen. Production, increasingly social, also clashed with the private appropriation of wealth. Finally, the revolutionary organization of the working class would break away from its shackles and install communism, a political project which, as Marx and Engels (1845, 38) observed in another text, followed the "real movement of things" (that is, the processual trend of modern society). Generalized social cooperation would replace the chaos and competition of the capitalist market.

It is not appropriate to require too much precision from Marx and Engels at this stage, for they are at the beginning of the development of their work, although its first results are truly impressive. And, in spite of the more or less significant changes underwent by their ideas, the general lines of their argument would remain unaltered in the following decades, including for those who ended up being known as "Marxists," although conflicting interpretations soon emerged. In other texts, Marx and Engels were concerned with eminently political issues. This was highlighted by the uprising that led to the Paris Commune (1871), with the construction of the "dictatorship of the proletariat," a radically democratic state that would mediate the transition to the "evanescence" of this very form of domination and the arrival of communism. The mechanism of realization of this process would at first be the revolutionary subjectivity of workers, leading to socialism as a transitional stage (still counting on labor as a measure and on individual rights, although increasingly egalitarian), which would eventually flow toward a classless and stateless society, but with a planned economy (Marx 1871, 1875). These are themes that later became central to Marxist thought.

Marx, however, did not truly articulate his view of the developmental trends of the capitalist "mode of production" systematically, though also there with a certain amount of ambiguity, until his economic writings. Those trends shaped what he defined as "natural laws" which guided – save for circumstantial variations – the processes and direction of capitalist accumulation.

In the first volume of *Capital* (1867) Marx makes these arguments, beginning with the shift from "absolute surplus-value" (linked to the duration of the workday) to "relative surplus-value" (as a function of the defensive struggles of the working class and the capitalists' own competition with each other, the machinery and the direct "real subsumption" of the worker to capital). He outlines a number of other cases along the way. Among them, the increase in the "technical composition" of capital – with more technology and productivity – which implies an increase in its "organic composition," with an increase in "constant capital" (instruments of production and raw materials, though it is not always clear whether Marx speaks of this in terms eminently physical or of accumulated labor-value, "sucked out" by capital with its "vampire-like" essence), to the detriment of "variable capital" (labor-power transformed into capital through its purchase). The result would thus be an excess of workers – a ceaselessly growing "superpopulation." He also points to the increasing "concentration" and "centralization" of capital, presciently outlining trends in the formation of large monopoly enterprises in advanced capitalism, which implied their growing socialization. The "enlarged reproduction" of capital was at the basis of this growing accumulation of surplus-value in the hands of an ever smaller or at least associated number of capitalists. But since only "variable capital" is capable of restoring the invested value and creating more value by overcoming the needs of its own reproduction, this continuous change in the composition of capital would tend to lead to a "fall" in the rate of profit, against which there are counter-tendencies, which imply the reduction of the cost of constant capital, as well as the increase in the rate of surplus-value, with the question ultimately ending up in the form of a spiral, that is, the problem being resumed at higher levels. Finally, expropriated by "primitive accumulation" and permanently maintained in this situation of deprivation of control of the means of production, workers would expropriate the expropriators, at which point, in transplanting the discussion to the realm of revolutionary political action, Marx interrupts his argument.

In the following volumes of *Capital*, left incomplete and edited by Engels, Marx (1883, 1894) takes up several of these themes. He adds in particular to them the problem of the "metamorphoses of capital," from money to constant and variable capital, hence to products in the form of commodities that have to be sold in the market for capital to be realized, that is, to return, under the money-form, with a profit in relation to what had been invested. All other elements concerning extended reproduction were resumed. It is also worth noting that the issue of social polarization returns to the core of his concerns. Marx did not seem to know what to do with the middle classes – whose presence is too significant and is ever growing, to the point it complicates any simplistic scheme of the class antagonisms that he and Engels had introduced in the *Manifesto* –, leaving notoriously unfinished the chapter that he proposed to write about classes. Marx pointed out, however imprecisely and hesitantly, in speaking of the "third persons" who appropriated surplus-value – in addition to capitalists and workers, and even landowners –, the importance of the middle classes, as well as consumers in the framework of this mode of production.

These are the fundamental ideas that can be found in *Capital*, in terms of historical trends that are basically "infrastructural" (that is, economic), with direct reflections in other social dimensions. Before analyzing some of its repercussions on the developments of Marxism after the death of Marx and Engels, it should be emphasized that if Marx spoke abstractly of "natural laws" – which seemed to dispense with the subjectivity of agents, which would, as stated in the "Preface" to the first volume, be merely *persona*, supports of capital, in its operation beyond the contingent perturbations that could concretely cloud its identification –, in other passages the question arises at variance with this characterization. After all, in all economic struggles between the bourgeoisie and the proletariat, it is not only in the immediate sphere of production, even in circulation, but also in politics and in the legislative sphere that the fate of capitalism is at stake. Obviously, the social revolution is contingent upon the consciousness of the working class, but capitalists daily fight to maintain and increase their rates of surplus-value and profit, directly affecting the state, through laws and violence, to guarantee their success, as Marx fully demonstrates in several passages of his masterpiece.

Thus, it is very difficult to argue that it would be only those "natural laws" that underlie the historical process of capitalist accumulation. On the contrary, it is necessary to analytically and concretely split the processes Marx refers to in two categories. First and foremost, the issue is the uncontrollable and opaque composition of individual actions and collective movements – not indeed "natural" phenomena, the rationale with which Marx lets show the influence of positivism on his scientific conceptions. Acting on the basis of more immediate goals, workers and capitalists generate tendentially-oriented processes – as if they were trapped in a "path dependence" that cannot be shaken off – that escape their knowledge and capacity of control –, what is conventionally called "unintentional consequences of action." But it should not be overlooked that, even from the point of view of economics, conflicts and regulations that come directly into the state, more or less intentionally carried out by individuals and collective subjectivities (classes and other agents, at the head of and within the State) play a decisive role in the unfolding of the historical trends of capitalist accumulation (for example, of the Victorian factory inspectors famously celebrated by Marx).

It must also be noted that in the *Grundrisse*, Marx (1857–58) underlines – in passing and indeed very incongruously – the growing, directly productive role of science and the "general intellect" as well as the "collective worker," whose emergence and strengthening receive the characterization of a historical trend. This ends up being excluded from *Capital* in part probably because it would open space to identify the capitalist's organizing work as itself a producer of wealth – which, in a way, on the other hand, he does by portraying, in the later work already written for publication, how capitalists are fundamental for the labor process to find its own capitalist form, with increased productivity and (relative) surplus-value. But even more relevant is that Max lacked a clear concept of "abstract labor." It was this that allowed him to take up again these themes in the writings of the following decade, as a long and consistent discussion has demonstrated from a systematic re-reading of his work and in particular after the publication in the 1980s of the preparatory manuscripts for the three volumes of *Capital* (see in particular Heinrich 2003, 2013, and for the *Grundrisse*, Bellofiore, Starosta and Thomas 2013). Marx was thus able to precisely define his concepts of "value" (use and exchange), surplus-value (absolute and relative) and labor process, constant and variable capital and organic composition of capital, as well as to reformulate his vision of crises (something to some extent hidden in the Engels' edition of volumes 2 and 3 of *Capital*).

It is crucial to emphasize the reformulation of his vision of the role of science, which does not, on the contrary, oppose the production of surplus-value by labor-power – it in fact drives it. The importance and positive effect of Marx's preliminary and confusing hypotheses in Negri's work will be made clear below, but it is not justified, it should be noted at the outset, in terms of political motivation and method of approach to the history of thought. It is worth noting, however, that Marx, though incapable of adequately theorizing the question of value, science and the destinies of capitalism, spoke of the subsumption of labor to "fixed capital" (machinery, etc.), embodying the material and spiritual production of the species. Capitalism would be poised in opposition to the worker and generates contradictions that only under communism would be solved, never under capital, our only choice being to while away until it cracked. This was what could be seen as the "rational core" of his perception at that moment. Only labor would continue to generate value, albeit magnified and excessively potent in the face of the narrowness of the consumption capacity of bourgeois society, a problem that would be solved under communism.

In the Second Workers' International and in particular in the powerful and organized German Social-Democracy, already in the twentieth century, a multitude of debates were carried out (see Aricó 1976–77, for a panorama of the discussion). The most notorious was the one that ensued after Bernstein's (1899) revisionist proposals, which denied both the inexorability and the positivity of revolution, and which called into question many aspects of Marx's own theory more generally, with the claim of socialism as a fundamentally ethical project. On the part of the Marxists – led by the orthodox Kautsky (for example, 1909) – the answer was simply to reiterate the key points of what was then defined as Marxism, expressed either in the *Manifesto* or in *Capital*, or in other texts of a more political nature. In practice, and in spite of the formation of Marxist parties to the left of Social-Democracy, it did indeed follow the path Bernstein advised, embracing a strongly state-oriented electoral and trade-union reformism, as articulated initially by Hilferding. The very idea of socialism, let alone communism, eventually disappeared amidst this process. The question of imperialism, as formulated in various ways, especially by Luxemburg and Lenin, with the mobilization by the former of Marx's schemes of "reproduction" – "simple" and "expanded" – in a manner that earned her strong criticism, was another issue in the controversy. With regard to the theme I am trying to address here, namely the idea of trends in the development of capitalism and modernity, it is interesting to point to the debate on the (in)avoidable "collapse" of bourgeois society, which would be resolved under communism.

The dispute focused on Marx's theses on the increase of the organic composition of capital and the law of the tendency of the rate of profit to fall (see Sweezy 1946). Luxemburg (1913) defended the thesis that, if the possibility of profits at the necessary levels were blocked, the collapse of capitalism would be inevitable. In addition, it was indispensable to support this determinism, otherwise the very viability of the socialist movement would be threatened, for it would have, one might say, to deal with contingency should this "law" fall short of a trend that in the long run would lead to impasses insuperable in the limits of that mode of production, thus undermining the confidence and enthusiasm of the revolutionary militants. Others, especially Grossmann (1929), criticized the way in which Luxemburg articulated her arguments, but rejected the perspectives of her critics, like Bauer, reaffirming the inevitability of the collapse of capitalism, whereas Kautsky oscillated between the two positions (possibly because he knew Marx's original preparatory texts for volumes 2 and 3 of *Capital*, in which the theme was treated much more smoothly than in the tenor in which they were published by Engels – as pointed out by Heinrich 2013). What role would the revolutionary collective subjectivity of the working class play in the face of this is a topic that remained pending in this discussion. Lenin himself seems to never have accepted the validity of the catastrophic perspective, emphasizing the need on the other hand of a revolutionary party to operate the overthrow of capitalism, even though concentration and centralization of capital, as well as its export and the colonization of the periphery by the European states, were at the foundations of imperialism and the general crisis of the system (Lenin 1917). The Marxist debate unfolded systematically at least until the 1950s with varying positions.

Today many of these debates seem to belong to a very distant past, to a world that has nothing to do with ours, in which people spoke of revolutions and laws of social development, two themes problematic contemporaneously, in times of much weaker reformism than anything German Social-Democracy could suggest at that historical moment and of the accentuation of the contingency of social development. Although, as I mentioned earlier, a re-reading of Marx's political economy has taken place in the last decades (see Heinrich 2013, for example), few remain in line with Marxist political economy systematically.

This is, however, notably the case of Harvey (2003, 2009). This includes his original concept of "accumulation by dispossession," his resumption of the concept of imperialism and his emphasis on the expropriation of contemporary, state, pre-capitalist, and non-capitalist pockets, etc. On the other hand, nothing or almost nothing of those debates about the collapse of capitalism, or anything similar to such thesis, is found in his works (although Harvey 1990, collects from Luxemburg the idea of the necessary geographic expansion of capital to overcome its crises). The diagnosis of the present remains in the framework of traditional Marxism, but when it comes to building alternatives what Harvey (2014) highlights is a restricted Lefebvrian perspective, pointing to everyday life as the decisive sphere of struggle against capitalism (unlike Lefebvre himself, it is worth stressing, who saw this path as a complementary aspect strategically). And this is where we stop, with nothing much left other than vague proclamations about the inevitability of the socialist revolution. It is true that it can be argued that the global expansion of capitalism will further restore the very problems that the Marxism of the early twentieth century emphasized. This literature could even be reborn and serve as a source of inspiration for the future, when eventually the whole world is subsumed into capital, without room for "accumulation by dispossession," such as highlighted by Harvey as a way of valuing the finance-steeped global capital of our times. It is a plausible idea, but on the wrong grounds, for it does not take into account the change in many aspects of social reality, which, even if those factors remain in operation, is quite distinct from that which Marx and Engels, Bernstein and Kautsky, Luxemburg and Lenin knew and theorized.

Contemporary Alternatives

We must now briefly examine two contemporary alternatives within the field of critical theory, with quite different views. Both identify developmental trends that would operate strongly today, but of an entirely different character and with political consequences also with divergent directions. I do not intend here to analyze their whole theories, an effort that is justified in both cases, but merely to outline some basic questions in terms of the procedural and teleological alternatives that can be expected from an emancipatory opening of modernity. As noted in the introduction and the previous section, apart from ritual repetitions and small advances, Marxism as such has not dwelt in the last decades on its theoretical aspects and neo or post-Frankfurtian authors no longer care about this subject.

Boaventura de Sousa Santos produced a body of work that has evolved systematically over time, but some fundamental elements can be found in his writings (basically here discussed through Santos 1995, 1999, 2000, 2007). He began with a perspective in which, in a postmodernist vein, the criticism of Western rationalism was emphasized, its vision gradually expanded. He has long identified a "paradigmatic transition," especially epistemological in character – this is the true working trend today, which includes even critical theory, taking us beyond Marx. He initially framed it by postmodernism and, finally, increasingly and combined with it, post-colonialism. Thus, it is the homogenizing and strongly future-oriented nature of modernity that he refuses, including the modern state, whose project would be based on the idea of a homogenous and exclusive nation. Contemporary spaces of experience – versus the futurist orientation of critical theory to this day –, he argues, must be valued, refusing the eschewing away of the former, particularly on the plane of epistemology, as opposed to scientific, Western reason. The same goes for social pluralism, and law, especially with the rejection of Western solutions, part of the modern agenda, according to him, as well as a new realistic utopia that enhances and promotes these alternatives. This is where movement is to be found, it is in this direction that he wants to bet, in order to surpass the impasses and excesses of regulation, especially state-based, and the placement of community in a secondary position, such as has been the case in the West since the emergence of modernity. He also affirms the need for an expansion of democracy and an openness to social experimentation, even if in very limited scales.

Seeking a substitute for the Marxist proletariat, Santos takes up the pluralism of the theory of social movements of the 1980s, radicalizing it and finally bringing to the core of his statements the idea that the "global South" – breaking with its own internal imperialist crust – may have a privileged role to play in the "paradigmatic transition" that is under way. For example, the constitutions and multi-national states of Bolivia and Ecuador, reversing the historically liberal logic of constitutionalism "from below," would be at least in some measure an expression of postmodernism and decolonization, still in the long run transitional process (which would include, he suggests, the decline, or something similar, of capitalism). In any case, Santos interestingly observes that the state is itself a field of struggle and thus must be disputed by popular movements, driven in an inclusive and experimental democratic direction.

Critically, it can be suggested that the main problem of his theses is that the diagnosis of contemporary social processes ends up subordinated to an all too general view – in addition to an aprioristic direction and, like Weber, unified by a conception of reductive rationalization. At the same time, the very social processes that underlie their production receive secondary treatment. In particular, Santos forgets the theme that in Marx and Engels would be fundamental, that is, the definition of critical theory as emancipating not only generically, but for being able to point out the ways of realizing, outside of modernity, the values that it itself promised to materialize, without its institutions permitting it. Moreover, he loses sight of how pluralism – as it has been the case with emancipatory homogenizing efforts in the past – may not challenge or even bother contemporary systems of domination, which have in fact already learned very well how to deal with such sort of social development, just as they knew how to deal with the projects of emancipation based on homogenization, whether of citizenship or of the working class as a universal subject. It thus ends up reifying difference, without inquiring about its contextual meaning, since it should never be seen as positively absolute, and not even when it is.

Moreover, the new epistemologies to which he refers are never concretely presented. The "ecology of knowledge" and "intercultural translation" are supposedly and specifically the instruments of the epistemologies of the South, argues Santos (2010, 108–109). But regarding actual knowledge operations he is not at all clear, let alone the caricature that is drawn of the modern social sciences. Nor is it explained why mere pluri-nationality (with its plurality) would take us beyond the West and modernity (existing for example for decades in India, without contradicting at all its modern national character and the modernization of this large Asian country in general). These are exaggerated arguments and of little use to overcome current impasses. Finally, that there are excesses and impasses of regulation does not imply that a paradigmatic transition is under way, supposing or not that it would be the solution for such problems. In any case, his motto – "prudent knowledges for a decent life" – has the virtue of assigning a more modest position to reason and theories about the present and the future (although its overarching view casts doubt on whether it applies to himself, a most general problem of postmodernism), as well as the emphasis stands out, for the sake of the truth today a consensus at least rhetorically, on the demand for a deepening of democracy, and especially on social experimentation.

In turn, Antonio Negri clearly points out several times, in a direct way when he prefaces a second edition of one of his works in which he presents for the first time a systematic view of the new "social worker" and resumes the core of his arguments in other occasions, that Marx's texts are all articulated by the identification of "trends" in the development of modernity (Negri 2005, 10). This is exactly what he wants to reiterate, and in this sense his relation to Marxism is rather narrow and indeed tributary of a worldview that many would like to relegate to the nineteenth and twentieth centuries, notwithstanding the growing influence of Nietzsche and of the French Nietzscheans in his totalizing conception of social life and its transformation. Strictly speaking, Negri goes further than Marx and radicalizes the approach of trends, dealing with an enormous number of subjects in a framework of this kind, even when Marx does not do so or does only partially.[1]

Negri's argument is based on the thesis of the transition from the "mass" worker to the "social" worker, which took place around the 1970s in the West. The former was typical of disqualifying Fordism, the latter is a producer of communication, culture and affections, with strong weight of science. This reading seeks to mobilize, as already pointed out, the *Grundrisse*, emphasizing the role of subjectivity immediately, by proposing a naive and reductionist reading of Marx, curious if it were not politically motivated also immediately and did not inevitably generate serious distortions, which will be examined below (Negri 1979, 2005; see also Hardt and Negri 1994). As a result of class struggles (without giving any importance to competition among capitalists), in this new framework capitalism would attain the "real subsumption" of the social totality and would appropriate a largely "immaterial" value, which ultimately Negri would define as "bio-political," generated generically in society, no longer only in the factory or by labor in a strict sense. Moreover, there would no longer be "civil society" to support a reformist project.[2] The de-territorialized empire that emerged at the turn of the millennium would generalize this form (more recently recognizing the role of national states, rendering the unsustainability of that thesis incongruous).

Negri changes his position from the margins of his proposal to try to deal implicitly with the objections of his critics, but a central theme persists in his thinking: the organization of the proletariat (and its various synonyms throughout his work: "multitude" as its political expression, and finally the "poor") immediately sticks to its "social composition" (in which it revisits and transforms the Marxist discussion analyzed above). He vehemently denies autonomy to politics (and the division of labor that accompanies it), a position

---

1   See Murphy 2012, for a general discussion of Negri's work and his political trajectory. It should be noted that themes such as the "social worker" were quite widespread in the Italian "operaismo" of the 1960s and 1970s; as in Mario Tronti, in particular, who arrives at conclusions opposed to those of Negri regarding the "autonomy of the political," returning to the Italian Communist Party. See also Gentili 2013. For a more general view of the time, by another left current within that party, see Magri 2009.

2   Contrary to this view of value theory, Offe (1973) emphasized the contradictions and conflicts that arose due to the tendency to expand forms of work that were not based on the commodity form and wages, but on the production of use value and "income," basically in the second phase of modernity, erected upon the strengthening of the state. Neoliberalism and "accumulation by dispossession" have, from the point of view of capital, come to attack this type of problem to a large extent. Another key reference in the debate on the theory of value is the work of André Gorz, which I cannot discuss here. See, however, Silva 2007.

that sprung forth at the very beginning of his clash with the Italian Communist Party. On the other hand, he simply dismissed socialism as a phase of transition to communism. This would be immediately available and should be carried out in an absolute and immediate way, against obviously the perspective of Marx himself. The state as such, for decades already converted into a mere agent of capital, is an enemy with which there could be no conciliation. Above all, the labor process would be, according to Negri, fundamentally independent of capital at this point – capital and empire itself becoming mere "parasites." Not only do they nourish themselves with the energies of the worker and the multitude, but they contribute nothing to the organization of production, contrary to what happened in previous periods. With this, communism is already a reality that expects only to discard the useless and corrupting crust of the dominant forces (with at least in *Empire* the pure and simple defense of an "exodus" from institutions, embodied by the global immigrants at that time). The multitude, a difficult and rather diffuse concept, is once again a direct mix between singularities – monadological, irreducible – and generality, conforming an absolute totality, without intermediate collectivities intervening in their composition (what is not explicitly said but implied). It would be the agent of this transition without intermediate stops.

If some of these elements are not yet fully developed, and it is not clear in their works which are and which are not, what matters to Negri – and Michael Hardt, his main collaborator since the 1990s – is precisely to indicate which trends rule the development of modernity and its overcoming. This would be done today through the re-appropriation of the "commons," in which some kind of mediation within the multitude intervenes, albeit in a restricted way – always with the refusal of any scheme of political representation. In this revolutionary process, some of the characteristics that constitute particular groups (which are linked to the criticisms that Hardt and Negri received, but also sometimes with academic fads), such as women, races and the colonized, are marked but dissolved by a policy of "liberation" that goes beyond its mere emancipatory but conservatively frozen affirmation.

Santos points outs the problems of elevating social fragmentation as the solution of the problems that the blockade of the socialist overcoming of modernity engendered throughout the twentieth century, but Negri, on the contrary, shows himself to be the direct heir of the Third International and its totalizing vision. More curiously, he deploys a brutal economic and sociological determinism by deriving from the "social composition" of the working class its political realization, although, aware of the criticisms that have been addressed to it, he tries to reject, without any real argument, this characterization (Negri 2011, 354). If this is a rather strange operation (combining economism with a theory of totalizing value, generic and of debatable precision), even more problematic and potentially deleterious political consequences have the series of rhetorical equivalents between proletariat, multitude and finally the "poor," whose constitution is exclusively positive, as opposed to the parasitism and corruption on which capital and empire are grounded. In addition to this, things become worse due to the lack of political mediations and particularizations regarding the collective subjectivities that weave the possible projects of emancipation. It does not really matter here to follow in detail his involvement in the politics of the Italian ultra-left in the 1980s – despite the bureaucratic and reformist limitations of the Communist Party at that time –, which Negri (1998, for example) came at least in part to recognize later, a problem that is reiterated in similar situations. It is only necessary to emphasize that his conception of a spontaneous totality, bereft of mediations, cannot but summon disaster in the ranks of the Left, in spite of his distancing from offensive violence and the introduction of a minimum of mediation in his recent work, with respect to the (re)construction of the common (Hardt and Negri 2011, 353ff).[3] In this regard, despite his flirtation with French Nietzscheism, the weight of a version that radicalizes Marxian ontology is excessive and strictly outdated, while his simplistic opposition between constituent and constitutive power, or bio-politics and bio-power (Negri 1992), supposedly drawing upon Spinoza and Foucault, actually reproduces already commonplace traits in Western thought, radicalized unilaterally in constituent power or in exodus.

Much would have to be done so that we would be able to account in greater detail for the Santos' and Negri's work. These, however, consist in the main lines of their thinking. Above all, they serve to screen the fundamental elements to which a critical, transformative social theory, open to the twenty-first century, must respond.

Tasks of Critical Theory – or Late Twentieth Century Communism

For many decades, Marxism was the almost uncontested theory of all the anti-capitalist movements in the world, although several were the readings that sprung from it. Today, it is patently insufficient, although it should not be underestimated how much it still serves to diagnose many aspects of the reality of capitalism. If this is true, there is no way to salvage central features

---

3 For a critique and enlargement of the concept, which assumes the countenance of a general alternative, in a mixture of Marx and, to a degree, Proudhon, see Dardot and Laval 2014, especially Chap. 5.

of its constitution as social theory. The first is relative to the very definition of historical materialism, to which the economy and interests derived from it are the causal and therefore analytical point of departure of social life and its understanding. I do not want to elaborate this theme here, because there is a wide debate, especially in sociology, that poses queries and offers more or less adequate solutions to this question. In the context of this article, if one must say that in Marx the problem is complicated, its reverberations in Negri are worse, with their identification between social worker and communism in a practical state, with the absolute refusal to accept a dynamic of political practices in which a certain degree of autonomy has to be recognized, including the formation of identities that refer directly to them. On the other hand, Marx emphasized the role of collective subjectivities that mediate between the general and the singular, which Negri's idea of the multitude totally discards, in addition to the radicalization of a conception of social life in which subjectivity (it is not clear whether centered or decentered, intentional or otherwise) acquires absolute pre-eminence.

Especially in a social formation or civilization in which there is increasing complexity – of identities, spheres, practices – this has to be recognized. This is what Laclau and Mouffe (1989) dealt with before, mainly the latter, sliding toward a simplifying apology of "populism" (Laclau 2005; see also Chapter 8 of this book) as an absolute instance of unification of popular subjectivities, something rare and improbable in contemporary conditions, which can only happen through the "articulation" they themselves discussed in relation to the, transformed, category of hegemony in Gramsci. On the other hand, it is precisely there that the virtues and mystifications of Sousa Santos' work reside, in affirming and making an excessive apology, in the name, in part, of an epistemological plurality, of a multiplication of particular collective subjectivities, without offering criteria around which it can and should be fit in an emancipatory project, as well as at this point with little sociological analysis of what they rest upon, hence naturalizing them.

In other words, it is a matter of recognizing the increasing pluralization of social life and the need to create emancipatory (or liberating, if one wants to distinguish between what is in reality indistinct) mediations to produce alliances based on concrete themes and to promote democracy setting on from its political dimension. This does not mean that one should lose sight of the immediate social dimension and the radical transformation of modern society beyond itself. Even here there are difficulties, for the Marxist vision of communism, or its substitute in Negri, the "common," does not happen immediately in a supposed dispensability of organizers and of a certain level of hierarchy. This is inevitable, as we know, in organizations, which never articulate in a simply networked, or "rhizomatic" way, which generates a permanent problem of democratic institution, control and de-institution in order to overcome the impasses of the "iron law of the oligarchy," according to Michels (1915). The problem is dramatic, but there is no magic trick that will make it disappear, as Negri expects, even in the inevitability of representation in a highly complex global social formation like ours. Of course, an even thornier problem arises with regard to large corporations, the basis of what would be via socialization of monopolies the very construction of socialism, toward communism, in accordance exactly with the tendential laws of capitalist accumulation. It is hard to rely, due to bureaucratic problems and scope of action, on the national state to do so, let alone the grassroots support and popular mobilization that would be required to operate such a policy, not to mention the enormous reach of transnational corporations. On the other hand, however, it must be questioned whether we are content with small steps in daily life, as Harvey suggests, or with the claim of citizenship which, surprisingly, such as put forward in the proposals or practical demands of the writings published in the new millennium by Hardt and Negri (2000, 2005, 2011).

In a sense, it is a priority to identify exactly in what aspects of political systems one should intervene to break with what appears to be the inexorable and insurmountable logic of liberal democracy as the guardian of capitalism and partly of other forms of social oppression. What I have called in other contexts equal freedom – that is, the egalitarian distribution of power among agents capable of intervention in their life and in the collective dimension – is a value and *telos* that should guide this perspective. This is a criterion that is after all lacking in Santos, at most being implicit and modernly smuggled into his arguments about emancipation, although in Negri's work it appears in one form or another also implicitly but more positively. But this in itself does not tell us how to engender these openings of democracy, nor what could come up beyond this move, for example and especially, in the case of large capitalist enterprises, which are by no means simply parasitic in what concerns production, a strong but not empirically corroborated assertion in Negri's analysis, or mere postulation, which has in part grounded his ultra-leftist, revolutionary vision for a long time, by overflowing onto the political plane. We cannot simply invent what these transformations might be, but we must at least look at current trends of development – especially in politics as a relatively autonomous system of modernity, even though it appears as a reification that largely defines the division of power especially in what concerns the state. Little is done today in this direction, apart from the limited or problematic efforts of the authors directly mentioned here, although on a more general and more political plane, other examples of this can be pointed out in the critical tradition, in its derivation, in good will or grudgingly, toward the vicinity of liberalism (see Habermas 1992; Cohen and Arato 1992; Kalyvas 2005).

That there is an inevitable, whether we like it or not, dialectic between instituting and instituted we have known at least since Marx and his "Theses on Feuerbach" (1845), which Sartre (1960), among others, also reaffirmed for us, stressing, lest we forget, collective constructions and mediations, even though he aimed excessively at the dialectical totalization of history. Besides, this is something that Negri is not unaware of. Obviously, this dialectic engenders the problems that autonomous crystallizations of power imply for the construction of democracy, without there being magic solutions for them, even in processes of radical transformation. What is to be considered is what directions this takes today and which points should be strained to push it toward its instituting dimension (or, rather, the word "constituent," provided it is not homogenized, monodologized and/or absolutized). This applies to political systems in general, as well as to popular organizations, and we do not know how to build systems of mediation that do not destroy what is mediated. These systems do indeed have a degree of autonomy in relation to other social systems and thus must be treated, namely, as a system of mediations in complex societies, which does not mean that their independence should be promoted in relation to popular struggles and creativity or that in another type of civilization we would remain with the same institutional design.

From the point of view of a renewal of critical theory, it is a matter of advancing a research agenda that is indispensable today, at the center of which the republic and the affirmation of the masses, including their autonomy (which today is expressed in various and insufficient forms of explicit and declared neo-anarchism, sometimes as a mostly diffuse inspiration), can only appear with centrality. In this sense, if the global space is increasingly affirmed as a necessary sphere of emancipation, national states remain the most accessible and immediately productive locus of social struggles, irreplaceable for the time being, although links across their borders are also increasingly important. It is equally essential to re-emphasize the issue of capitalism, above all in the case of large corporations. It is, of course, necessary to return to the discussion of transformative collective subjectivities, not those posited by any generic philosophy, but those that can be empirically located in their concrete developmental trends, just as Marx assumed it in *Capital* and today we have assented in losing sight of. If it is not possible to stay on Derrida's side of the river, nor is it the case of radicalizing Adorno's negative dialectic or simply embracing the Deleuzian philosophy of difference. The crisis of metaphysics, long ago, beginning with Marx, has indicated the exhaustion of philosophy in the classical sense. Only the scientific analysis of social phenomena can effectively guide us, even though it must in its own way incorporate and respond to the great questions of the philosophical tradition, without succumbing to it.

The defeat of socialism, as configured in "real socialism," but not only in it, imposes the revision of all expectations of this tradition, without giving in to its abandonment. Communism – more than capitalism, in the Frankfurt School version – is a late project in today's modernity, in the sense that it is delayed and perhaps has reached a frustrated climacteric. Nothing tells us, apart from optimistic proclamations without support in any way unequivocal in reality, in the style of which Luxemburg emphasized, that its hour will come. If we want to realize, however, the equal freedom that modernity has promised us and cannot itself accomplish, by virtue of the systems of domination that cut across and constitute it, we must embrace the contingency of its possible fulfillment and seek the developmental trends that could suggest ways in which this civilization may be overcome. They do not in any event constitute "natural laws," not even in economics, even less in politics, although this is not really subject to the totality of the agents that weave it. If social and human emancipation will ever be effected, it depends therefore on our will, expressed today, albeit limitedly, in a wide range of social contestations that no longer reproduce simply the golden age of the revolutionary workers' movement; although, as we know, a long time passed before the human desire to fly became a reality, in ways unimagined and unimaginable for almost the entire course of its evolution, as Brecht and others have pointed out. In its plurality and possible convergence, it needs to be pushed forward and pursue more radical ways so as to continue advancing at least as a trend that can unfold toward the future. For this scientifically informed social theory may be instrumental.

Modesty is necessary in this respect. There is no longer place for formulations that resemble totalizing cosmologies, nor do we lack them, even more if they are derived from a simple, almost emanationist principle. It is debatable even if Marx espoused something of the like, despite his commitment to the idea of totality and its historical economic one-sidedness, whatever qualifications may be adduced. In any case, it is important for politics to move forward propelled by social agents – which in my opinion need a more advanced theorization, such as the one I have tried with concepts such as that of collective subjectivity, including unintended consequences, and social creativity –, although theory may be also operative in combining with social practices and helping to organize them, in dialogue with the multiplicity of collectivities that in one way or another carry out projects of social emancipation. This should be done today with the theory set in a more circumscribed, empirical and scientific way, as well as with the maintenance of its autonomy. This can produce, in effect, bold and incisive knowledge, with clear emancipatory criteria, but then and only then, more prudently, as Santos would have it, without losing itself in empiricism and in localism, without compromising in addition with plurality for its own sake.

We would thus move forward with Marx's spirit, although without fully incorporating his excessively strong commitment to a vision of totality, which we should not, however, within certain limits and considered the mediations of scientific practice, discard. This remains a challenge for critical theory: to shed light on the tendencies that point to the future, to think how to exploit them in the direction of emancipation and to search for totality, for sure, but without ever supposing that it has reached it, therefore always remaining wary of projecting too broad and a priori scenarios for social change. Transformative politics dispenses and must refuse anything beyond this.

References

Abaza, Mona (2006) *Changing Consumer Cultures of Modern Egypt: Cairo's Urban Reshaping* (Leiden and Boston: Brill).

Adams, Susan (ed.) (2014) *Cornelius Castoriadis: Key Concepts* (New York: Bloomsbury).

Adorno, Theodor W. and Horkheimer, Max (1944–45) *Dialektik der Aufklärung* (Frankfurt am Main: Suhrkamp, 1984).

Agamben, Giorgio (1997) *Homo sacer. Il potero sovrano e la vita nuda* (Turin: Einaudi).

Agamben, Giorgio (2003) *Stato di eccezione* (Turin: Bollati Boringhieri).

Alexander, Jeffrey C. (1988) *Action and its Environments* (New York: Columbia University Press).

Alexander, Jeffrey C. (2003) *The Meanings of Social Life: A Cultural Sociology* (Oxford and New York: Oxford University Press).

Alexander, Jeffrey C. (2006) *The Civil Sphere* (Oxford and New York: Oxford University Press).

Almond, Gabriel A. (1960) "Introduction: a functional approach to comparative politics," in Gabriel A. Almond and James S. Coleman (eds), *The Politics of Developing Areas* (Princeton, NJ: Princeton University Press).

Althusser, Louis (1965) *Pour Marx* (Paris: La Découverte, 1996).

American Political Science Association Task Force on Inequality and American Democracy (2004) *American Democracy in an Age of Rising Inequality* (www.apsanet.org).

Amin, Samir (1973) *L'Imperialisme et le development inegal* (Paris: Minuit).

Amin, Samir (1988) *L'Eurocentrisme* (Paris: Economica).

Anderson, Perry (1995) "Balanço do neoliberalismo," in Emir Sader and Pablo Gentile (eds), *Pós-Neoliberalismo* (São Paulo: Paz e Terra).

Ansaldi, Waldo and Giordano, Veronica (2012) *América Latina. La construcción del orden*, vols. 1–2 (Buenos Aires: Ariel).

Araujo, Kathya (2016) *El miedo a los subordinados* (Santiago: Lom).

Araujo, Kathya and Martuccelli, Danilo (2012) *Desafíos comunes. Retrato de la sociedad chilena y sus individuos* (Santiago: Lom).

Archer, Margaret, Bhaskar, Roy, Collier, Andrew, Lawson, Tony and Norrie, Alan (eds) (1998) *Critical Realism: Essential Readings* (Oxon and New York: Routledge).

Arditi, Benjamin (2005) "Populism as the internal periphery of democracy," in Francisco Panizza (ed.), *Populism and the Mirror of Democracy* (London and New York: Verso).

Aricó, José (1976–77) *Nueve lecciones sobre economía y política en el marxismo* (Mexico: Fondo de Cultura Económica and El Colegio de México, 2012).

Ariza, Marina and Oliveira, Orlandina de (2001) "Familias en transición y marcos conceptuales en redefinición," *Papeles de Población,* no. 28.

Arriagada, Irma (2002) "Changes and inequality in Latin American families," *Cepal Review*, no. 77.

Arriagada, Irma (2004) "Transformaciones sociales y demográficas de las familias latinoamericanas," *Papeles de población,* no. 40.

Austin, John (1861) *Lectures on Jurisprudence or the Philosophy of Positive Law* (London: John Murray, 1885).

Auyero, Javier (2001) *La política de los pobres. Las prácticas clientelares del peronismo* (Buenos Aires: Manancial).

Beck, Ulrich (1986) *Risk Society: Towards a New Modernity* (London: Sage, 1992).

Becker, Gary S. (1991) *A Treatise on the Family: Enlarged Edition* (Cambridge, MA: Harvard University Press).

Bell, Daniel (1978) *The Cultural Contradictions of Capitalism* (New York: Basic Books, 1996).

Bellofiore, Ricardo, Starosta, Guido and Thomas, Peter D. (eds) (2013) *In Marx's Laboratory: Critical Interpretations of the Grundrisse* (Leiden: Brill).

Bendix, Reinhard (1964) *Nation-Building and Citizenship: Studies of our Changing Social Order* (Berkeley and Los Angeles: University of California Press, 1996).

Bendix, Reinhard (1978) *Kings and People: The Mandate to Rule* (Berkeley and Los Angeles: University of California Press, 1980).

Benhabib, Seyla (1986) *Critique, Norm and Utopia: A Study of the Foundations of Critical Theory* (New York: Columbia University Press).

Bernstein, Eduard (1899) *Evolutionary Socialism: A Criticism and Affirmation* (New York: Schocken, 1961).

Bhaskar, Roy (1975) *A Realist Theory of Science* (Leeds: Leeds Books).

Bhaskar, Roy (1979) *The Possibility of Naturalism* (New York and London: Routledge, 1998).

Boltanski, Luc (2009) *De la Critique. Précis de sociologie de l'émancipattion* (Paris: Gallimard).

Boltanski, Luc and Chiapello, Ève (1999) *Le Nouvel esprit du capitalisme* (Paris: Gallimard).

Boltanksi, Luc and Thévenot, Laurent (1991) *De la Justification. Les economies de la grandeur* (Paris: Gallimard).

Botton Beja, Flora (1999) "La familia y el Estado en China y Singapur: algunos puntos de comparación," *Estudios de Asia y África,* vol. 34.

Boudon, Raymond (1984) *La Place du désordre* (Paris: Presses Universitaires de France, 2014).

Boyer, Robert (1986) *La Théorie de la regulación. Une analyse critique* (Paris: La Découverte).

Brandão, Gildo Marçal (2007) *Linhagens do pensamento político brasileiro* (São Paulo: Hucitec).

Brenner, Robert (2006) *The Economics of Global Turbulence: The Advanced Capitalist Economies from Long Boom to Long Downturn, 1945–2005* (London and New York: Verso).

Browne, Craig (2008) "The end of immanent critique?," *European Journal of Social Theory*, vol. 11.

Bruce, Steve (1996) *Religion in the Modern World: From Cathedrals to Cult* (Oxford: Oxford University).

Buarque de Hollanda, Sérgio (1936) *Raízes do Brasil* (São Paulo: Companhia das Letras, 1977).

Burawoy, Michael (2005) "For public sociology," *American Sociological Review*, vol. 70.

Butler, Judith, Laclau, Ernesto and Zizek, Slavoj (2000) *Contingency, Hegemony, Universality: Contemporary Dialogues on the Left* (London and New York: Verso).

Canovan, Margaret (2002) "Talking politics to the people: populism as the ideology of democracy," in Yves Mény and Yves Surel (eds), *Democracies and the Populist Challenge* (Basingstoke and New York: Palgrave).

Casanova, José (1994) *Public Religions in the Modern World* (Chicago: Chicago University Press).

Casanova, José (2011) "Erkundungen des Postsekulären. Role und Bedeutung der Religion in Europa," *Westend*, vol. 8.

Casanova, José (2012) "Rethinking public religions," in Timothy Samuel Shah, Alfred Stepan and Monica Duffy Toft (eds), *Rethinking Religion and World Affairs* (Oxford: Oxford University Press).

Castells, Manuel (1996) *The Information Age: Economy, Society and Culture*, vol. 1. The Rise of Network Society (Malden, MA and Oxford, Blackwell, 2000).

Castells, Manuel (2013) *Networks of Outrage and Hope: Social Movements in the Internet Age* (Cambridge: Polity).

Castoriadis, Cornelius (1975) *L'Institution imaginaire de la société* (Paris: Seuil).

Castoriadis, Cornelius (1994) "Modes of being and problems of knowledge of the social-historical," in *Philosophy, Politics, Autonomy* (New York: Oxford University Press).

Chakrabarty, Dipesh (2000) *Provincializing Europe* (Princeton, NJ: Princeton University Press, 2007).

Chatterjee, Partha (1993) *The Nation and its Fragments: Colonial and Postcolonial Histories* (Princeton, NJ: Princeton University Press).

Chatterjee, Partha (2004) *The Politics of the Governed: Reflections on Popular Politics in Most of the World* (New York: Columbia University Press).

Clausewitz, Carl von (1832) *Vom Krieg* (Bonn: Dümmler, 1991).

Cohen, Jean and Arato, Andrew (1992) *Civil Society and Political Theory* (Cambridge, MA: The MIT Press).

Cohn, Gabriel (1978) *Crítica e resignação. Fundamentos da sociologia de Max Weber* (São Paulo: T.A. Queiroz).

Cohn, Gabriel (2003) "A sociologia e o novo padrão civilizatório," in Barreira, Cesar (ed.), *A sociologia no tempo* (São Paulo: Cortez).

Collins, Randall (1986) *Weberian Sociological Theory* (Cambridge: Cambridge University Press).

Collins, Randal (1995) *Macrohistory: Essays in the Long Run* (Stanford: Stanford University Press).

Cooley, Charles H. (1909) *Social Organization: The Study of the Larger Mind* (Ithaca, NY and London: Cornell University Press, 2009).

Cooper, Frederick (2005) *Colonialism in Question: Theory, Knowledge, History* (Los Angeles and Berkeley: University of California Press).

Coser, Lewis (1956) *The Functions of Social Conflict* (New York: Free Press).

Crouch, Colin (2004) *Post-Democracy* (Cambridge: Polity).

Dahl, Robert (1972) *Poliarchy: Participation and Opposition* (New Haven, CO and London: Yale University Press).

Dahl, Robert (1989) *Democracy and its Critics* (New Haven, CO and London: Yale University Press).

Dardot, Pierre and Laval, Christian (2014) *Commun. Essai sur la revolution au XXIe sciècle* (Paris: La Découverte).

Davis, Deborah S. and Friedman, Sara L. (2014) *Wives, Husbands and Lovers: Marriage and Sexuality in Hong Kong, Taiwan, and Urban China* (Stanford, CA: Stanford University Press).

Debés Valdés, Eduardo (2012) *Pensamiento periférico. Una tesis interpretativa global* (Santiago de Chile: Idea-Usach).

Delamata, Gabriela (2008) "Luchas sociales, gobierno y estado durante la presidencia de Néstor Kirchner," in Maria Regina Soares de Lima (ed.), *Desempenho de governos progressistas no Cone Sul* (Rio de Janeiro: Edições IUPERJ).

Delamata, Gabriela (ed.) (2009) *Movilizaciones sociales: ¿nuevas ciudadanías? Reclamos, derechos, Estado en Argentina, Bolivia y Brasil* (Buenos Aires: Biblos).

Derrida, Jacques (1966) "La Structure, le signe et le jeu dans le discours des sciences humaines," in *L'Écriture et la différence* (Paris: Seuil).

Descola, Phillipe (2005) *Par-delà nature et culture* (Paris: Gallimard).

Diehl, Paula (2011) "Die Complexität des Populismus. Ein Plädoyer für ein mehrdimensionales und graduelles Konzept," *Totalitarismus und Demokratie*, vol. 8.

Domingues, José Maurício (1992) "A América. Intelectuais, interpretações e identidades," in *Do Ocidente à modernidade. Intelectuais e mudança social* (Rio de Janeiro: Civilização Brasileira, 2003).

Domingues, José Maurício (1995a) *Sociological Theory and Collective Subjectivity* (Basingstoke: Macmillan Press and New York: Saint Martin's Press – Palgrave).

Domingues, José Maurício (1995b) "The space-time dimension of social systems," *Time & Society*, vol. 4.

Domingues, José Maurício (2000a) *Social Creativity, Collective Subjectivity and Contemporary Modernity* (Basingstoke: Macmillan and New York: Saint Martin's Press – Palgrave).

Domingues, José Maurício (2000b) *"The City*: rationalization and freedom in Max Weber," *Philosophy and Social Criticism*, vol. 26.

Domingues, José Maurício (2006a) *Modernity Reconstructed* (Cardiff: University of Wales Press).

Domingues, José Maurício (2006b) "Instituições formais, cidadania e 'solidariedade complexa,'" in *Aproximações à América Latina. Desafios contemporâneos* (Rio de Janeiro: Civilização Brasileira, 2007).

Domingues, José Maurício (2008) *Latin American and Contemporary Modernity: A Sociological Interpretation* (New York and London: Routledge).

Domingues, José Maurício (2009) "Modernity and modernizing moves: Latin America in comparative perspective," *Theory, Culture & Society. Annual Review*, vol. 26.

Domingues, José Maurício (2010) "Ashis Nandy e as vicissitudes do self. Crítica, subjetividade e civilização indiana," in *Teoria crítica e (semi)periferia* (Belo Horizonte: Editora UFMG, 2011).

Domingues, José Maurício (2012) *Global Modernity, Development, and Contemporary Civilization: towards a Renewal of Critical Theory* (New York and London: Routledge).

Domingues, José Maurício (2013) "Democratic theory and democratization – in Brazil and beyond," *Thesis Eleven*, vol. 114.

Domingues, José Maurício (2015) *O Brasil entre o presente e o futuro. Conjuntura atual e inserção internacional* (Rio de Janeiro: Mauad, 2ª. edition, revised and enlarged).

Dun, John (1979) *Western Political Theory in the Face of the Future* (Cambridge: Cambridge University Press).

Durkheim, Emile (1893) *De la Division du travail social* (Paris: Presses Universitaires de France, 1973).

Durkheim, Emile (1897) *Le Suicide. Etude de sociologie* (Paris: Presses Universitaires de France, 2013).

Easton, David (1965) *A Framework for Political Analysis* (Englewood Cliffs, NJ: Prentice-Hall).

Ebrey, Patricia (1991) "The Confucian family and the spread of Confucian values," in Rozman Gilbert (ed.), *The East Asian Region: Confucian Heritage and its Modern Adaptation* (Cambridge: Cambridge University Press).

Eisenstadt, Shmuel N. (1973) *Traditional Patrimonialism and Modern Neopatrimonialism* (Beverly Hills, CA and London: Sage).

Eisenstadt, Shmuel N. (2001) "The civilizational dynamic of modernity: modernity as a distinct civilization," *International Sociology*, vol. 16.

Elias, Nobert (1939) *The Civilizing Process: Sociogenetic and Psychogenetic Investigations* (Oxford: Blackwell, 2000).

Elster, Jon (1985) *Making Sense of Marx* (Cambridge: Cambridge University Press).

Elster, Jon (2009) *Alexis de Tocqueville: The First Social Scientist* (Cambridge: Cambridge University Press).

Engels, Friedrich (1884) *Der Ursprung der Familie, des Privateigentum und des Staats*, in Karl Marx and Friedrich Engels, *Werke*, vol. 21 (Berlin: Dietz, 1975).

Evans, Peter, Rueschemeyer, Dietrich and Skocpol, Theda (1985) *Bringing the State back in* (Cambridge: Cambridge University Press).

Foucault, Michel (1976) "Cours de janvier 1976," in *Dits et écrits*, vol. 2 (Paris: Gallimard, 2001).

Foucault, Michel (1982) "Le sujet et le pouvoir," in *Dits et écrits*, vol. 2 (Paris: Gallimard, 2001).

Fraser, Nancy (2009) *Scales of Justice: Reimagining Political Space in a Globalizing World* (Cambridge: Polity).

Fraser, Nancy and Honneth, Axel (2003) *Redistribution or Recognition: A Political-Philosophical Exchange* (London and New York: Verso).

Freud, Sigmund (1900) *Die Traumdeutung*, in *Studienausgabe*, vol. 1 (Frankfurt am Main: S. Fisher, 1972).

Freud, Sigmund (1915) "Das Unbewusste," in *Studienausgabe*, vol. 3 (Frankfurt am Main: S. Fisher, 1975).

Freud, Sigmund (1923) *Das Ich und das Es*, in *Studienausgabe*, vol. 3 (Frankfurt am Main: S. Fisher, 1975).

García, Brígida and Lorena Rojas, Olga(2002) "Cambios en la formación y disolución de las uniones en América Latina," *Papeles de población,* no. 32.

García Canclini, Néstor (1995) *Consumidores y ciudadanos. Conflictos multiculturales de la globalización* (Mexico: Grijalbo).

Gentili, Dario (2013) "Una crisi italiana. Alla radice della teoría dell'autonomia del politico," *Il rasoio de Occam*, 27 de fevereiro.

Germani, Gino (1965) *Política y sociedad en una época de transición* (Buenos Aires: Paidós).

Giddens, Anthony (1976) *New Rules of Sociological Method* (London: Hutchinson).

Giddens, Anthony (1984) *The Constitution of Society* (Cambridge: Polity).

Giddens, Anthony (1985) *The Nation State and Violence* (Cambridge: Polity).

Giddens, Anthony (1990) *The Consequences of Modernity* (Cambridge: Polity).

Giroux, Henry A. (2004) *The Terror of Neoliberalism: Authoritarianism and the Eclipse of Democracy* (Boulder, CO and London: Paradigm; Aurora, Ontario: Garamond).

Go, Julian (2012) "For a postcolonial sociology," *Theory and Society*, vol. 42.

Godelier, Maurice (1973) *Horizon, trajets marxistes en anthropologie* (Paris: Maspero).

Godelier, Maurice (2010) *Métamorphoses de la parenté* (Paris: Flammarion).

Goode, William J. (1963) *World Revolution and Family Patterns* (New York: Free Press, 1970).

Graeber, David (2011) *Debt: The First 5.000 Years* (New York and London: Melville House, 2014).

Gramsci, Antonio (1929–35) *Quaderni del carceri*, vols 1–3 (Turin: Einaudi, 2001).

Grossmann, Henryk (1929) *Das Akkumulation- und Zusammenbruchgesetz des kapitalistischen Systems* (Frankfurt am Main: Neue Kritik, 1967).

Habermas, Jürgen (1976) *Für Rekonstruktion historischen Materialismus* (Frankfurt am Main: Suhrkamp).

Habermas, Jürgen (1980) "Das unvollendete Projekt der Moderne," in *Philosophisch-politische Aufsätze, 1977 – 1990* (Leipzig: Reclam, 1994).

Habermas, Jürgen (1981) *Theorie des kommunikativen Handelns*, vols 1–2 (Frankfurt am Main: Suhrkamp).

Habermas, Jürgen (1992) *Faktizität und Geltung* (Frankfurt am Main: Suhrkamp).

Habermas, Jürgen (2001a) *Die Zukunft menschlichen Natur* (Frankfurt am Main: Suhrkamp).

Habermas, Jürgen (2001b) *Glauben und Wissen* (Frankfurt am Main: Suhrkamp).

Habermas, Jürgen (2011) *Eine Verfassung Europas. Ein Essay* (Frankfurt am Main: Suhrkamp).

Hadden, Jeffrey K. (1987) "Toward desacralizing secularization theory," *Social Forces*, vol. 65.

Halevy, Elie (1901–04) *The Growth of Philosophical Radicalism* (New York: Augustus M. Kelley, 1970).

Hardt, Michel and Negri, Antonio (1994) *Labor of Dyonisius: A Critique of the State Form* (Minneapolis, MN: University of Minnesota Press).

Hardt, Michael and Negri, Antonio (2000) *Empire* (Cambridge, MA: Harvard University Press).

Hardt, Michael and Negri, Antonio (2005) *Multitude: War and Democracy in the Age of Empire* (New York: Penguin).

Hardt, Michel and Negri, Antonio (2011) *Commonwealth* (Cambridge, MA: Harvard University Press).

Harvey, David (1990) *The Condition of Postmodernity* (Malden, MA and Oxford: Blackwell).

Harvey, David (2003) *The New Imperialism* (Oxford: Oxford University Press).

Harvey, David (2009) *The Enigma of Capital and the Crisis of Capitalism* (New York: Oxford University Press).

Harvey, David (2014) *Seventeen Contradictions and the End of Capitalism* (New York: Oxford University Press).

Hayek, Friedrich A. (1944) *The Road to Serfdom* (London: Routledge & Kegan Paul, 1979).

Hedström, Peter and Swedberg, Richard (eds) (1998) *Social Mechanisms: An Analytical Approach to Social Theory* (Cambridge: Cambridge University Press).

Heinrich, Michael (2003) *Die Wissenschaft vom Wert. Die Marxsche Kritik der politischen Ökonomie zwischen wissenschaftlicher Revolution und klassischer Tradition* (Münster: Westfälisches Dampfboot).

Heinrich, Michael (2013) "Crisis theory, the law of the tendency of the profit rate to fall, and Marx's studies in the 1870s," *Monthly Review*, vol. 64.

Hirschman, Albert O. (1976) *The Passion and the Interests: Political Arguments for Capitalism before its Emergence* (Princeton, NJ: Princeton University Press).

Hobbes, Thomas (1651) *Leviathan* (Cambridge: Cambridge University Press, 1996).

Hobsbawm, Eric (1964) "Introduction," in Karl Marx, *Pre-Capitalist Economic Formations* (New York: International Publishers).

Ho-fung Hung (2008) "Rise of China and the global overaccumulation crisis," *Review of International Political Economy*, vol. 15.

Honneth, Axel (2008) "Verflussigungen des Sozialen: Zur Gesellschaftstheorie von Luc Boltanski und Laurent Thévenot," in *Das Ich in Wir. Studien zur Annerkennungstheorie* (Frankfurt am Main: Suhrkamp, 2010).

Honneth, Axel (2010) *Das Ich in Wir. Studien zur Anerkennungstheorie* (Frankfurt am Main: Suhrkamp).

Honneth, Axel (2011) *Das Recht der Freiheit. Grundrisse eine demokratischen Sittlichkeit* (Frankfurt am Main: Suhrkamp).

Honneth, Axel (2014) "Die moral im 'Kapital.' Versuch einer Korrektur der Marxschen Ökonomiekritik," in Rahel Jaeggi and Daniel Loick (eds), *Nach Marx. Philosophie, Kritik, Praxis* (Frankfurt am Main: Suhrkamp).

Honneth, Axel (2015) *Die Idee des Sozialismus* (Frankfurt am Main: Suhrkamp).

Huntington, Samuel P. (1968) *Political Order in Changing Societies* (New Haven, CO and London: Yale University Press, 2006).

James, Daniel (1990) *Resistance and Integration: Peronism and the Argentine Working Class, 1946–1976* (Cambridge: Cambridge University Press).

Jameson, Fredric (1991) *Post-Modernism, or the Cultural Logic of Late Capitalism* (Durham, NC and London: Duke University Press).

Jay, Martin (1986) *Marxism and Totality: The Adventures of a Concept from Lukács to Habermas* (Berkeley and Los Angeles: University of California Press).

Jessop, Bob (1990) *State Theory: Putting Capitalist States in their Place* (Cambridge: Polity).

Jessop, Bob (2008) *State Power* (Cambridge: Polity).

Jhabvala, Renana and Standing, Guy (2010) "Targeting the 'poor': clogged pipes and bureaucratic blinkers," *Economic and Political Weekly*, vol. 45, nos. 26–27.

Joas, Hans (2012) *Glaube als Option: Zukunftsmöglichkeit des Christentums* (Freiburg: Herder).

Kalyvas, Andreas (2005) *Democracy and the Politics of the Extraordinary: Max Weber, Carl Schmitt, and Hannah Arendt* (Cambridge: Cambridge University Press).

Karatani, Kojin (2004) "Introduction: the Eighteenth Brumaire of Louis Bonaparte," in *History and Repetition* (New York and Chichester: Columbia University Press, 2011).

Karatani, Kojin (2005) *Transcritique: on Kant and Marx* (Cambridge, MA: MIT Press).

Karatani, Kojin (2010) *The Structure of World History: from Modes of Production to Modes of Exchange* (Durham, NC and London: Duke University Press, 2014).

Kautsky, Karl (1909) *The Road to Power* (Alameda, CA: Center for Socialist History, 2007).

Knöbl, Wolfgang (2001) *Spielräume der Modernisierung* (Weilerwist: Velbrück).

Knöbl, Wolfgang (2007) *Die Kontingenz der Moderne: Wege in Europa, Asien und America* (Frankfurt am Main and New York: Campus).

Kowarick, Lucio (1977) *Capitalismo e marginalidade na América Latina* (Rio de Janeiro: Paz e Terra).

Laclau, Ernesto (2005) *On Populist Reason* (London and New York: Verso).

Laclau, Ernesto and Mouffe, Chantall (1985) *Hegemony and Socialist Strategy* (London and New York: Verso).

Lange, Hellmuth and Meier, Lars (eds) (2009) *The New Middle Classes: Globalizing Lifestyles, Consumerism and Environmental Concern* (Dordrecht: Springer).

Laplanche, Jean and Pontalis, Jean-Bertrand (1967) *Vocabulaire de la psicanalyse* (Paris: PUF, 2000).

Lechner, Nobert (1997) "Tres formas de coordinación social," in *Obras Escogidas*, vol. 2 (Santiago: Lom, 2007).

Lefort, Claude (1981) *L'Invention democratique. Les limites de la domination totalitaire* (Paris: Fayard).

Leledakis, Akis (1995) *Society and Psyche: Social Theory and the Unconscious Dimension of Social Life* (London: Berg).

Lenin, Vladimir (1917) *Imperialism, the Highest Stage of Capitalism: A Popular Outline*, in *Selected Works*, vol. 1 (Moscow: Progress, 1963).

Lerner, Daniel (1958) *The Passing of Traditional Society: Modernizing the Middle East* (New York: Free Press).

Lévi-Strauss, Claude (1969) "The family," in Harry L. Shapiro (ed.), *Man, Culture, and Society* (Oxford: Oxford University Press).

Lezama, José Luis (1993) *Teoría social, espacio y ciudad* (Mexico: Colegio de México, 2005).

Lipset, Seymor M. (1959) "Some social requisites of democracy: economic development and political legitimacy," *The American Political Science Review*, vol. 53.

Lukács, Gyorg (1923) *Geschichte und Klassenbewusstsein. Studien über Marxistische Dialektik*, in *Werke*, vol. 2 (Darmstadt: Luchterhand, 1977).

Luxemburg, Rosa (1913) *Die Akkumulation des Kapitals. Ein Beitrag zur ökonomischen Erklärung des Imperialismus* (Berlin: Institut für Marxismus-Leninismus, 1975).

Lyotard, Jean-François (1979) *La Condition postmoderne. Rapport sur le savoir* (Paris, Minuit).

Macfarlane, Alan (1978) *The Origins of English Individualism* (Cambridge: Cambridge University Press).

Madan, T.N. (1987) "Secularism and its place," in *Images of the World: Essays on Religion, Secularization, and Culture* (Nova Deli: Oxford University Press, 2006).

Madan, T.N. (1997) *Modern Myths, Locked Minds: Secularism and Fundamentalism in India* (Nova Deli: Oxford University Press).

Madsen, Richard (2010) "Religious revival," in You-tien Hising and Kwan Ching Lee (eds), *Reclaiming Chinese Society: The New Social Activism* (New York and London: Routledge).

Magri, Lucio (2009) *Il sarto di Ulm. Una posibilie storia del PCI* (Milan: Il Saggiatore).

Maneiro, María (2012) *Encuentros y desencuentros. Estado y movimientos de trabajadores desocupados del Gran Buenos Aires (1996–2005)* (Buenos Aires: Biblos).

Manicas, Peter T. (2006) *A Realist Philosophy of the Social Sciences* (Cambridge: Cambridge University Press).

Manin, Bernard (1997) *The Principles of Representative Government* (Cambridge: Cambridge University Press).

Mann, Michael. (1986) *The Sources of Social Power*, vol. 1. A History of Power from the Beginning to A.D. 1760 (Cambridge, Cambridge University Press).

Mann, Michael (1993) *The Sources of Social Power*, vol. 2. The Rise of Classes and Nation-States, 1760–1914 (Cambridge: Cambridge University Press).

Mann, Michael (2013) *The Sources of Social Power*, vol. 4. Globalizations, 1945–2011 (Cambridge: Cambridge University Press).

Marshall, T.H. (1950) "Citizenship and social class," in *Class, Citizenship and Social Development* (Garden City, NY: Double Day & Co, 1964).

Martin, David (1978) *A General Theory of Secularization* (New York: Harper & Row).

Martín-Barbero, Jesús (1987) *De los medios a las mediaciones. Comunicación, cultura y hegemonía* (Barcelona: G. Gilli).

Martínez, Tomás E. (2003) *Requien por un país perdido* (Buenos Aires: Aguilar).

Martuccelli, Danilo (2006) *Forgé par l'éprouve. L'individu dans la France contemporaine* (Paris: Armand Collin).

Martuccelli, Danilo (2010) *La Société singulariste* (Paris: Armand Colin).

Marx, Karl (1844) *Zur Judenfrage*, in Karl Marx and Friedrich Engels, *Werke*, vol. 1 (Berlin: Dietz, 1956).

Marx, Karl (1845) "Thesen über Feuerbach," in Karl Marx and Friedrich Engels, *Werke*, vol. 3 (Berlin: Dietz, 1956).

Marx, Karl (1852) *Der achtzehnte Brumaire des Louis Bonaparte*, in Karl Marx and Friedrich Engels, *Werke*, vol. 8 (Berlin: Dietz, 1976).

Marx, Karl (1857–58) *Ökonomische Manuskripte 1857/58 (Grundrisse)*, *Mega 42* (Berlin: Dietz, 1983).

Marx, Karl (1859) "Vorwort," in *Zur Kritik der politischen Ökonomie,* in Karl Marx and Friedrich Engels, *Werke,* vol. 13 (Berlin: Dietz, 1971).

Marx, Karl (1867) *Das Kapital. Kritik der politischen Ökonomie,* vol. 1 (Berlin: Dietz, 1968).

Marx, Karl (1871) *The Civil War in France,* in Karl Marx and Friedrich Engels, *Collected Works,* vol. 22 (Moscow: Progress Publishers, 1986).

Marx, Karl (1875) *Kritik der Gothaer Programms,* in Karl Marx Karl and Friedrich Engels, *Werke,* vol. 19 (Berlin: Dietz, 1973).

Marx, Karl (1883) *Das Kapital. Kritik der politischen Ökonomie,* vol. 2 (Berlin: Dietz, 1963).

Marx, Karl (1894) *Das Kapital. Kritik der politischen Ökonomie,* vol. 3 (Berlin: Dietz, 1983).

Marx, Karl and Engels, Friedrich (1845) *Die deutsche Ideologie,* in *Werke,* vol. 3 (Berlin, Dietz, 1969).

Marx, Karl and Engels, Friedrich (1848) *Manifest der kommunistischen Partei,* in *Werke,* vol. 6 (Berlin: Dietz, 1959).

Mead, Georg H. (1927–30) *Mind, Self and Society* (Chicago: The University of Chicago Press, 1962).

Medina Echevarría, José (1964) *Consideraciones sociológicas sobre el desarrollo económico* (Buenos Aires: Solar y Hachette).

Merton, Robert K. (1968) *Social Theory and Social Structure* (New York: Free Press).

Michels, Robert (1915) *Political Parties: A Sociological Study of the Oligarchical Tendencies of Modern Democracy* (New York: Simon & Schuster, 1968).

Mignolo, Walter D. (2000) *Local Histories/Global Designs: Coloniality, Subaltern Knowledges, and Border Thinking* (Princeton, NJ: Princeton University Press).

Mignolo, Walter D. (2005) *The Idea of Latin America* (Oxford: Blackwell).

Mill, John Stuart (1843) *System of Logic, Ratiocinative and Inductive, being a Connected View of the Principles of Evidence, and the Methods of Scientific Investigation* (New York: Harper and Brothers, 1882).

Milliband, Ralph (1971) *The State in Capitalist Society: The Analysis of the Western System of Power* (London: Quarter).

Moore Jr., Barrington (1967) *Social Origins of Democracy and Dictatorship: Lord and Peasant in the Making of the Modern World* (Boston, MA: Beacon).

Morgenthau, Hans J. (1949) *Politics among Nations: The Struggle for Power and Peace* (New York: Alfred A. Knopf, 1967).

Müller-Doohm, Stephan (2005) "How to criticize: convergent and divergent paths in critical theories of society," in Gerard Delanty (ed.), *Handbook of European Social Theory* (London and New York: Routledge).

Murillo, Sonia (2008) *Colonizar el dolor. La interpelación ideológica del Banco Mundial en América Latina. El caso argentino desde Blumberg a Cromañon* (Buenos Aires: CLACSO).

Murmis, Miguel and Portantiero, Juan Carlos (1972) *Estudios sobre los orígenes del peronismo* (Buenos Aires: Siglo XXI, 2006).

Murphy, Timothy S. (2012) *Antonio Negri* (Cambridge: Polity).

Nanda, Meera (2004) *Prophets Facing Backwards: Postmodernism, Science, and Hindu Nationalism* (Delhi: Permanent Black).

Nandy, Ashis (1978) "Towards a Third World utopia," in *Traditions, Tyranny, and Utopias: Essays in the Politics of Awareness* (New Delhi: Oxford University Press, 1992).

Nandy, Ashis (1985) "An anti-secularist manifesto," in *The Romance of the State and the Fate of Dissent in the Tropics* (New Delhi: Oxford University Press, 2003).

Nandy, Ashis (1990) "The politics of secularism and the recovery of religious tolerance," in *Times Warp: Silent and Evasive Pasts in Indian Politics and Religion* (New Brunswick, NJ: Rutgers University Press, 2002).

Navarro, Marysa (1977) "The case of Eva Perón," *Signs*, vol. 3.

Negri, Antonio (1979) *Marx oltre Marx. Quaderno di lavoro sui Grundrisse* (Roma: Manifestolibri, 2003).

Negri, Antonio (1992) *Il potere constituente. Sagio sulle alternative del moderno* (Roma: Manifestolibri, 2002).

Negri, Antonio (1998) "Reviewing the experience of Italy in the 1970s," *Le Monde Diplomatique*, English edition, September.

Negri, Antonio (2005) *The Politics of Subversion: A Manifesto for the Twenty-First Century* (Cambridge: Polity, 2nd edition).

Neri, Aldo et al. (2010) *Asignación universal por hijo. Ciclo de conferencias* (Buenos Aires: AAPS).

Nobre, Marcus (2008) "Teoria crítica hoje," in Daniel Tourinho Peres et al (eds), *Tensões e passagens. Filosofia crítica e modernidade* (São Paulo: Singular).

Nun, José (2001) *Marginalidad y exclusión social* (Buenos Aires and Mexico: Fondo de Cultura Económica).

O'Donnell, Guillermo (1991) "Delegative democracy," *Journal of Democracy*, no. 5.

Offe, Carl (1973) *Strukturprobleme des kapistalistischen Staates* (Frankfurt am Main: Suhrkamp).

Ortiz, Renato (1994) *Mundialização e cultura* (São Paulo: Brasiliense).

Panitch, Leo and Gindin, Sam (2012) *The Making of Global Capitalism: The Political Economy of the American Empire* (London and New York: Verso).

Panizza, Francisco (2005) *Populism and the Mirror of Democracy* (London and New York: Verso).

Parsons, Talcott (1937) *The Structure of Social Action* (New York: The Free Press, 1966).

Parsons, Talcott (1951) *The Social System* (London: Routledge & Kegan Paul, 1979).

Parsons, Talcott (1955) "The American family: its relations to personality and to the social structure," in Talcott Parsons and Robert F. Bales (eds), *Family: Socialization and Interaction Process* (New York: Free Press).

Parsons, Talcott. (1967) *Sociological Theory and Modern Society* (New York: Free Press).

Parsons, Talcott (1971) *The System of Modern Society* (Englewood Cliffs, NJ: Prentice-Hall).

Pasukanis, Evgeny B. (1926) *La Théorie generale du droit et le marxisme* (Paris: EDI, 1969).

Patel, Sujata (2006) "Beyond binaries: a case for self-reflexive sociologies," *Current sociology*, vol. 54.

Patel, Tulsi (ed.) (2005) *The Family in India: Structure and Practice* (New Delhi: Sage).

Pateman, Carol (1988) *The Sexual Contract* (Stanford, CA: Stanford University Press).

Piaget, Jean and García, Rolando (1983) *Psychogenèse et histoire des sciences* (Paris: Flammarion).

Pierson, Paul and Skocpol, Theda (eds) (2007) *The Transformation of American Politics: Activist Government and the Rise of Conservatism* (Princeton, NJ: Princeton University Press).

Piketty, Thomas (2013) *Le Capital au XXIe siècle* (Paris: Seuil).

Pitkin, Hannah F. (1967) *The Concept of Representation* (Berkeley and Los Angeles: University of California Press).

Pleyers, Geoffrey (2011) *After Globalization: Becoming Actors in the Global Age* (Cambridge: Polity).

Polanyi, Karl (1944) *The Great Transformation: The Political and Economic Origins of our Time* (Boston: Beacon, 2002).

Poulantzas, Nicos (1968) *Pouvoir politique et classes sociales* (Paris: Maspero).

Poulantzas, Nicos (1978) *L'Etat, le pouvoir, le socialisme* (Paris: Presses Universitaires de France).

Quijano, Aníbal (1977) *Imperialismo y marginalidad* (Lima: Mosca Azul).

Quilodran Julieta (2003) "La familia, referentes en transición," *Papeles de población*, no. 37.

Riley, Alexander T. (2005) "'Renegade Durkheimianism' and the transgressive left sacred," in Jeffrey A. Alexander and Philip Smith (eds), *The Cambridge Companion to Durkheim* (Cambridge: Cambridge University Press).

Riley, Patrik (1982) *Will and Political Legitimacy: A Critical Exposition of Social Contract Theory in Hobbes, Locke, Rousseau, Kant, and Hegel* (Cambridge, MA: Harvard University Press).

Robbins, Lionel (1932) *An Essay on the Nature and Significance of Economic Theory* (London: Macmillan).

Rock, David (1987) *Argentina, 1516–1982: From Spanish Colonization to Alfonsín* (Berkeley and Los Angeles: University of California Press).

Rodriguez Vignoli, Jorge A. (2004) "¿Cohabitación en América Latina: modernidad, exclusión o diversidad?," *Papeles de población*, no. 40.

Ronen, Ruth (1997) "Description, narrative and representation," *Narrative*, vol. 5.

Rouanet, Sérgio Paulo (1985) *A razão cativa* (São Paulo: Brasiliense).

Sahlins, Marshall (1960) "Evolution: specific and general," in E.R. Service et al (eds), *Evolution and Culture* (Ann Arbor, MC: The Michigan University Press, 1982).

Santos, Boaventura de Sousa (1995) *Pela mão de Alice. O social e o político na pós-modernidade* (São Paulo: Cortez).

Santos, Boaventura de Sousa (1999) "Por que é tão difícil construir uma teoria crítica?," *Revista crítica de Ciências Sociais*, no. 54.

Santos, Boaventura de Sousa (2000) *A crítica da razão indolente. Contra o desperdício da experiência* (São Paulo: Cortez).

Santos, Boaventura de Sousa (2002) "Para uma sociologia das ausências e uma sociologia das emergências," *Revista crítica de ciências sociais*, vol. 63.

Santos, Boaventura de Sousa (2007) *Renovar a teoria crítica e reinventar a emancipação social* (São Paulo: Boitempo).

Santos, Boaventura de Sousa (2010) *Refundación del Estado en América Latina. Perspectivas desde una epistemología del Sur* (Lima: Instituto Internacional de Derecho y Sociedad).

Saraceno, Chiara (1976) *Anatomia della famiglia* (Bari: De Donato).

Sarlo, Beatriz (2011) *La audacia y el cálculo: Kirchner 2003–2010* (Buenos Aires: Sudamericana).

Sarmiento, Domingo F. (1845) *Facundo. Civilización y barbarie: vida de Juan Facundo Quiroga* (Caracas: Biblioteca Ayacucho, 1977).

Sartre, Jean-Paul (1960) *Critique de la raison dialectique* (Paris: Gallimard).

Sassen, Saskia (2006) *Territory, Authority, Rights: from Medieval to Global Assemblages* (Princeton, NJ: Princeton University Press, 2nd edition).

Sassen, Saskia (2007) *A Sociology of Globalization* (New York: W.W. Norton & Co).

Schmidt, Volker H. (2007) "One world, one modernity," in Volker H. Schmidt (ed.), *Modernity at the Beginning of the 21st Century* (Newcastle: Cambridge Scholarly Publishing).

Schmidt, Volker H. (2009) "Modernity and diversity: reflections on the controversy between modernization theorists and multiple modernists," *Social Science Information*, vol. 49.

Schumpeter, Joseph A. (1942) *Capitalism, Socialism, and Democracy* (New York: Harper, 2008).

Schutz, Alfred (1962–66) *Collected Papers*, vols 1–3 (Dordrecht: Martinus Nijihoff).

Senén González, Santiago and Lerman, Gabriel D. (2005) *El 17 de octubre de 1945: antes, durante, después* (Buenos Aires: Lumiere).

Sewell Jr., William H. (2005) *Logics of History: Social Theory and Social Transformation* (Chicago: University of Chicago Press).

Shah, A. M. (1998) *The Family in India: Critical Essays* (Himayatnegar, Hyderabad: Orient Longman).

Sidicaro, Ricardo (2010) *Los tres peronismos: Estado y poder económico* (Buenos Aires: Siglo XXI, 2nd edition).

Sigal, Silvia and Verón, Eliseo (2003) *Perón o muerte: los fundamentos discursivos del fenómeno peronista* (Buenos Aires: Eudeba).

Silva, Josué Pereira da (2007) *André Gorz. Trabalho e política* (São Paulo: Annablume).

Simmel, Georg (1908) *Soziologie. Untersuchungen über die Formen der Vergesellschaftung* (Frankfurt am Main: Suhrkamp, 1992).

Singh, Yogendra (1986) *Modernization of Indian Tradition* (Nova Delhi: Rawat, 2009).

Skocpol, Theda (1979) *States and Social Revolutions: A Comparative Analysis of France, Russia, and China* (Cambridge: Cambridge University Press).

Smelser, Neil J. (1959) *Social Change in the Industrial Revolution: An Application of the Theory to the British Cotton Industry* (Chicago: The University of Chicago Press).

Smith, Adam (1776) *The Wealth of Nations* (Oxford: Oxford University Press, 2014).

Smith, Dennis (1992) *The Rise of Historical Sociology* (Philadelphia, PA: Temple University Press).

Spivak, Gayatri C. (1988) "Can the subaltern speak?," in Cary Nelson and Lawrence Grossberg (eds), *Marxism and the Interpretation of Culture* (Urbana, IL: University of Illinois Press).

Stepan, Alfred (2009) "Multiple secularisms," *Seminar*, #593 (http://www.india-seminar.com/2009/593.htm).

Streeck, Wolfgang (2011) "The crisis of democratic capitalism," *New Left Review*, no. 71.

Streeck, Wolfgang (2013) *Gekaufte Zeit. Die vertagte Krise des demokratischen Kapitalismus* (Frankfurt am Main: Suhrkamp).

Svampa, Maristella (2005) *La sociedad excluyente. La Argentina bajo el signo del neoliberalismo* (Buenos Aires: Taurus).

Svampa, Maristella (2006) *Barbarie o civilización. El dilema argentino.* (Buenos Aires: Taurus, 2nd edition).

Svampa, Maristella (2008) *Cambio de época. Movimientos sociales y poder político* (Buenos Aires: Siglo XXI and CLACSO).

Sweezy, Paul (1946) *The Theory of Capitalist Development* (New York: Monthly Review).

Swingewood, Alan (1991) *A Short History of Sociological Thought* (Basingstoke: Macmillan).

Taylor, Charles (2007) *A Secular Age* (Cambrigde, MA and London: The Karnap Press of Harvard University Press).

Tenbruch, Friedrich H. (1980) "The problem of thematic unity in the works of Max Weber," *British Journal of Sociology*, vol. 31.

Therborn, Göran (2004) *Between Sex and Power: Family in the World, 1900–2000* (New York and London: Routledge).

Therborn, Göran (2009) *From Marxism to Post-Marxism* (London and New York: Verso).

Tilly, Charles (1984) *Big Structures, Large Processes, Huge Comparisons* (New York: Russel Sage Foundation).

Tilly, Charles (1992) *Coercion, Capital and European States: Ad 990–1992* (Oxford: Willey-Blackwell, revised edition).

Tilly, Charles (2004) *Contention and Democracy in Europe, 1650–2000* (Cambridge: Cambridge University Press).

Tilly, Charles (2007) *Democracy* (Cambridge: Cambridge University Press).

Ungpakorn, Giles (2006) "The impact of the Thai 'sixties' on the People's Movement today," *Critical Asian Studies*, vol. 7.

Vanaik, Achin (1997) *The Furies of Indian Communalism: Religion, Modernity and Secularization* (London and New York: Verso).

Velho, Otavio Guilherme (1976) *Capitalismo autoritário e campesinato* (São Paulo: Difel).

Wagner, Peter (1994) *A Sociology of Modernity: Liberty and Discipline* (London and New York: Routledge).

Wagner, Peter (2008) *Modernity as Experience and Interpretation: A New Sociology of Modernity* (Cambridge, Polity).

Wagner, Peter (2012) *Modernity: Understanding the Present* (Cambridge: Polity).

Wainwright, Hilary (1994) *Arguments for a New Left: Answering the Free-Market Right* (Oxford and Cambridge, MA: Willey-Blackwell).

Wallerstein, Immanuel (1974, 1980, 1989) *The Modern World System*, vols 1–3 (New York: Academic Press).

Weber, Max (1904a) "Die 'Objekivität' sozialwissenschaftlicher Verursachung in der historischen Kausalbetrachtung," in *Schriften zur Wissenschaftslehre* (Stuttgart: Philiph Reclam, 1991).

Weber, Max (1904b) *Die Wirtschaftsethik der Weltreligionen. Die Protestantischen Ethik und der Geist der Kapitalismus* in *Gesammelte Aufsatze zur Religionssoziologie*, vol. 1 (Tübingen: J.C.B. Mohr [Paul Siebek], 1988).

Weber, Max (1913) "Ueber einige Kategorie des verstehenden Soziologie," in *Gesammelte Aufsätze zur Wissenschaftslehre* (Tübingen: J.C.B. Mohr [Paul Siebeck], 1951).

Weber, Max (1919) "Wissenschaft als Beruf," in *Gesammelte Aufsätze zur Wissenschaftslehre* (Tübingen: J.C.B. Mohr [Paul Siebeck], 1951).

Weber, Max. (1920a) "Vorbemerkung," in *Die Wirtschaftsethik der Weltreligionen*, in *Gesammelte Aufsätze zur Religionssoziologie*, vol. 1 (Tübinbgen, J.C.B Mohr [Paul Siebeck], 1988).

Weber, Max (1920b) *Die Wirtschaftsethik der Weltreligionen. Zwischenbetrachtung: Theorie der Stufen und Richtungen religiöser Weltablehnung*, in *Gesammelte Aufsätze zur Religionssoziologie*, vol. 1 (Tübinbgen, J.C.B Mohr [Paul Siebeck], 1988).

Weber, M. (1920c) *Die Wirtschaftsethik der Weltreligionen. Konfuzianismus und Taoismus*, in *Gesammelte Aufsätze zur Religiossoziologie*, vol. 1 (Tübingen: J.C.B. Mohr [Paul Siebek], 1988).

Weber, Max (1920d) *Die Wirtschaftsethik der Weltreligionen. Zwischenbetrachtung: Theorie der Stufen und Richtungen religiöser Weltablehnung*, in *Gesammelte Aufsätze zur Religionssoziologie*, vol. 1 (Tübingen: J.C.B. Mohr [Paul Siebek], 1988).

Weber, Max (1921–22) *Wirtschaft und Gesellschaft. Grundriß der verstehenden Soziologie* (Tübingen: J.C.B Mohr [Paul Siebeck], 1980).

Weber, Max (1923) *General Economic History* (Masfield Center, CT: Martino, 2013).

Werneck Vianna, Luiz (1975) *Liberalismo e sindicato no Brasil* (Rio de Janeiro: Paz e Terra).

West, Cornel (1989) *The American Evasion of Philosophy: A Genealogy of Philosophy* (Madison, WI: The Wisconsin University Press).

White, Harrison (1992) *Identity and Control: A Structural Theory of Social Action* (Princeton, NJ: Princeton University Press).

Williamson, Oliver E. (1983) *Markets and Hierarchies* (New York: Free Press).

Winckelmann, Johannes (ed.) (1995) *Die protestantische Ethik*, vol. 2. Kritiken und Antikritiken (Mohn: Guesteloher).

Zavaleta Mercado, René(1990) *El Estado en América Latina* (Cochabamba and La Paz: Los Amigos del Libro).

Zeng Yui (1991) *Family Dynamics in China: A Life Table Analysis* (Madison, WI: The University of Wisconsin Press).

Index

www.ingramcontent.com/pod-product-compliance
Lightning Source LLC
Chambersburg PA
CBHW070930030426
42336CB00014BA/2613